Seattle's Women Teachers

OF THE INTERWAR YEARS

Seattle's Women Teachers

OF THE INTERWAR YEARS

Shapers of a Livable City

DORIS HINSON PIEROTH

A McLellan Book

UNIVERSITY OF WASHINGTON PRESS

Seattle and London

This book is published with the assistance of a grant
from the McLellan Endowed Series Fund, established
through the generosity of Martha McCleary McLellan
and Mary McClellan Williams.

Copyright © 2004 by University of Washington Press
Designed by Pamela Canell
Printed in the United States of America
10 09 08 07 06 05 04   5 4 3 2 1

University of Washington Press
P.O. Box 50096, Seattle, WA 98145, U.S.A.
www.washington.edu/uwpress

Library of Congress Cataloging-in-Publication Data
can be found at the back of this book.

The paper used in this publication is acid-free and recycled from 10 percent
post-consumer and at least 50 percent pre-consumer waste. It meets the
minimum requirements of American National Standard for Information
Sciences—Permanence of Paper for Printed Library Materials,
ANSI Z39.48-1984.♾♽

Cover illustration: Pupils from a wartime overcrowded T. T. Minor School
received a happy send-off from their teachers on the last day of school in 1943.
Photo courtesy of Museum of History and Industry, PI 25660.

Contents

Preface   vii

Maps   x–xii

Introduction   3

1 / New Century, New City, New Schools   11

2 / 1920 and Beyond   37

3 / Quality of Life: Home, School, Transportation   63

4 / Perpetuating the Seattle Way:
Cadets and a Demonstration School   87

5 / Principals: Saints, Ogres, and Legends   102

6 / Dealing with Diversity   131

7 / Genteel Militants   151

8 / Beyond the Classroom   174

9 / Leaving the Classroom   199

Epilogue   216

Notes   221

Bibliography   257

Index   269

Preface

I n *The Ideal Teacher,* a slender volume published in 1910, the education philosopher George Palmer wrote that a teacher "must have an
aptitude for vicariousness . . . an already accumulated wealth . . . an
ability to invigorate life through knowledge . . . [and] a readiness to be forgotten." Although few if any were ever wealthy, Seattle's school women
of the interwar years enjoyed a wide range of experience vicariously and
certainly invigorated life through knowledge. Perhaps through the pages
that follow they will not be forgotten.

This book rests on the premise that the influence of women who taught
in its public schools between the two world wars made modern Seattle
the livable place that it remained through the twentieth century. World
War II had a tremendous impact on Seattle—population mushroomed,
demographics changed, city boundaries expanded. But in the immediate
postwar decades of growth and change, the charitable, philanthropic, volunteer, municipal, and civic leadership of what was still a rather provin-
cial and insular city remained firmly in the hands of men and women
who had attended Seattle's public schools before 1941.

The careers of these interwar teachers did not consistently follow the
pattern set by those who taught elsewhere in the United States. Seattle
drew women bent on professional careers and in most instances held them
for long tenures. Most taught through at least one world war and the Great
Depression. They enjoyed amiable relations with administrators and
supervisors. The evidence shows that, although never suitably paid, these

teachers considered themselves fortunate and thought their lives tremendously fulfilling.

This is the story of those women—who they were, whence they came, what they did both in and out of the classroom, and what they bequeathed to the city, their successors, and their students. It is not a treatise on education theory or the history of education but rather an account of women teachers set against the backdrop of a developing city. The Introduction and Chapters 1 and 2 are a chronological review of Seattle's growth and of major events that affected its schools and teachers. Other chapters cover specific topics pertaining to the experience of the interwar teacher cohort. Biographical sketches of teachers appear throughout to illustrate events and trends.

In addition to published sources, this study is based on documents in the archives of the Seattle Public Schools, material in the special collections at the University of Washington Libraries, and interviews with and materials lent by some of those women, their family members, students, and fellow teachers. Statistics came from the school district records of seven hundred women who taught at some point between 1919 and 1940; the sample includes all applicable records from a collection known as A-96-9 and from every tenth legible applicable record from the much larger microfilm collection.

More than eighty interviews with members of the interwar cohort of teachers, their former students and later colleagues, and others active in Seattle's school sphere have enriched this book. Talking with these considerate, thoughtful people was both informative and a true pleasure; I am grateful to all of them for the time they were willing to spend with me and for written materials they lent me. I am indebted to Olaf Kvamme and Paul Horlein for providing me with tapes of interviews conducted for the oral history project of the Seattle Retired Teachers Association.

In researching and writing, I incurred many other debts of gratitude as well. Thanks go first of all to Eleanor Toews, the Seattle Public Schools archivist who directed me to records for the interwar cohort and provided invaluable assistance in the use of those and other collections. Richard Berner and Howard Droker shared unpublished manuscripts, and Louis

Fiset provided me transcripts of interviews he conducted in his own work; I thank all three historians for their generosity. The book's excellent maps are the creations of Fred Bird; my friend Laura Arksey contributed the index. I am grateful to the staff of the University of Washington Libraries Special Collections for assistance and suggestions. Materials from the Plymouth Congregational Church Archives and those of the Seattle Education Association proved invaluable, and I appreciate the privilege of using them. I benefited enormously from the superb editorial skill of Carol Zabilski; for this I remain in her debt.

Over the course of years devoted to this book, other obligations mounted. I enjoyed greatly the interest and enthusiasm that friends and family have shown, and I gained much from their support. I want especially to thank Pauline and Charles LeWarne, Joanne Torney Rehfeldt, Suzanne Hittman, and Margaret Hall, all of whom encouraged the project from its beginning. My husband, John, provided technical advice and moral support that made the undertaking possible. Perhaps my greatest debt is to the interwar teachers themselves—those I came to know personally and others I met only in the archives; without them there would truly have been no book.

DORIS H. PIEROTH
Seattle, Washington
October 2003

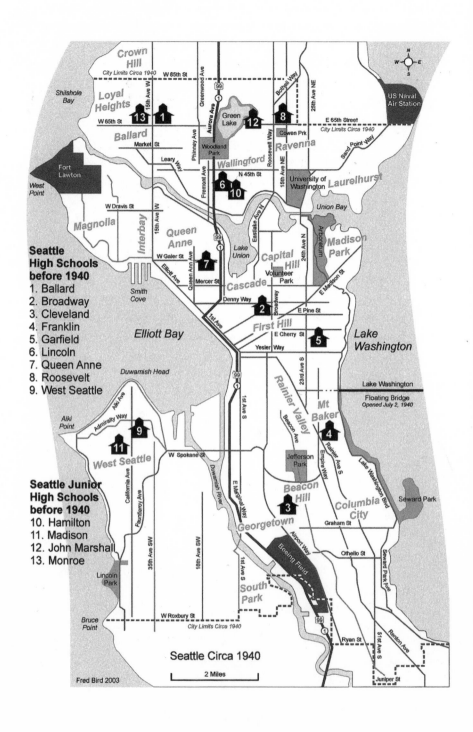

Seattle
High Schools
before 1940
1. Ballard
2. Broadway
3. Cleveland
4. Franklin
5. Garfield
6. Lincoln
7. Queen Anne
8. Roosevelt
9. West Seattle

Seattle Junior
High Schools
before 1940
10. Hamilton
11. Madison
12. John Marshall
13. Monroe

Seattle Circa 1940

2 Miles

Fred Bird 2003

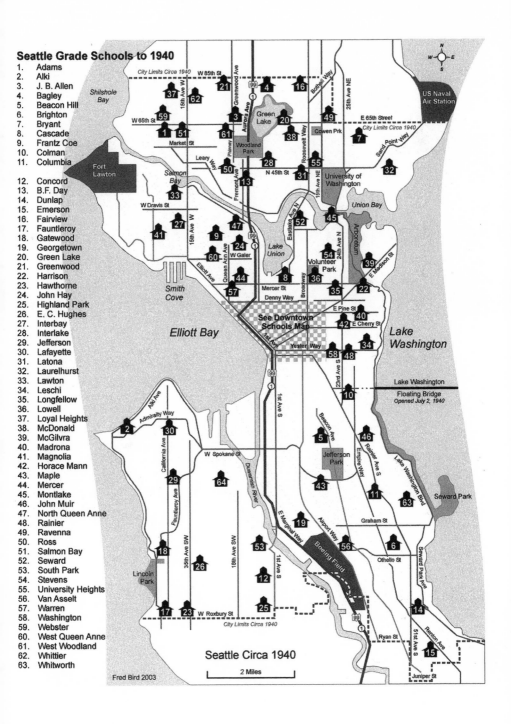

Seattle Grade Schools to 1940

1. Adams
2. Alki
3. J. B. Allen
4. Bagley
5. Beacon Hill
6. Brighton
7. Bryant
8. Cascade
9. Frantz Coe
10. Colman
11. Columbia
12. Concord
13. B.F. Day
14. Dunlap
15. Emerson
16. Fairview
17. Fauntleroy
18. Gatewood
19. Georgetown
20. Green Lake
21. Greenwood
22. Harrison
23. Hawthorne
24. John Hay
25. Highland Park
26. E. C. Hughes
27. Interbay
28. Interlake
29. Jefferson
30. Lafayette
31. Latona
32. Laurelhurst
33. Lawton
34. Leschi
35. Longfellow
36. Lowell
37. Loyal Heights
38. McDonald
39. McGilvra
40. Madrona
41. Magnolia
42. Horace Mann
43. Maple
44. Mercer
45. Montlake
46. John Muir
47. North Queen Anne
48. Rainier
49. Ravenna
50. Ross
51. Salmon Bay
52. Seward
53. South Park
54. Stevens
55. University Heights
56. Van Asselt
57. Warren
58. Washington
59. Webster
60. West Queen Anne
61. West Woodland
62. Whittier
63. Whitworth

City Limits Circa 1940   W 85th St

Shilshole Bay

W 65th St

Green Lake

US Naval Air Station

E 65th Street

City Limits Circa 1940

Cowen Prk

Sand Point Way

Market St

Woodland Park

Leary Way

Salmon Bay

N 45th St

University of Washington

Union Bay

W Dravis St

Fort Lawton

15th Ave W

Lake Union

Arboretum

W Galer

Volunteer Park

Elliott Ave

Smith Cove

Mercer St

Denny Way

Broadway

E Pine St

See Downtown Schools Map

E Cherry St

Elliott Bay

Yester Way

Lake Washington

Lake Washington

Floating Bridge
Opened July 2, 1940

Alki Ave

Admiralty Way

California Ave

Beacon Ave

W Spokane St

Jefferson Park

Rainier Ave S

Lake Washington Blvd

Seward Park

Fauntleroy Ave

Lincoln Park

35th Ave SW

16th Ave SW

Duwamish River

E Marginal Way

Airport Way

Boeing Field

Graham St

Seward Park Ave

W Roxbury St

City Limits Circa 1940

Othello St

Ryan St

51st Ave S

Renton Ave

Juniper St

Seattle Circa 1940

Fred Bird 2003

2 Miles

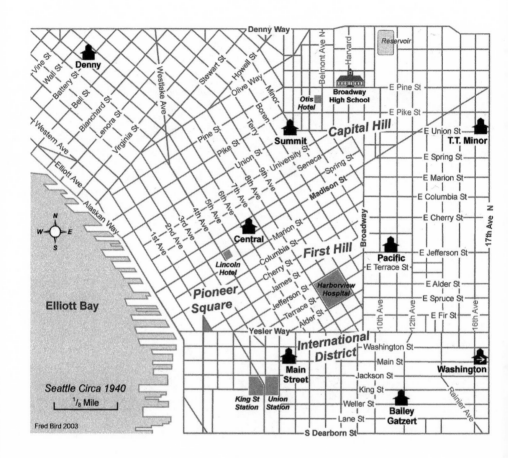

Downtown Seattle Schools before 1940

Seattle's Women Teachers

OF THE INTERWAR YEARS

Introduction

E lementary school teaching in the United States was a male occupation through most of the nineteenth century, until growing demands for mass education in the industrial age helped to open the door for women. With the subsequent growth of large urban school districts, women came to dominate grade school teaching. Urban districts offered them opportunities for professional growth[1]; during the Progressive Era, Seattle and other cities drew outstanding women teachers who carved careers of very long tenure.

School boards tapped a prime talent pool, no doubt hiring single women because they were "mobile, more docile and manipulable, and because they could be hired at a much lower price than the man whose family responsibility was acknowledged." As more women entered the teaching profession, men exited the classroom to become administrators and education theorists.[2]

In 1900, public school teachers in America earned, on average, 75 percent of the wage paid to workers in manufacturing and less than half the salary of federal employees and postal workers.[3] Women teachers earned less than their male colleagues and had fewer opportunities to improve their lot, but limited alternative employment possibilities made teaching attractive. Salary was ever a leading grievance of teachers and a spur to organize the profession. Other motives for organizing lay in the area of reform and teacher empowerment. Historians of education generally consider Progressive Era reforms to have given "power to newly emergent administrators bent on scientific meritocratic management of the schools" and to have changed a teacher from "being a recipient of political patronage to being a worker who was expected to follow orders."[4]

The Chicago teacher Margaret A. Haley, an early leader in organizing, worked to secure improvements of vital concern to women such as salary, class size, pensions, and a more democratic role for the classroom teacher. In a landmark address to the male-dominated National Education Association in 1904, Haley virtually set the agenda that women teachers would pursue for decades as they faced rising living costs, overcrowded classrooms, lack of tenure, and uncertainty after retirement. She spoke for the many women for whom teaching was not just a temporary stop on the road to marriage but a career on a par with other professions.[5]

Viewing the history of American education in the twentieth century from a vantage point early in the twenty-first, it is difficult to disagree with the historian David Tyack:

> The concept of a golden age in the past is untenable. . . . Teachers have been young and poorly paid. They came in and out of the occupation as though they were passing through a revolving door. Women bore the largest share of the work, but faced many kinds of discrimination. . . . In cities, teachers often had little voice in planning their work and were closely supervised to ensure that they, like their pupils, toed the line. . . . If one looks at the characteristics and daily lives of average teachers in the past, it is hard to discover any golden age.[6]

If not during a golden age, the careers of Seattle's women teachers of the interwar years might be said to have occurred during a latter-day bronze age. Because of precedent set by an extraordinary superintendent—Frank Cooper, known as a "teachers' superintendent"—they fared better than most. They *did* face salary discrimination and sexism; they had bleak retirement prospects; they paid the penalty of dismissal when they married; and they had little recourse regarding salary or reinstatement. But these strong, independent, proud professional women relished their jobs and took advantage of every opportunity that came their way.

When Frank B. Cooper joined a legion of other newcomers to Seattle in 1901, the entire nation embraced Progressive reforms in government and education. Seattle matured as a city during the Progressive Era, and its Progressive business and professional leaders served on the school board. The board maintained a Progressive hue until World War I, all the while tolerating a longtime socialist member and, between 1916 and 1918, a future Communist, Anna Louise Strong.

In hiring Cooper, the school board chose a remarkable administrator and supported him for twenty years. An Illinois native and graduate of Cornell, Cooper had served as superintendent in Des Moines, Iowa, and then in Salt Lake City. He hired the district's teachers himself, championed them and their interests, and created a spirit between teachers and administration that, for the most part, appears to have been one of mutual respect and even affection.[7] Seattle gave Cooper an "extraordinary opportunity to develop a new urban school system, essentially unencumbered by the past." Together he and the board built many neighborhood grade schools and established comprehensive high schools in which women taught across the curriculum.[8]

Cooper essentially standardized the curriculum citywide, and new teachers were more or less indoctrinated in the "Seattle Way." "Subject matter supervisors went from school to school, and even held Saturday teacher meetings. . . . [T]eachers not only knew what to teach but how to teach it."[9] Like much in progressivism, the Seattle Way was something of a paradox. While expanding to include new subjects, and with nebulous "character development" as a goal, elementary schools hammered home the basic core subjects. The high schools continued to provide solid preparation in the liberal arts, while vocational and commercial classes, physical education, home economics, music, and art became integral parts of the curriculum. As an education Progressive, Cooper reflected that movement's general concern with the "whole child" and its belief that all children were entitled to be educated to their greatest potential.

John Dewey, who symbolized Progressive education, had abandoned "such historic philosophical dualisms as those of individual and community, body and mind, and ideal and actuality," and his philosophy of education showed that. He saw the school "as a social institution designed to immerse children in an embryonic social life especially organized to nurture intellectual, moral, and aesthetic development," with curriculum that unified "newer studies (drawing, music, nature study, manual training) with the older (the three R's)." The Seattle Way does not trace directly to Dewey, but much that Cooper promulgated in his first decade in the city suggested Dewey and his learning-by-doing approach. Such programs as domestic science, manual training, and gardening were installed in each school. Cooper followed Dewey in the matter of moral instruction, holding that it was integral to all teaching and "went on through out the day and could not be separated from other parts of the curriculum. . . . [It] was neither a formal subject nor a religious education."[10] By the mid-twenties, the Seattle Way embraced Dewey's view of the school as a laboratory for democracy.

As the traditional curriculum of science, mathematics, language, and history expanded to include new subject matter, Cooper appointed committees of teachers and principals to help develop curricula. By involving teachers he "not only produced better results, but promoted teacher morale."[11] Seattle soon became a magnet district that attracted experienced teachers who came mainly from the Midwest, the East Coast, and the Pacific Northwest.

Many of the interwar cohort of women teachers began their Seattle careers during this period. By 1920, the city's population had reached 315,312;[12] its schools and their women teachers had helped to shape that growth. Cooper resigned in 1922, but teachers he had personally hired continued teaching for two or more decades. Although somewhat frayed during the late twenties and thirties, much of the Seattle Way and its esprit de corps survived until World War II.

One of the first Seattle teachers hired by Frank Cooper came with him from Salt Lake City. Trella Belle Logan had thought there must be more to see in life than what Plymouth, Indiana, offered, and as the nineteenth century drew to a close, with normal school certificate in hand and some rural teaching to her credit, she "blind-folded herself and chose a place" to move by pushing a pin into a map of the West. By the following autumn she had moved to Salt Lake City. She later told her daughter that she loved her teaching job, but her principal would come in after school and "chase her around the desk." When she complained to the superintendent he asked her to bear with the situation for the rest of the year, told her he was going to Seattle, and asked her to consider coming along as a member of the teaching corps he would assemble there.[13]

Trella Logan came to Seattle in autumn semester 1902, to a city that had not yet thrown off its image as a young, raw, male-dominated, roughneck spot. It was far from being a cultured or sophisticated place—downtown streets were unpaved or planked, mud remained a constant, and such urban amenities as plumbing and street lighting left much to be desired. But the city still reaped financial benefits from the Alaska gold rush of 1897, and it nurtured a sense of the common good. Seattle had recovered from the disastrous fire that had nearly destroyed it in 1889; growth and expansion had made real estate a prime investment; and turn-of-the-century speculation had brought eastern money for development of new downtown business blocks. Near-boom conditions would continue through 1910, and civic confidence remained high.[14]

Trella Logan taught seventh grade at Mercer School and lived in the same boarding house on Sixth Avenue as an architect, Clayton B. Wilson. After her second school year in Seattle had passed, they married and moved to a small house on Alki Beach.[15] School district policy, though less socially restrictive than that of many rural and small-town districts, always held that "marriage of a woman teacher during the period of her employment shall automatically terminate" her contract. Thus Trella Logan Wilson left teaching; she returned as a substitute during the 1920s, and in 1927 her daughter, Alma Wilson, joined the Seattle corps.[16]

As it had since its founding in 1852, Seattle differed from other American cities in a number of respects. Because it was difficult and expensive to reach the far northwest corner of the nation, "only certain individuals ever came to Seattle"—those who could afford the trip. Solidly middle class by 1910, the city had an economy that rested on providing services, trans-shipping goods to the hinterland, and the fishing and timber industries. Both of the latter operated at some remove, resulting, according to the historian Janice Reiff, in "an absence of unskilled or semi-skilled workers" in the city; they simply passed through instead of settling permanently. The citizenry was primarily white collar and skilled, with "no lower class or large unassimilated ethnic population." Most immigrants came to Seattle only after "years in America and after accumulating at least limited assets."[17]

In 1910 there were 237,000 residents, overwhelmingly Caucasian and native born. Fewer than 5 percent of the residents were nonwhite, and only 27 percent foreign born. Early Seattle was not composed of ethnic neighborhoods in the mode of its eastern counterparts; residential patterns ran more along economic lines and reflected the gap between settled residents and the large transient population.[18]

Schooling had developed slowly in the city. The territorial legislature named Seattle the home of the University of Washington, which laid its cornerstone on May 20, 1861, on a plot of land that became the heart of the downtown commercial district. The first public school opened in 1870, when the number of school-age children had climbed above one hundred. Before that, students had attended either the "primary school" at the university or one of a few small private schools. The university would become a significant factor in the lives of the city's teachers.[19]

What had brought people to Seattle before the Alaska gold rush in 1897? Men had come to start business enterprises, to find jobs in the lumber mills, to escape service in the Civil War, or perhaps just because it was farther west than the last place. Some worked for a railroad that would make it much easier for a flood of others to follow. Promotional brochures touted Washington Territory nationwide, stressing that "nature had blessed Washington with her gifts and beauties. . . . [and] nowhere else could one find such magnificent scenery." Whatever their reasons, people came in growing numbers. Most in that in-migration were young, single men; they outnumbered women three to one; the ratio still stood at two to one through 1900.[20]

Most women who arrived in Seattle before gold fever hit came with husbands or fathers. Among the few who moved to Seattle alone, Julia A. Kennedy came to visit and stayed to serve as superintendent of schools from 1888 through 1890. Julia Kennedy had graduated from an Illinois normal school and studied in Germany; as head of a growing school system, she drove her own horse-drawn buggy on her rounds to visit the three schools and prided herself in that "not one of the teachers she selected ever, involuntarily, lost her position."[21]

In the early 1890s, Eunice Copeland came to Seattle as a youngster with her father, a superintendent with the newly completed Great Northern Railroad. She graduated from the city's lone high school in 1895. Three years later she applied to teach elementary students in the public schools, though she lacked a normal school credential. An inveterate member of the interwar cohort, Eunice Copeland became a school principal in 1922; she retired in June 1946, at the age of seventy.[22]

Another longtime Seattle teacher and an 1894 graduate of its high school began her career in the city in 1900. Ada J. Mahon had immigrated with her family from New Brunswick. She, too, lacked a normal school certificate, but she went on to serve as one of Seattle's most important elementary school principals in the interwar years, retiring in 1945.[23]

Twenty-seven-year-old Letta Nason, another early arrival who had a long career, graduated from Wisconsin's Stevens Point Normal School, taught primary grades in that state and in Montana, and came on west to Seattle in 1899, teaching at Central School until 1903. After a short leave that fall when her mother died, she returned to teach at Longfellow School, where she remained until her own death in 1933 at the age of sixty-two.[24]

Coming late to the ranks of urban education, the Seattle School District did not carry much of the political baggage borne by cities in the East. Its school board, an autonomous body with taxing authority, was separate from city government and made appointments free of overt political influence. The board's selection of Frank Cooper insured better conditions than in other cities and a benign chain of command for teachers, who soon "identified themselves with their managers, especially with their chief advocate Superintendent Cooper."[25]

Yet Seattle's women teachers were not entirely docile, compliant employees. Even before Margaret Haley's 1904 speech to the men of the NEA, "Why Teachers Should Organize," they had gathered after school to establish "an association, the aim of which is to be the promotion of educational interests . . . and the advancement of the teacher's work as a profession." That first meeting, on March 26, 1897, indicates that attaining professional status clearly stood as a top priority. A vocal solo opened the program, followed by a discussion of how to obtain the best results in spelling—they voted in favor of the "use of diacritical marks." Reading came next, in a presentation "by Misses Hart, Fisken, and Goodspeed" on "how to obtain the best results in reading." Both Nell Hart and Bella Fisken taught throughout the interwar years.[26]

Adopting a constitution and electing officers came last on the agenda. No copy of the constitution can be found, but the secretary's minutes indicate much discussion and rescinding of motions to table before adoption of its eight articles. On one point of major concern they voted "that sections pertaining to sick benefits be laid on the table till next meeting." Nominees showed great reluctance to accept office,[27] but Sara Waughop, who continued teaching into the 1930s, was in charge a year later. That was the last recorded meeting. The teachers tabled a communication from the Pedagogical Club "pertaining to the teaching of morals in the schools" and agreed to meet again in three months.[28] But Seattle was changing: seven months earlier, the S.S. *Portland* had arrived with its ton of gold from the Yukon and virtually transformed the city. Almost two decades would pass before women teachers formed an organization that endured.

When Trella Logan arrived to teach at Mercer School in 1902, Seattle had twenty-two grade schools and six school annexes located mainly in churches and at the synagogue. Eunice Copeland was then teaching third grade at T. T. Minor School on the city's First Hill; Ada Mahon taught fourth grade at the magnificent Denny School, near what became Seattle Center; and Letta Nason had been assigned to teach primary grades at Central School on the corner of Sixth and Madison downtown. In the next decade, by growth and annexations to the city, the number of schools would more than double to fifty-seven with only one annex; five new high schools would join the original, now named Broadway High School; and the teacher corps would grow proportionately.[29]

1 / New Century, New City, New Schools

B
y 1900, Seattle was the most important city in the Pacific Northwest and beginning a decade of transformation. The forest still came close to the edge of town that year; logging operations, shingle mills, and sawmills continued to hum; and, although "gold fever finally abated in 1907," an aura lingered that sustained a "sense of newness and unlimited opportunity common to a frontier." The whole city fit the 1901 description that Dean Frederick Padelford gave of the university's neighborhood: it was "distinctly a town in the making . . . almost entirely made up of people . . . from somewhere else, and all ambitious and confident of achievement. The atmosphere was electric, charged with youth and energy."[1]

Those people from somewhere else were joined by women who came to staff new schools being built to keep pace with the city as it grew and expanded north along the waterfront and spread outward onto the surrounding hills. Suburban annexation transformed the city into the hourglass shape it still retains. The limits of the city and the school district in 1910 were Eighty-fifth Street on the north, Roxbury Street on the southwest, and Ryan Street in the southeast sector. These boundaries remained through World War II, contributing to the stability that marked the city and its schools during the interwar years.

Annexations included the town of Ballard and the neighborhoods of Ravenna, Laurelhurst, Green Lake, Wallingford, and the University District; southward expansion took in Columbia City, Van Asselt, Georgetown, and South Park; each name would adorn a public school.[2] The street-car system kept pace and became a determining factor in the lives of Seattle's teachers. By 1910 the school district's personnel directories listed streetcar routes to each school from locations throughout the city.

Beginning in the 1890s, Seattle undertook a series of massive regrading projects that completely altered its hilly topography. Regrading created level ground for business development, but streets torn up in the process meant dislocation for the populace. Women teachers en route to school endured dust and dirt at the beginning and end of the school year and decorously lifted long skirts above high-button shoes to slog through muck and mire during the long rainy season. The Denny Hill regrade at the north edge of downtown started in 1910, opening a wound akin to an open-pit mine; sluicing of the 234–foot-high hill into Elliott Bay lasted until 1930.[3] No regrading project affected teachers' lives more than that which leveled Denny Hill and destroyed a landmark school in the process.

Promoters and developers met the demand for residential expansion, and where homes rose, schools soon followed. The city's elite had established the first neighborhood beyond the downtown core—on First Hill, just up Madison Street from the waterfront.[4] The south slope of Queen Anne Hill would attract a newer elite, and former First Hill residents would move on to new, exclusive enclaves beyond the city limits.

Early arrivals to the city had already moved toward Queen Anne, which soon developed a well-defined sense of community. The family of Erik Soderback, a tailor who had come from San Francisco in 1890 after the fire, moved from the heart of downtown into a home built on the west side of Queen Anne Hill. His daughter, Florence, born there on December 6, 1904, started school in 1910, walking along the plank surface of Fifteenth Avenue West to Interbay School. There her fifth-grade teacher, Nina Moore, a 1903 arrival in Seattle, would inspire her to become a teacher. Florence Soderback began teaching in Seattle in 1927 and taught seventh- and eighth-grade reading until she retired in 1971.[5]

New neighborhoods appeared, old ones changed, and the city's earlier spirit of openness changed, too. In his classic study *Seattle Past to Present*, Roger Sale makes the point that rich and poor lived in close proximity in the 1890s, with "constant mixing of people and types of activity." He found, however, that in the early twentieth century "the 'democratic' mixing of rich and bourgeois and settled poor was replaced by a more self-conscious sorting out of neighborhoods into good and not so good."[6]

In the first decade of the century, an elite neighborhood developed on Capitol Hill near Volunteer Park, joining those on Queen Anne and First hills, and blue-collar areas materialized—near Lake Union, in Ballard, Georgetown, and south Seattle for example. Society became increasingly structured along economic lines.[7] This sorting out, which also followed ethnic lines, would define the careers of many of the interwar cohort of women teachers.

By 1910 Seattle ranked twenty-fifth on the list of major American cities. Its population was still overwhelmingly white, and immigrants still arrived after first locating elsewhere. Early immigrants had settled near the waterfront, but as the historian Richard Berner puts it, "Once their countrymen established enclaves elsewhere, subsequent newcomers tended to bypass the downtown area and gravitate" directly to outlying neighborhoods. He cites the movement of Scandinavians to Ballard. Italian immigrants, a fast-growing ethnic group, settled in and around the Rainier Valley and sent their children to Colman School.[8]

In the 1890s, "Seattle's first Jews lived mixed in with their Gentile neighbors" along Yesler Way. A growing number of Eastern European Jewish immigrants settled between Ninth and Fourteenth avenues, Yesler Way and King Street, where they were joined by Sephardic Jews who began arriving around 1903. By 1910, the Jewish population stood at just under 2 percent of the city's total, and as families began to move east up the hill along Main and Yesler toward Nineteenth Avenue, Washington School "absorbed the children of the immigrants."[9]

Among Seattle's nonwhite population at the start of the twentieth century, Japanese predominated. Japanese workers had helped build Great Northern Railway lines and had provided labor for the area lumber mills. Recruited for those jobs, some of the new immigrants later bought farm land or invested in city property, where they owned hotels, cafés and small shops. The Nikkei had settled originally around Fifth Avenue between Main and Jackson streets, and their children attended Main Street School, which the school district replaced in 1920 with a building named for the longtime school board member Bailey Gatzert.[10] The community gradually spread eastward, and Nikkei children in growing numbers also attended Washington and Pacific schools.

In that first decade of the new century, Seattle's African-American population grew from 406 to 2,296. The migration to Washington Territory had begun before emancipation; in addition to escaping bondage and growing racial oppression, African Americans came for the same reasons that other immigrants did.[11]

Although they held property throughout the city and lived in every part of Seattle, as the nineteenth century ended they had begun to concentrate their residences east of First Hill along Madison Street. From the beginning, African-American children attended Seattle's public schools without restriction. The family of Mattie Vinyerd Harris, who was born in Seattle in 1894, lived near the foot of Queen Anne Hill and would have attended Denny, Warren Avenue, or Mercer schools. Priscilla Maunder Kirk's family lived in the newly annexed Green Lake district, where children "walk[ed] through cow pastures and wooded trails to get to school" until as late as 1917.[12]

To keep pace with change, growth, and annexation, the school district engaged in a flurry of high school acquisitions and construction. Seattle High School, which produced some of the city's long-tenured teachers, had no building of its own. Its students shared quarters with grade classes in Central School downtown until they outnumbered those in the grades, and the need for a separate building could not be ignored. The school board acquired lots at Pine Street and Broadway, and in 1902 Broadway High School started its long run as the city's premier secondary institution. Florence Adams, a legendary English teacher who taught there until 1940, recounted its day of dedication as a

> gloomy Saturday, darkened by a pall of smoke from forest fires, whe[n] the grand new building was opened. No lights being available in the still not quite finished building, the [dedication] exercises were held in the Christian Church . . . on the opposite side of the street. Following this, we groped our way across the newly plowed grounds to rooms lighted only by kerosene lamps, or candles stuck into ink-wells.[13]

The district built Lincoln High School in 1906, to meet rapid growth around the site north of Lake Union to which the University of Washington had moved in 1895. With annexation, Ballard High School became part of the Seattle district in 1907. The city annexed West Seattle in 1908, but its high school students shared space with elementary pupils until the present West Seattle High School building was completed in 1917. In 1909 Thomas Jefferson High School opened, but pressure from neighborhood citizens soon had it renamed Queen Anne High School. In 1912, Franklin High School occupied a new building in the Mount Baker Park district.[14]

Seattle and its school district differed in a number of ways from many of the nation's cities in the Progressive Era. A Seattle grade teacher did not face a crush of "immigrant children profoundly dependent on her for their introduction into American language and culture," nor did she contend with "increasingly professional and elite administrators who dared to think of her as if she were a factory hand." Secondary teachers did not find a predominance of men in the high schools as those in other cities did. When Broadway opened, women outnumbered men on its faculty thirty-two to nineteen.[15]

Women coming to Seattle to teach did find a superintendent who championed his teachers, supervisors, and administrators. When Frank Cooper arrived in July 1901, the school district boasted one woman among its supervisors—Emma Small, supervisor of drawing. By 1910 she had the company of four more women supervisors—including Clara P. Reynolds, manual training, and Georgia McManis, penmanship. The tenures of all three extended into the interwar decades.[16] Emma Small retired in 1923; Clara Reynolds had attained the position of director of art by the midtwenties, a post she still held in 1941. Georgia McManis continued to oversee the penmanship of Seattle children until 1933.

Frank Cooper recalled arriving to find meager provisions for equipment, but he was welcomed by a cooperative corps of teachers with a good "working spirit." He built on this foundation and seized on the board's inclination "to employ only the best teachers without regard to connections or residence." Cooper inherited a teacher corps of 350.[17] By 1910, the total was 838, including male principals in the six high schools where women teachers outnumbered men 106 to 81. Grade teachers, all women, found women principals in twelve of their fifty-two schools.[18]

During Cooper's first decade, as Seattle assumed greater stability and acquired the trappings of a more mature, commercial city, teaching was not "an elite profession . . . [but] it seems to have been a solidly middle-class one." Middle-class Seattle and its Progressive schools drew women for a number of reasons. The amenities and opportunities of a city and the anonymity of an urban system attracted some. Although the declining ratio of men to women in the city stood at 1.36 to 1 by 1910, some may have come seeking better marriage prospects. Others were lured by natural beauty, recreational opportunities, and adventure. Some followed siblings who had settled earlier. Most hoped to build professional careers and to earn good salaries. Whatever their individual reasons, they were part of the ongoing westward movement, perhaps drawn by a perception of unlimited opportunity on a far frontier.[19]

During that 1900–1910 decade of growth, the number of grade teachers increased by 340. Among those who taught into the interwar years, experience was an important factor in their selection: 26 percent had at least five years of experience; 52 percent had taught between six and ten years; 14 percent, between eleven and fifteen years; and another 5 percent for more than fifteen years. Experience seems to belie their ages—22 percent were less than twenty-five years old, 43 percent between twenty-six and thirty, 29 percent between thirty-one and thirty-five; and 6 percent were older than thirty-six.[20]

An overwhelming majority of Seattle's new grade teachers applied from other towns in Washington, but the normal schools they attended show that most hailed from other states. Normal schools in Illinois and Michigan each had prepared 9 percent of the new teachers, Wisconsin 12 percent, Iowa 17 percent, and Minnesota 6 percent. Other midwestern and western states sent a total of 10 percent, and 17 percent came from schools in the East. Washington's own newly opened normal schools in Bellingham (1899) and Ellensburg (1891) sent only 10 percent of Seattle's new teachers. At some point, 12 percent of grade teachers hired between 1900 and 1910 earned bachelor's degrees.

Long tenures marked their careers; the vast majority taught until retirement. Only 1 percent stayed less than ten years; 37 percent taught between twenty-six and thirty-five years. Twenty-seven percent spent thirty-six to forty years in the classroom, and an amazing 18 percent of those dedicated women taught for more than forty years. That merely 5 percent resigned to be married calls into question husband hunting as a major motive for moving to Seattle.

Applications to teach in Seattle's six high schools in the same period show similar patterns. The main difference between the two groups was the requirement of a college degree for high school teachers, which the district rarely waived. The significance of the University of Washington in Seattle is readily apparent; 41 percent of the high school applicants had earned bachelor's degrees there; 18 percent would at some point earn a master's degree. At this early stage, the Seattle School District had already begun to hire its own graduates; 18 percent of the high school sample had graduated from Broadway High School. On average, secondary candidates applied at an earlier age than grade applicants, with 41 percent under twenty-five. Their tenures ranged from only two to forty years, and 30 percent taught for more than thirty years.

Salaries were fairly high but far from munificent. The matter of salary loomed large for most who came. Money mattered to thirty-four-year-old Kate Adams, who applied from Evanston, Illinois, in January 1908. A graduate of Cook County Normal School, she had taught in two other towns and wrote on her application form, "Must know by last of March at latest as we have to sign our contracts very early. Couldn't think of accepting less than $840, as I have a supposedly ideal position here." No salary record exists, but she began that fall at Webster School in north Ballard, then transferred the next year to University Heights School, near the new university campus. When she retired on June 12, 1942, she still ruled the school's fourth-grade classroom for an annual salary of approximately $3,000.[21]

Ida Ahlgren of Littlefalls, Minnesota, may or may not have been influenced by possibly enhanced marriage prospects when she applied in Seattle. Born in 1887, she had earned a diploma from Wisconsin's Superior State Normal School and taught in Spokane for two years. Hired by Frank Cooper in 1908, she taught in five different schools over the next seventeen years and resigned only in 1925 to be married.[22]

Those who followed siblings to Seattle include Ellen Powell Dabney, who applied with the district in May 1907. In her early forties, she had spent that school year at Columbia University's Teachers College. As a niece later wrote, "left a widow with five children [and] being without formal training for making a living, [she undertook] . . . to study the then new subject of 'Home Economics'." Her application listed Illinois as her permanent address, but a handwritten note directed correspondence to a Seattle location: "37th Ave North and E Aloha, care John H. Powell." John Powell, her brother, was an influential and respected Seattle attorney and regent of the University of Washington. With a new credential in home economics, Ellen Dabney began teaching at Lincoln High School in the fall of 1907. Promoted to supervisor of home economics by 1915, she held that position until her death in 1937.[23]

More typical perhaps than Ellen Dabney, Margaret Kane followed her sister, Anna, to Seattle in 1910. Anna had come in 1901 after teaching five years in Grand Forks, North Dakota, and another year in Montana. Both Kanes had attended River Falls, Wisconsin, Normal School. Anna began her Seattle career teaching at Cascade School; in 1912 she was named principal of Colman School. Margaret had taught eight years in Wisconsin; after "caring for my mother during last illness" and attending summer school at the University of Minnesota, she joined Kate Adams at University Heights for a year. From then on, she received centrally located assignments. The Kane sisters shared a home on Capitol Hill until Margaret died in 1929. When Anna retired from Colman in 1940 she was one of the longest serving and strongest principals of the interwar years.[24]

Whatever her motives for moving to the Northwest, the career of Edith Page Bennett ranks among the longest tenures of any high school teacher in the interwar teacher cohort. An Illinois native, she completed her bachelor's degree at the University of Illinois in 1900, with a major in classics. She taught Latin, Greek, and English for eight years at Ottawa Township High School; she applied in Seattle in April 1908 but, as many others did, had to renew her application the following spring. That autumn, just shy of her thirty-third birthday, she joined the faculty of Franklin High School. Greek was taught only at Broadway, so she taught Latin and English composition at Franklin until retiring in 1945. By the end of her forty-five-year teaching career, thirty-six of which were in Seattle, Edith Bennett commanded a salary of $2,600.[25]

Agnes Parker's path to high school teaching differed considerably from Edith Bennett's. Her early career anticipated the model followed by many who taught in the twenties and thirties. She prepared at Iowa State Normal School and, after nine years of teaching grades in rural Iowa and Sioux City, in 1904 she applied in Seattle. She taught at Ross and T. T. Minor schools. And she took full advantage of the University of Washington's presence in the city, earning a bachelor's degree in 1926. After a year-long sabbatical leave "to travel and study," she returned to Broadway High School where she taught history until 1945, when her salary was $3,300. Agnes Parker and Edith Bennett retired the same year at the same age; there is no explanation for the $700 difference in their salaries.[26]

Another grade teacher from the early years who would earn a B.A. from the University of Washington, Marie Nettleton graduated from Seattle High School in 1900, did normal school work in Bellingham, and then taught in rural schools and at Aberdeen. Beginning in 1908, she taught in six different Seattle schools. In 1938, when she was fifty-eight, she completed her bachelor's degree while teaching at Concord Elementary. She retired in 1942 but returned to teach two more years during the World War II teacher shortage.[27]

Another graduate of Iowa State Normal School, Lavinia Mowry applied in August 1909 at the age of thirty-eight, listing Lake City, Iowa, as her address. From a Seattle address in the University District, she wrote on her application form, "I am traveling at present." She had spent two summers at the University of Chicago and also earned University of Washington credits. With nine years of experience, she began fall semester 1910 teaching intermediate grades at University Heights School; in 1922 she earned $1,950, more than twice her original expectation. She taught in four other schools before retiring in 1937.[28]

The adventurous who came for natural beauty and recreational opportunities found both thanks to the Seattle Mountaineers, founded in 1906. This "association of kindred spirits who love the out-of-doors and to whom the wildwood, the flowery mead and the mountain fastness afford a rest, a solace, and an inspiration" sponsored summer outings that included climbs of Mount Olympus, Mount Baker, and Mount Rainier. Its members included Seattle school women, such as Winona Bailey and Lulie Nettleton, both of whom made the 1907 trek up Mount Olympus.[29]

Regardless of their motives for coming to Seattle during the century's first decade, women teachers would have been caught up in the euphoria and excitement surrounding the Alaska Yukon Pacific Exposition, staged in 1909 to celebrate the city's growing stature. The AYP brought throngs of people to town and its displays and exhibits widened residents' horizons. The school board endorsed the AYP and even allowed teachers to voluntarily attend Children's Day with their pupils.[30] Surely teachers responded and joined in the festivities.

The AYP capped the city's transition from frontier status. Seattle would retain much of its 1910 profile for decades; Janice Reiff's study of the city's social structure underscores this stability. She concludes, "Although the city in 1910 was half the size . . . in fundamental ways, [it] looked very much like Seattle in 1980."[31] It looked even more like the Seattle of 1950, when students of those first-decade teachers and their pre-1940 colleagues assumed the city's leadership.

In the afterglow of the exposition, Frank Cooper's Progressive programs continued to attract teachers and offer opportunities for professional growth and success. The teachers' superintendent himself would have been a draw; he happily credited "whatever excellence the schools may have achieved" to the spirit, work, and cooperation of the corps of teachers.[32]

The city itself became more attractive. More or less in accord with a 1903 plan developed for Seattle by the Olmsted Brothers, work had begun on the creation of parkways that would link current and future parks and green belts. By 1913, twenty-five miles of improved roadway had been realized along the estimated fifty-mile projected route.[33]

A woman teacher thinking of relocating would see freedom and opportunity in Washington's passage of women's suffrage in 1910. It had been a fifty-six-year struggle, but in November 1910, men in Washington voted 52,299 to 29,676 to make theirs the fifth state in the union to grant women citizens the right to vote in all elections.[34]

Adella Parker took part in the politics of progressivism and suffrage; she had moved into the new Broadway High School building in 1902 and continued to teach civics, history, and economics there until 1922. A graduate of the University of Washington's Law School, she fiercely supported women's suffrage and openly advocated Progressive politics. While still disenfranchised, with her father as something of a voting surrogate partner, she embarked on a crusade for municipal ownership of utilities and drafted the amendment to the city charter providing for recall of elected officials. Adella Parker helped shape the thinking of a growing number of the city's high school graduates who themselves became Seattle teachers. Of the women high school teachers hired in the second decade of the century, 36 percent had graduated from Broadway.[35]

Railroads played a vital role in the settlement of the Northwest and especially in the migration of single women to Seattle. The Chicago, Milwaukee & St. Paul came into Seattle in 1909, joining the Great Northern and the Northern Pacific. In addition to bringing them to Puget Sound, the three lines allowed teachers to maintain their ties to home and family. Both Union Station and the depot on King Street hummed with activity at school vacation time. Teachers headed for hometowns in northern tier states, the upper Midwest, and elsewhere; they made connections in Chicago. Perhaps apocryphal, school district lore credits a railroad timetable with setting school schedules. Today districts may dismiss classes at noon on the day before a vacation, but Seattle adopted the practice early. The Northern Pacific's North Coast Limited departed daily for Chicago at 4:30 in the afternoon; teachers were intent on catching that train.[36]

Renewed by vacationing with families and perhaps enjoying the advantages of older and larger cities, in the years before World War I, teachers returned to a city rapidly acquiring more urban amenities. Seattle continued to advance as a center of culture that would appeal to an educated woman. Popular entertainment included traveling theater productions and the best vaudeville available; a new entertainment medium would soon produce a bevy of movie houses. There was notable development both in music and the visual arts.[37] In 1891 Seattle women had formed the Ladies Musical Club, which presented monthly concerts. In 1903, the Seattle Symphony Orchestra had debuted to appreciative support. The Seattle Fine Arts Society, founded in 1908, together with the Fine Arts Department at the University of Washington, nurtured and encouraged local artists.[38]

In 1914, Nellie Cornish further expanded prospects for the arts when she opened the Cornish School. She began with the teaching of piano but soon included instrumental and vocal instruction. An added dance curriculum benefited from interest generated in 1917 by the modern dance pioneers Ruth St. Denis and Ted Shawn with the Denishawn troupe, which was held over for an additional week.[39]

The opportunity to attend performances by such avant-garde artists as St. Denis and Shawn would have thrilled Eva Jurgensohn or perhaps even inspired the direction her teaching career would take. In the spring of 1917, Miss Jurgensohn, a Washington native and graduate of Bellingham Normal School, was teaching physical education at Bagley School in the Green Lake area. In 1919 she began a four-year stint in the administrative office, and, when Garfield High School opened in 1923, she moved in to create a strong program in dance and physical education. Jurgensohn's reputation as an authority on dance—and the respect of colleagues and students—endured until her retirement in 1961.[40]

The Seattle Way directed teachers and principals toward goals commensurate with Progressive values—democracy, patriotism, obedience, hard work, and civic responsibility. In addition to their attending school "assiduously," Cooper wanted elementary students to achieve academically: to read intelligently, write legibly, spell correctly, calculate readily, and express themselves "clearly and truthfully." He wanted them to "take perplexities and hardships as they come and make the best of them. . . . cultivate self-denial and a spirit of helpfulness . . . be heedful of behests— Whether they come from school, home, country or conscience. . . . [and] esteem what is right, and to do it."[41]

Adhering to the Progressive philosophy of the whole child, in 1908 Cooper added a program of medical inspection in the schools, which he also saw as a way to retain students and improve school attendance. By 1914, the board hired Ira C. Brown, a former army physician experienced in dealing with large-group health concerns, under whose leadership the program encompassed the health of teachers as well as students; the district established a downtown clinic and built a school nurse program that reached into all the elementary schools.[42]

Education Progressives held that all children had the right to instruction and to proceed to "the highest development possible for them," including those outside the mainstream. Early in his tenure, Cooper created schools for exceptional children, with women teachers and principals. A school for the deaf came first. What would become the Child Study Laboratory followed next, at Cascade School, just north of downtown; it began on a small scale to work with students whose mentality was, in the era's terminology, "below the normal and yet above the imbecile type." In cooperation with the juvenile court, separate parental schools for boys and girls were established for serious delinquents. The district supplied teachers for children whose physical disabilities confined them in the new Orthopedic Hospital. So-called auxiliary teachers worked in three selected schools with students who had for whatever reason "fallen behind pupils of their own age and need especial attention."[43] Many of the interwar cohort of teachers served as auxiliary teachers at some point in their careers.

The annual Teachers Institute, which survived well past World War II relatively unchanged, brought all teachers together each autumn for orientation and in-service work sessions. Cooper saw it as a chance "to give stimulus and infuse ardor for work by means of one or two inspirational lectures . . . [to] the whole body of teachers." For their part, teachers saw this singular time when the entire corps came together as the opportunity for reunion—to greet current and former colleagues and renew long-standing friendships.[44]

After five years at the helm, Cooper had induced the school board to revise salary schedules. Teachers and principals would receive an annual salary based on two hundred days of service and payable in twelve installments. The July and August "vacation" salary would be based on a percentage of total days served. The matter of sick leave, which had been discussed by primary teachers at their March meeting in 1897, also received Cooper's attention. The board voted to allow "one-half salary for absence from duty on account of sickness up to twenty days" in any year. The superintendent considered it "justifiable both for humane and administrative reasons."[45]

Not content with that provision, in 1911 Cooper asked the teachers themselves to address the matter of sick leave. They responded by forming the Seattle Teachers' Association to deal with "not only pecuniary benefits for the sick, but mutual acquaintance and professional betterment as well." The STA soon had funds sufficient for teachers "to receive $10.00 per week during enforced illness."[46]

The 1907 schedule established five salary levels based on years of service. A brief flirtation with a form of merit pay, undertaken by the board against Cooper's advice, ended badly when teachers awarded the bonus learned "that conditions were such that [the board] could not, at this time, grant it." Those 1907 changes also established a salary differential between grade and high school teaching, a point of irritation and contention that would fester until 1928.[47]

The November 1912 establishment of the Seattle Grade Teachers' Club, which will be discussed in detail later, added a persistent voice to the marathon struggle over salary. At countless meetings of the school board from that point on, the club requested increases or amelioration of other inequities in the district pay schedule. But the board reiterated that it "could not see its way to grant increase of salaries, owing to the general financial condition of the District," an oft-repeated mantra.[48]

In 1912, as teachers strove for professional recognition, Arthur C. Perry, Jr., wrote *The Status of the Teacher,* in which he opined that the "salary factor" was a minor one in determining professional status. He went on to say, "No man or woman of sanity would for a moment think of entering the teaching vocation as a method of reaching financial prosperity. . . . teaching, like virtue, is its own reward."[49] Theorists and salary improvements made since 1900 aside, job candidates continued to specifically address money in their applications.

In 1910, after teaching in her hometown of Erie, Pennsylvania, for ten years, thirty-one-year-old Etta Minnig decided to move West. Holding a permanent certificate, she requested $840 per year as a starting salary. Reliable figures do not consistently appear in school district records until 1922, by which time Etta Minnig earned $1,950 teaching sixth grade in a school soon to be renamed for a pioneer in education—Horace Mann. After fourteen years as Van Asselt School's head teacher, a category that included the responsibilities of a principal as well as a teacher, in 1937–38 she received $2,700. Her salary remained the same until she retired in June of 1943, a veteran of forty-three years in the classroom.[50]

Ella Albright had also said she would "not accept less than $840" when she applied in 1909. An Iowa native and graduate of Council Bluffs High School, she had prepared for teaching with "Part of one summer at Chautauqua, N.Y." and correspondence work at Northwestern University.

Cooper placed high priority on experience, and most teachers he brought to Seattle came with more professional education than the national mean for urban districts. Ella Albright's scant training must have been offset by glowing letters of recommendation from her ten years of experience. She later took courses at the University of Washington and completed the two-year course at Bellingham Normal School. The record does not show her salary at the time she resigned for health reasons in 1946, but in 1931 she earned only $2,300, and Depression-era reductions would cut that. Miss Albright taught throughout the interwar years; she died in 1947, just short of her sixtieth birthday.[51]

Experienced teachers found Seattle's salaries competitive, but the prized figure of $840 did not become the minimum salary for elementary teachers until May 23, 1917. In December 1918, substitutes received the minimum $840 plus a $216 bonus, paid to help meet the rising wartime cost of living. Salaries of new elementary teachers elected that month ranged from $1,092 to $1,320, but inflation and still rising costs more than consumed any increases.[52]

If teaching, like virtue, is its own reward, virtue, like teaching, was a school board concern in early twentieth-century Seattle. Although the city provided them anonymity in the larger context, in the network of neighborhood grade schools, teachers were well-known and visible to the immediate community. They were expected to dress properly, live in acceptable places, and radiate respectability. Smoking and drinking in public were definite taboos. Parents had high expectations; as the historian Bryce Nelson puts it, "They wanted their teachers virtuous, dedicated, and on a pedestal."[53]

Many teachers lived in downtown rooming houses; some moved into residential hotels as those evolved. An acceptable domicile in 1914 would have been run by an "aunt and widowed mother. . . . ladies to the core," and the rooming house would have been "respectable and impeccable." But the school board was inordinately concerned. In September 1913, it addressed the topic of "Teachers—Place of Abode" by directing Cooper "to convey to the teaching force of the city, the desire of the Board of Directors that in so far as possible, the teachers secure rooms and board in the private homes of the city."[54]

The board had the right to dismiss teachers for cause but seldom exercised it. In a sample of 205 women grade teachers hired between 1900 and 1920, two were dismissed, but on grounds more likely related to teaching performance. One of them, dropped in 1927, had teaching evaluations ranging from "doubtful" to satisfactory and back to fair.[55]

The morals of students also came under the board's protective scrutiny from time to time. Cooper "thought [his] staff was doing a good job of 'giving pupils right motives for good conduct,'" but the board worried about outside factors, and in 1909, moved into the area of student activities. It decreed that a small girls club started by the YWCA at Broadway High School should become a schoolwide organization without the outside influence of the Y. Over the next three years, responding to what Cooper termed "a well defined need," the board voted to designate a teacher to serve as "an adviser of girl students, along general welfare lines" and to "give two or three periods a day for such work in the B'way High School."[56] Elizabeth Rowell, Broadway history department head, first had that responsibility; the head French teacher, Lila Lawrence, soon took over.

The Seattle Federation of Women's Clubs quickly saw the importance of a girls adviser, and the social, educational, and vocational aspects of her work. The federation, which enjoyed a cordial relationship with the school board, urged the members to appoint an adviser in all the high schools. The High School Women's League, the teachers' advocacy group, made the same request. Soon all high schools had girls clubs and girls advisers.[57]

Margaret McCarney, who taught biology at Franklin, was the first girls adviser there. In her view, the girls club's concerns related to "philanthropy, social life, athletics, indeed anything in which any girl might be interested," but its chief purpose was to maintain "the democratic spirit of the school."[58] These aims and purposes would remain throughout the interwar years and beyond.

Seattle had reached its full physical expansion in 1912. The center of the city shifted north from Pioneer Place toward the university's former site on Fifth Avenue between Union and University streets, where "department stores, smaller shops, and hotels [mingled with] office buildings and apartment houses." Population growth continued, and improvements, alterations, and demographic changes marked the years remaining until the United States entered World War I.[59]

The outbreak of that war in August 1914 pushed Seattle's economy to boom proportions much as the Alaska gold rush had seventeen years earlier; the cost of living rose and the atmosphere changed. Soon after the assassination in Sarajevo, the school board addressed the matter of the war and the classroom. It directed that "teachers in the Seattle Public Schools should not refer to the questions involved in the European War."[60] But in the next three years, as America turned away from neutrality, public sentiment shifted, and Seattle's schools experienced great pressure and traumatizing change.

As one who was then a pupil at Warren Avenue School put it, even a boy "could not miss the excitement in the air after . . . war broke out in Europe. It seemed as if the newspapers issued extras on the hour, with black headlines two inches high." By 1916, "old and new shipyards south of town were coming to life." Many trained shipbuilders and their families moved from the East Coast, and rumor had it that they received "fabulous wages of seven to ten dollars a day."[61]

Women continued to move to Seattle to teach the children of workers who flocked to jobs in the shipyards and other defense-related enterprises. The school board raised "the question of men teachers for service in grade schools, and . . . point[ed] out the desirability of employing men teachers" in what constituted a female bastion. In 1912 it had considered a proposal "to establish a retirement system as a way to attract and hold men," but no program materialized.[62] The board seemed not to know it, but women teachers had always been as concerned about retirement prospects as any man.

An earlier legislative attempt to create a teacher retirement program had been thwarted at the polls in referendum, but during the 1917 session the legislature granted larger school districts the right to establish local retirement systems. The legislation required a school board to consider written petitions for such a fund if signed by a majority of teachers and required a board majority to establish the fund. Within two months of the legislation's passage, Cooper presented a petition signed by 87 percent of the teaching corps.[63] Although it provided for an annual annuity of only $480 after thirty years of teaching, the first retirement system would have been a significant draw for the professional teacher.[64] For this and other reasons, the city and its schools continued to attract women for the same reasons they had in the past.

The war decade saw the return of more of Seattle's own high school graduates to teach; 5 percent of the grade teachers hired had attended Broadway. A Lincoln graduate who came home, Ella Fahey began her long career in 1919 at Jefferson Elementary in West Seattle, after teaching two years in Grays Harbor County. She transferred twice before settling in for fourteen years with first-graders at Ravenna School; in 1948 she moved to Laurelhurst, where she remained until she retired on July 15, 1964, a sixty-eight-year-old veteran of forty-five years in Seattle classrooms.[65]

The Buckley sisters represent the family migration pattern. Nellie Buckley began teaching in the old Central School in 1903, with a certificate from Minnesota's Winona State Normal School. She took a leave of absence for the 1908–1909 school year to complete her bachelor's degree at the University of Washington, and when Queen Anne High School opened that fall she was on its first mathematics faculty. Her younger sister, Catherine, a graduate of the University of Minnesota, applied to join her in 1917. Catherine began at Ballard High School, also teaching mathematics; she moved to newly opened Garfield High School in 1925, and stayed there through retirement in 1948. Nellie retired from Queen Anne in 1937.[66]

Experience continued to count heavily in the school district's hiring: 72 percent had taught five to ten years, down slightly from 78 percent of first-decade hires. They, too, were older when they applied, with 34 percent over the age of thirty. When they made application, 69 percent lived within Washington or in the Pacific Northwest; an additional 9 percent lived elsewhere in the West. Normal schools again provide a clue about the origins: Michigan, Minnesota, and Wisconsin again had trained the largest percentage (33), but 12 percent had come from schools in other eastern or midwestern states. Washington's own normal schools had trained 32 percent, up from 10 percent of Frank Cooper's first-decade recruits.[67]

These grade teachers had slightly shorter tenures than their predecessors: 41 percent stayed in the district for twenty-one to thirty years, and 34 percent stayed longer. Of those who resigned before retirement,

26 percent gave no reason, but a vastly increased number, 48 percent, resigned to be married.

Sample figures for high school teachers hired in the decade show that, like the grade teachers, about two-thirds applied from within Washington and the Pacific Northwest. Underscoring the importance of the University of Washington to the city's public school teaching corps, 43 percent had received bachelor's degrees there, and 11 percent would eventually hold a master's degree. No one taught less than three years; 76 percent taught twenty-one years or more.

Frank Cooper's Seattle Way gained further credibility with professionally motivated women in 1912 with the appointment of Almina George as assistant superintendent. Born December 15, 1870, Almina George graduated from a New York normal school and studied further in the Midwest and in Germany. Before serving as president of the Washington Education Association in 1919, she had played a major role in the formation of the National Council of Administrative Women in Education, which elected her its first president. In a 1922 administrative reorganization following Cooper's resignation, she became head of the Department of Intermediate Grades. She continued in that role until her retirement in June of 1931.[68]

The 1916 election of Anna Louise Strong to the school board finally catapulted a woman into the forefront of school district politics after previous failed campaigns by others. A graduate of Oberlin College who earned her Ph.D. in philosophy from the University of Chicago in 1908, Anna Louise Strong had directed popular Progressive Era child welfare exhibits, both in New York for the Russell Sage Foundation and in Washington, D.C., for the Children's Bureau. In 1915 she joined the Anti-Preparedness League and arranged antiwar rallies in the Midwest. That same year she came to Seattle, following her pacifist father, the Reverend Sidney Strong, pastor of Queen Anne Congregational Church.[69] She was elected to the school board just as political winds shifted; the school election the next year returned the archconservative Ebenezer Shorrock to the board by a decisive margin and signaled that "public sentiment . . . is inclining at this time toward a very marked conservatism."[70]

Patriotism, that prime underpinning of progressivism, took an ugly turn toward nativism when the United States entered the war in April 1917. Anna Louise Strong's antiwar stance and her increasing defense of known radicals made her an easy target for reactionary critics.[71] At polling places on election day, her opponents circulated petitions for her recall. The following March, voters recalled her by a vote of 27,163 to 21,447.[72] She promptly appeared before the school board to request that a woman be selected to replace her. Other groups present also asked that a woman be appointed but insisted that, unlike Strong, "the woman should be a mother, and preferably one with children in the schools, whose patriotism is absolutely unquestioned." On April 22, the men on the board named Mrs. Evangeline C. Harper to fill the vacancy until the next regular school election.[73]

Evangeline Harper had served as president of the Federation of Women's Clubs in 1914 and cast one of her earliest school board votes in the cause of equal salary for women. Her male colleagues had proposed offering a bonus to dissuade men from leaving the classroom for more lucrative war industry jobs; they had dismissed a unanimous petition from women high school teachers to receive the same bonus. On May 29, 1918, the board authorized the men's bonus with Evangeline Harper's the lone dissenting vote.[74]

Nativist critics had other objectives and targets within the schools, from ridding the district of teachers deemed not supportive of the war to banning the teaching of German as a foreign language. Teacher loyalty had already come into question. Cooper fought to retain German language classes as essential for college requirements, but anti-German sentiment intensified; finally he submitted to pressure and in April 1918 agreed to drop German from the curriculum.[75]

The well of good feeling that Cooper had maintained in the district soon appeared to be poisoned. In July, a delegation appeared at a board meeting to "urge the Board to make a careful search and examination of all text books used in the schools, and to eliminate any books that were found to contain German propaganda." This demand reopened a 1914 controversy over replacing outmoded history texts. Those that Cooper had recommended, Ginn and Company's *Outlines of European History*, "were alleged to be pro-German and the patriotism of the authors was suspect." The school board not only bypassed Cooper in textbook selection but also intruded into personnel matters, dismissing six teachers in a surge of war-related nativism.[76]

The First World War, a turning point that would define the rest of the century, received near total public support from Seattle's school women. Some took leaves of absence to serve in various support capacities both in this country and abroad. Those who served with the Red Cross and YMCA in France went with the enthusiastic backing of their colleagues. When Adelaide Pollock, principal of West Queen Anne School, left with the Red Cross, her fellow principals sent her off with "a big purse" and special gifts "for the boys in France." Others, considered "lucky enough to be sent to work in France," went as canteen workers and recreation directors for the Y.[77] Blanche Wenner, English and oral expression teacher at Broadway High School since 1908, served in France, "giving talks and coaching plays put on for soldiers" by the Y's entertainment service. Long after she retired in 1954, she remained a member of the Women's Overseas Service League.[78]

Among those recruited for service on the home front, Ellen Powell Dabney, supervisor of home economics, "was called to Washington D.C. to assist" in the food conservation program. A War Department commission sponsored a venture known as War Camp Community Service. Its programs included organized sports and games, social hours, and dances, and drew teachers such as Eva Jurgensohn, the physical education teacher, into active wartime service. As late as the summer of 1919, requests came to use school buildings and to engage "the services of Miss Jurgensohn . . . to assist in community recreation work for girls."[79]

The Red Cross benefited enormously from Seattle volunteers, and teachers did their part. Lincoln High School's Gertrude Streator and Queen Anne's Winona Bailey headed the Mountaineers' Red Cross activities. They worked with its "committee on sphagnum dressing at the University of Washington. . . . [where] sphagnum [was] made up into pads . . . [and] shipped directly to the American Red Cross in France." Among other instances of home front support, the Grade Teachers' Club voted to forgo its annual luncheon in the spring of 1917 and donate to the Red Cross the money that would have been spent on those festivities.[80]

Students were coopted into the war effort as well. Ellen Dabney reported that "approximately six thousand girls in the Home Economics [classes] . . . are able and anxious to do their 'bit' of patriotic service by sewing and knitting;" one project was making "European Orphan Clothing." Students in Bessie Bankhead's French classes at West Seattle High School "adopted" a French orphan, creating an ongoing correspondence with residents of one French town.[81]

A grade school pupil before 1920, Mary Desimone recalled decades later the war-related observances at Colman School under Anna B. Kane's principalship: "We would all bring flowers . . . [to] make wreaths . . . for the soldiers. . . . And we had a ceremony every Memorial Day." Few Seattle schoolrooms had displayed American flags until the school laws of 1915 required that "appropriate flag exercises be held in every school, at least once each week." The decree of the school board made previously rare flag saluting a daily ritual that endured. Students from throughout the interwar years recalled that the school day always began with the flag salute.[82]

Some women who came to Seattle to teach after the war had served in Europe. Irene B. Taake had taken a leave from her teaching job in Des Moines, Iowa, "to go into Y.M.C.A. work in France." She applied with the Seattle district while visiting the city in the fall of 1919, listing among her references the Y's Women's Department in New York City. First assigned to teach math and science at West Seattle High School, she could have shared her experiences with the French class that had adopted the orphan in France. She later taught at both Lincoln and Roosevelt, and while traveling and studying on sabbatical leave in the fall of 1938, the second world war of her lifetime erupted. She resigned in September 1943 for "other work." Perhaps American troops abroad had once again propelled Irene Taake into war-related endeavors.[83]

Alma Hawkins returned from France in 1919 to teach a few years in Kirksville, Missouri. The Bellingham High School graduate with a B.A. from Cornell returned to the Northwest and in the fall of 1927 began at Seattle's Roosevelt High School, where she taught French and German until retiring in 1960 at age seventy. On her Seattle application she listed among additional advantages, "A year's residence in France [and] Four summer schools of graduate work." Former Roosevelt students describe a teacher who was "very prim, very prim." Fifty years later some could still recite her entire opening dialogue in French that had started her every class. They had liked her: "We learned, no question, [but] she wasn't above the little anecdotal things." One anecdote related to her serving as an interpreter in General Pershing's office in France. "We got her . . . talking about being interviewed over the telephone . . . in French [when] . . . she simply could not figure out what the person was saying." That faux pas impressed one student, who has remained certain that "she was actually Pershing's [personal] interpreter."[84]

At the cessation of conflict on November 11, 1918, the school district declared a holiday, and in 1920 the board ordered "appropriate exercises" in the schools to commemorate the day.[85] Genuine patriotism and love of country inspired women teachers, who for more than twenty years observed each Armistice Day in their Seattle classrooms. Students joined them in standing for a moment of silence to mark "the eleventh hour of the eleventh day of the eleventh month."[86]

The Armistice brought peace on the battlefield, but fear that bolshevism would sweep across the Atlantic helped keep Seattle in turmoil a while longer. War industries had bolstered the city's economy, but teachers' salaries did not keep pace with the rise in the cost of living, and the board's decision to grant bonuses to male teachers created an open rift in the corps. In a city known for radical labor activity, industrial and labor relations smoldered and flared into strikes on several fronts.

At various times from 1917 on, steamboatmen, telephone operators, laundry workers, meatpackers, and streetcar workers, among others, struck. But it was in the shipyards that the greatest conflict originated. With the end of the war, the loss of jobs and high wages drove workers toward the first general strike in the history of the United States. Angry shipyard workers, 35,000 strong, walked out on January 21, 1919; organized labor succeeded in shutting down virtually the whole city on Thursday, February 6; the general strike began to fall apart on Saturday and was essentially over by Tuesday, February 11. It had caused considerable disruption, fear, and anxiety among the middle class. Anna Louise Strong had further fueled the fear of bolshevism on the day before the strike with an unsettling editorial in Seattle labor's *Union Record* that declared, "We are undertaking the most tremendous move ever made by LABOR in this country, . . . we are starting on a road that leads—NO ONE KNOWS WHERE!"[87]

Anticipating a long walkout, Cooper had told the board, "If the schools are operated, which I think they should be, provision will have to be made for the transportation of teachers who live at a distance from their schools." The board expected no strike trouble from middle-class women teachers, but the unionized school custodians were a concern (fortunately, the streetcar men were among the first to return to work). The board was determined to keep the schools open. Although Cooper was confident that many custodians would stay on the job with "proper protection," on February 7 all six high schools closed; four of the only five elementary schools that remained open were in middle-class neighborhoods.[88]

The postwar influenza epidemic proved to be of greater and longer-lasting consequence for Seattle's teachers than the general strike. Public facilities were closed in late fall of 1918, and the December school board election received little attention. An alarmingly low voter turnout produced a sea change in the school district's course. As Bryce Nelson points out, that election heralded "the virtual abandonment of the board by socially prominent progressives." The reactionary and ungenerous trend that the board set during the war gained strength. New board members received support from a faction that, flush with patriotic excess and antiradical fervor, remained intent on restricting the schools and cutting expenses. They "did not share the pre-war progressive spirit, that had considered schools as community facilities to be used 'by the people.'"[89]

The effects of the changed district philosophy were immediate: teacher salaries came under fire. In February 1919, the red scare claimed a victim from the teaching corps—Charles Niederhauser, a popular history teacher at West Seattle High School. His colleagues, 54 percent of them women, stood behind him; students and parents signed petitions in his behalf; and Frank Cooper defended him, but to no avail. On motion of the holdover reactionary, Ebenezer Shorrock, the board dismissed Niederhauser soon after the general strike.[90]

Even as the handwriting on the wall became clearer every day, Cooper kept to the Progressive course of the Seattle Way. Continuing as an advocate for his teachers, in March he recommended raising the minimum starting salary from $840 to $1,080 for grade teachers with two years' experience and from $1,020 to $1,230 for high school teachers with one year behind them.[91] His 1921 report to the board, with a nod to the Niederhauser episode, reiterated his belief that the purpose of geography, history, and civics remained "the development of a social being intelligently and sympathetically interested in his fellow-men and in the life about him."

But the postwar board heeded the dictates of a succession of tax-cutting groups—the Voters Information League, the Tax Reduction Council, and the Chamber of Commerce's Bureau of Taxation. The first of these came into being in 1921. Allied with the Chamber of Commerce, the VIL worked to force tax reduction and took the lead in forming the Tax Reduction Council, an amalgam of some fifty organizations representing a broad spectrum of interests in the city. The council would virtually dictate the school district budget. The Chamber of Commerce's own Bureau of Taxation spoke for such businessmen as Shorrock, school board member and president of Northwest Trust and Safe Deposit Company.[92]

The school election of 1920 cemented a board majority dedicated to dismantling most of Cooper's Progressive program. This group determined that

> urban schooling would offer a core of academic classes, and that was all. Those students who could attend, stay, and appreciate such an experience were to do so. Others were to leave school and do other things—which was not the business of the state through an agency like the schools.[93]

Class and administrative staff size, extracurricular activities, curriculum "frills," and teacher salaries came under relentless attack. The first cuts targeted maintenance workers' salaries and eliminated gardening, manual training, and home economics in the elementary schools. After hearing from the likes of the Voters Information League, the board recommended to Cooper "that the number of pupils per room be increased . . . [some] seventh and eighth grades be combined . . . and that in the high schools all vacant periods for department heads" be eliminated. Class size in many grade schools already approached forty pupils, and in spring of 1921, the board voted to hire no new teachers and, in an unprecedented move, to lay off some. The Tax Reduction Council issued a call to replace Cooper with a younger person.[94]

Less than a year later, the embattled Cooper refuted the VIL's suggestions for "improvements that could be made in educational methods in use in the schools"; he corrected comparisons with other cities and pointed out difficulties inherent in expanding the high school teaching day to eight periods.[95] On March 17, he did resign.

Cooper had defended his system and fought to the end for his faculty. But the board voted in June to reduce teachers' annual salaries by $150 and to make further reductions in the corps. It reduced the number of supervisors and special programs for the developmentally disabled, the deaf, and the blind. Cooper's successor, Thomas Cole, was charged with instituting a 25 percent rollback of all salary increases made since 1918.[96] Struggles over budget and salaries occupied the school district for the rest of the decade, leading Seattle teachers to undertake their first serious attempt to organize a union.

2 / 1920 and Beyond

Nationwide, World War I had virtually dismantled the Progressive movement's prewar agenda. In Seattle, a distorted and radical patriotism had seized otherwise sensible and restrained citizens, and by 1917, a divided school board disagreed on the role of the schools.[1] The reactionary faction gained control by 1920 and claimed Frank Cooper as its victim. Yet the Seattle Way and its spirit were sustained for another two decades by women teachers who had taught in Seattle since early in the century and now had as classroom colleagues many younger women who had been their students.

Interwar Seattle settled into comfortable stability even as its economy bordered on stagnation. The symphony languished, but there were some cultural developments: the little theater movement blossomed; a young Mark Tobey led the way toward international recognition in the visual arts; the number of movie theaters multiplied; and the city boasted the second commercial radio station in the nation when KJR went on the air in 1920.[2]

There seemed to be great promise for the New Woman in politics with the 1926 election of Bertha Knight Landes, the first woman mayor of a major city in the United States. She had come to public office by way of the presidency of the Federation of Women's Clubs, with which the Grade Teachers' Club had affiliated soon after its founding. An active participant in Parent Teacher Associations at Lincoln and University Heights schools, the mayor was no stranger to the city's teachers. But her support of such Progressive measures as enforcement of prohibition laws and municipal ownership of utilities led to her defeat for reelection in 1928.[3]

Dormant stability would hardly seem desirable, but lack of change in the city and its established neighborhoods had a positive side. In writing *Seattle, Past to Present,* Roger Sale interviewed Seattleites who came of age between the wars and found them agreeing that it "was a wonderful place in which to grow up." They inherited Progressive Era neighborhoods, parks, and boulevards and an urban milieu that was "simultaneously reassuring and exciting" during those great years of Seattle's high schools.[4] The optimistic women who taught in the public schools maintained stability even as they widened their students' horizons.

The gender composition of the nation's teaching force changed between the world wars; by 1925 the percentage of men in teaching had begun to rise. "The teaching profession was one area where women lost ground . . . [their total number] fell from 85 percent to 78 percent between 1920 and 1940." In Seattle, however, statistics for grade teachers show an increase for women in the twenties, from 92 percent to 94; nationally, by 1930, men composed 10.5 percent of grade teachers. In Seattle high schools, the percentage of women dropped very little in ten years—from 63 percent in 1920 to 62 in 1930.[5]

Why would women continue to seek teaching jobs in Seattle? The district's reputation as a good place for a young teacher to build a career continued to attract them. It motivated Velma Laccoarce to apply in 1926, as she finished her first year of teaching in Kellogg, Idaho. She wrote:

> I understand that you do not require two years' experience for cadet teachers. . . . I enjoy my work in Kellogg, but since I shall probably make teaching my profession, I should like to be in a larger system where there is a greater opportunity for properly guided growth and development along educational lines. So far as I have been able to ascertain, Seattle has one of the best systems for such progress.

That fall the graduate of Lewiston Normal School began teaching upper grades at E. C. Hughes School in West Seattle. Fortunately, she received a salary of $1,260 rather than the meager amount paid to cadets. With the professional encouragement she had sought, she completed her B.A.

at the University of Washington in 1930 and remained at Hughes until resigning to be married in June of 1935.[6]

Seattle had created its cadet teacher program in 1917—a rare exception to the rule of hiring experienced teachers only—to forestall a possible wartime teacher shortage. Perhaps the school board's desire to lower costs was another motivation. The state's normal schools submitted lists of their most promising graduates from which the district chose its cadets. Originally called "novitiate teachers," they taught their first year at austere and frugal salaries, $780 in 1918 and only $1,200 in 1935.

Frank Cooper's special classes for the less able student continued to attract women experienced in working with those pupils. Having heard "some interesting things" about such programs, and with a desire "to make [her] home in Seattle with [her] father who has settled there permanently," Marjorie Starks applied in 1925. She held a B.A. from the University of Missouri and had taught "low ungraded" in Kansas City since 1922. She taught such classes in two Seattle elementary schools before moving into Ballard High School's special classes. Her career reflects the trend toward shorter tenures and more resignations to marry; she resigned to be married in June of 1933.[7]

A sense of obligation to family, compelling among many single women, continued to lead some to Seattle. Sara Keegan, teaching in her hometown of Spokane in 1927, applied to the Seattle School District that April. A graduate of West Valley High School, she had completed the normal course in Cheney. The state's normal schools maintained close ties with alumnae, and the placement office director in Cheney was pleased to report that

> her reason for wishing to change systems is because she has lately lost her father and the Mother is moving to Seattle to be with a son. Miss Keegan is an attractive young woman with an excellent scholarship record here. I can strongly recommend her.

She did not let him down. Five years of evaluations from demanding principals at both Bryant and Ravenna schools show her as a "very good" to "superior" teacher. Another who left teaching for marriage, Sara Keegan resigned at the end of the 1932–33 school year.[8]

Nepotism had not reared its ugly head in Seattle, and the desire to join a sibling in the corps remained a motive for many women. Kellogg, Idaho, lost a principal in 1925 when Estelle Erickson joined the Seattle corps, writing, "I would much prefer being in a larger system. . . . My brother, Howard E. Erickson is teaching at the Adams school in Seattle. We would both like very much to be together." A graduate of Cheney Normal School, she had taught at Reardon in eastern Washington before moving to Kellogg. Her first evaluation in Seattle underscored her "progressive attitude among the pupils." She transferred to Laurelhurst School in 1936, where she was a favorite in the community and stayed until she retired in 1964. Her marriage to E. Mervin Flohr in June of 1946 occurred three years after wartime teacher shortages led the district to hire married women on a temporary basis. She was among the first to apply for permanent status when that became possible in 1948.[9]

The twenties brought social changes described by one scholar as catching teachers

> between nineteenth-century-middle-class standards of behavior and an expanding mass consumer culture that was mounting a strong challenge to the old mores. . . . films and magazines were presenting a new, sexually and socially "liberated" woman, who was not constrained as to the clothes, hairstyle, and makeup she wore and who had the freedom to smoke, drink, or dance as she pleased.

Somewhat paradoxically, advertising's commercial appeals also reinforced a homemaker stereotype that militated against the young woman who aspired to a profession. Still, many who began their long careers in Seattle in the 1920s emulated their nineteenth-century counterparts who had moved into teaching as an alternative to "woman's 'normal life course' of remaining at home until marriage and delaying or forgoing marriage in the process."[10]

The previously greater ratio of men to women in the city no longer existed, but one 1929 study of teacher supply and demand in Washington State asserted that the West "still has its lure, not only from the standpoint of climate and adventure, but in the female mind, of apparently superior matrimonial possibilities." Indeed, the number of resignations for marriage increased in the 1920s. Because "the immigrant teacher [was] one of the large sources of supply," the study recommended a policy of "restriction on the basis of quality" and protection of teachers with in-state normal certificates.[11]

Quality had always been a priority in Seattle's hiring considerations, and the number of the city's own high school graduates with in-state degrees and normal certificates continued to increase in the district. Some of these women had very long careers in their hometown.

Ruth Ostle was in the graduating class at West Seattle High School in 1919. With her two-year certificate from Bellingham Normal School, she followed the usual career pattern: after four years of teaching in small towns in eastern Washington (Harper and Grandview) she returned to the west side of the Cascades, teaching in Edmonds. She applied to Seattle in 1927 and again the next year, accepting a midyear appointment in January 1929. She went to Alki School in the fall of 1932 and retired from there in 1968; she had devoted forty of her sixty-eight years to teaching in the Seattle schools.[12]

The city's high schools, too, reclaimed their own as teachers. Jessie Orrell graduated in 1917 from Queen Anne, where such teachers as Jessie Lackey and the legendary Nellie Buckley had fostered her interest in mathematics. Majoring in math at the University of Washington, she earned a bachelor's degree and election to Phi Beta Kappa in 1921. She taught physics, algebra, plane and solid geometry, and general science for six years in Ferndale, near Bellingham. In September 1927, she began forty-one years at Lincoln High School, adding trigonometry, mathematical analysis, and calculus to her repertoire. She received superlative evaluations and in 1953 moved into the counseling ranks.[13]

By the time Jessie Orrell returned to her hometown, Seattle's teachers had experienced five years without Frank Cooper in the superintendent's office. Thomas Cole, concerned with efficiency in school management, fit the mold of the new "administrative Progressive." In 1925, he persuaded a still conservative board to reinstate the teaching of German in the high schools. He created the Department of Research, which used statistical analysis to reassess much that had been the heart of Cooper's philosophy.[14] Grade teachers anticipated retrenchment, and after a year as superintendent, Cole addressed them in regard to curriculum, saying, "We can well afford to sacrifice quantity for quality."[15]

Other changes in the 1920s can be traced at least in part to the severe budgetary restrictions, the mania for efficiency, and changing trends in education. The cadet teacher program expanded well beyond its early scope; new graduates of normal schools presented a pool of promising but inexperienced teachers from which the district could draw. Two newly opened high schools—Roosevelt in 1922, and Garfield in 1923—almost immediately became overcrowded. Junior high schools appeared to be an efficient solution, offering seventh- through ninth-grade instruction in larger buildings at a lower cost. Alexander Hamilton and John Marshall opened in 1927 in the city's north end, and many women who had taught in eighth-grade elementary schools staffed those new buildings for grade teacher salaries.

The high school curriculum changed in line with national trends toward vocational and career-oriented options. New commercial classes ranged from bookkeeping and typing through shorthand; girls were encouraged to follow the commercial track. A course in retail selling, which involved work experience, caught the imagination of many students captivated by the promise of a career in a local department store. A vocational education program had begun in 1919; under its director, Samuel Fleming, it grew in size and importance during the decade. The basic academic curriculum remained strong, with an occasional addition such as a high school social science course called "The Pacific Rim."

One imaginative young woman joined the Seattle teaching corps in the 1920s and combined the new vocational with the academic traditional. After Marion McMaster graduated from the University of Oregon, she taught high school English for two years in the Columbia River town of Stevenson, Washington. She attended the 1926 summer session at the University of Washington, and, along with courses in the English department, she enrolled in something called Vocational Guidance, taught by Samuel Fleming. She returned to Stevenson to inaugurate a class called "Vocations with English." Emulating the Seattle Way, she blended student research and writing assignments with Saturday trips to nearby paper mills and salmon and fruit canneries. Her students enjoyed the English class with practical applications in industry.[16]

As others had, Marion McMaster believed that Seattle's school system offered opportunities for advancement and for "doing original work in the field of teaching English." She applied in February 1927 and that fall began a nine-year teaching stint at Franklin High School. In 1936 she expressed the frustration of many: "I am planning to be married in June which entails the drastic step of resignation, according to a certain ominous little clause in our contract." After repeal of the marriage ban in 1948, she returned to the district in September 1954 and taught at Nathan Eckstein Junior High until her retirement twelve years later.[17]

Other changes in the 1920s, such as legislation regulating child labor and mandating longer school attendance and the burgeoning of radio and motion pictures, altered, expanded, and complicated the teacher's role. By the end of the decade the number of high school-age students who stayed in school had increased as much as eightfold since 1900. Motion pictures had entered the schools during the war; by 1923 principals were being queried on the use of movies in their schools—how often were they shown for educational or entertainment reasons, and did they feel pupils benefited educationally. Radios, too, gradually became school equipment; "appreciating the importance of the radio in education," the PTA of Horace Mann School installed a set in that building in 1928.[18]

Thomas Cole inherited an extraordinary corps of women from the Cooper decades. He acknowledged:

The Seattle teacher has had for years characteristics that are distinctly her own. She comes to us free of responsibility to anyone other than to herself for her appointment, because she was chosen on merit, . . . she enters into her work with an eagerness to do,—she knows her suggestions for the improvement of the schools are welcome . . . [and] has a personal interest in our system that makes it succeed and she succeeds with it.[19]

Although the description held true for the twenties, the composite picture of women teachers hired during the decade changed somewhat.

The school board noted in 1923 that the district had many career teachers: "About one-half the staff are forty years of age or over . . . [and] while the majority of these form the backbone of the system in devotion and efficiency, it is desirable that the schools shall also have the benefit of teachers with more recent normal school and college training."[20] As a result of this shift in hiring policy, 27 percent of women hired as grade teachers during the decade would earn a bachelor's degree, up from 12 percent the previous decade. As a whole, they were much younger than those hired previously; 58 percent were between twenty and twenty-five years old compared to 23 percent of the earlier group. Their record of experience reflects both the youth of the group and greater reliance on the cadet program: most notably, 11 percent of those hired between 1920 and 1930 had no teaching experience, and 27 percent had taught between six and ten years, down from 41 percent of those hired between 1910 and 1920.[21]

As in the previous decade, more than 60 percent applied from within Washington State and an impressive 51 percent had trained at Washington normal schools, up from 33 percent. Minnesota and Wisconsin normal schools combined sent a steady 17 percent of the decade's new teachers.

Teachers hired during the twenties had, on average, shorter tenures than those hired earlier: 26 percent, compared to 7 percent hired between 1910 and 1920, taught only one or two years. In both decades, 11 percent taught between eleven and twenty years; but the later sample shows only 32 percent teaching twenty-one to forty years compared to 68 percent earlier.

More teachers hired during the twenties were dismissed than before; more than half of them resigned, 66 percent of them to be married. One indication of growing opportunities for women appears in the number who resigned to pursue other work—21 percent. Those who stayed with the district until retirement tended to retire at an earlier age: 62 percent were between fifty-five and sixty-five years of age, and fewer taught beyond their sixty-fifth birthdays. A sample of high school records shows similarly changed patterns. These teachers were younger, and their tenures were not as long as their earlier counterparts': 49 percent taught more than twenty-five years, whereas 68 percent had earlier. The numbers for those serving more than thirty years differ less.

Behind the statistics stand real people. The career of Margaret Passage mirrors the changing landscape of the 1920s in a number of respects. A 1915 graduate of Seattle's Lincoln High School, she completed the two-year course at Bellingham Normal School, and summer terms at both Washington State College and the University of California. She renewed her 1923 application twice before the district hired her in 1925 to teach at Bailey Gatzert School. She resigned when she married in 1933, and in

1944 she returned to teach at Columbia School in the emergency service category. A five-year absence from Columbia classrooms, between June 1948 and September 1953, suggests that she may have elected to stay at home with her children. She retired June 6, 1960.[22]

Evelyn Brown emigrated from Rossland, British Columbia, and prepared for teaching kindergarten and primary grades at Ellensburg Normal School. Seattle selected her as a cadet from the normal school's list of promising candidates, and she taught in that capacity at Mercer School in 1925. She moved into Mercer's regular teaching ranks, with the attendant increase in salary, and on to West Queen Anne School in 1931. She spent the 1936–37 school year as an exchange teacher in Providence, Rhode Island, and finished her career in Seattle at Lowell Elementary. After forty years, she retired in June 1965, just before reaching her sixtieth birthday.[23]

Dorothy Kwapil twice seized the opportunity to teach in the exchange program; she spent 1938–39 in Providence, and 1947–48 in Springfield, Massachusetts. Born in Seattle in 1905, she had attended University Heights School, graduated from Lincoln in 1922, and gone right on to the University of Washington. She received a degree in English in 1927 and taught in Lake Stevens, Washington, until 1930, when Seattle hired her to teach English at West Seattle High School. She transferred to her alma mater in the fall of 1934 and taught at Lincoln until her retirement in 1968.[24]

In addition to her two years of exchange teaching on the eastern seaboard, Dorothy Kwapil also enjoyed spring semester 1955 on sabbatical leave in Europe. The district instituted a leave program in the mid-1920s, and most teachers who applied for sabbaticals pursued further study or traveled or both.

The Roaring Twenties had hit the Seattle Public Schools hard financially, but over time the board gradually restored salaries to earlier levels. It took other positive steps that enhanced the Seattle Way—instituting the program of sabbatical leaves, establishing a demonstration school, and salvaging the six-period day for high school teachers, to name three[25]—but its action did not stave off unionization efforts. Few teachers would have imagined themselves part of Seattle's radical labor scene; indeed, teachers held back until the salary situation became intolerable. In 1928, grade school teachers finally prevailed in their long quest for a single salary scale. High school teachers had always been more disposed to organize; when the Seattle High School Teachers' Union became a local of the American Federation of Teachers in 1927, labor battles began in earnest.[26]

In the aftermath of union and contract disputes, the teachers' influence on students became a high-priority concern for the school board. Emphasizing "the development in children of right social and civic attitudes, healthful outlooks, confidence in our institutions, and whole-hearted cooperation," the board sought "teachers who feel and express [qualities of citizenship] in their own relation to the system of which they are a part."[27] Even though the board inferred disapproval of the teachers' role in past disputes, generally cordial relations between administrators and teachers remained.

In 1929 Superintendent Thomas Cole, who had steered the school district through fiscal difficulties compounded by the intrusion of groups such as the Tax Reduction Council, resigned; his successor was Worth McClure. Frank Cooper had brought both men to Seattle as principals before World War I—Cole from Minnesota to Broadway High School, and McClure from Iowa to Youngstown Elementary. During his first year as Cooper's successor, Cole moved McClure into the Central Office as superintendent's assistant.[28] Together McClure and the corps of teachers prepared to carry much of the Seattle Way into the next decade.

But two months after the autumn semester began, the stock market crashed. In the Great Depression that followed, no city in the nation would suffer more than Seattle did, and it looked to the state for help.

Washington's constitution declares education the state's "paramount duty." The state had always prided itself on its schools, but as early as 1920 school funding, heavily dependent on property taxes, was problematic. Neither man who sat in the governor's chair between 1919 and 1932 championed the public schools. World War I inflation had contributed to a rise in school costs of more than 80 percent. School taxes rose about 40 percent between 1917 and 1920, but the lion's share went to higher education. The crisis in common school funding resulted in an initiative that made its way onto the ballot in 1922 to increase state school funding to $30 per child. Initiative 64, the state's first citizen-impelled school reform effort, lost by a 150,114 to 99,150 margin.[29] Against this background, the Seattle School Board had acquiesced to demands for draconian budget cuts.

When Washington slid into the depths of the Depression, a misanthropic Governor Roland Hill Hartley refused what little early aid became available from the federal government. Hartley railed against state appropriations for highways, education, libraries, parks, and the new state capitol building, and education took the full brunt of his attempts to bring state government under his control. His dismissal of Henry Suzzallo from the presidency of the University of Washington in 1925 produced an unsuccessful recall attempt by, among others, outraged supporters of the university. But perhaps Hartley's greatest disservice to Washingtonians lay in his reaction to the distress and misery of the Depression; as economic devastation wreaked havoc, he did virtually nothing about unemployment. Estimates of those out of work in Seattle climbed from nearly 15,000 in 1930 to 35,000 in the fall of 1933. When Hartley left office in January of 1933, the number of employed workers statewide was only 47.3 percent of what it had been six years earlier.[30]

By the summer of 1932, Seattle's unemployed citizens had reached a point of desperation. The Unemployed Citizens League, first in a succession of citizen organizations, worked in conjunction with municipal and county relief efforts. As the decade wound on, the UCL would be supplanted by the Commonwealth Builders, Inc., which would be displaced by the more militant Washington Commonwealth Federation. Each group proved more extreme than the one before, and issues of unemployment became grist for the mill of radical politics. Labor unrest characterized Seattle in the 1930s, and the Communist Party's unwelcome intrusion kept the city and state in political turmoil throughout the decade.[31]

The Roosevelt landslide of 1932 swept the Democrat Clarence Martin into the governor's office. It fell to Martin, a conservative former mayor of Cheney and head of his family's successful flour-milling operation in eastern Washington, to confront the deepening crisis in the state. In a special message to the legislature on February 6, 1933, he emphasized that "the relief of unemployment and the maintenance of the common schools system stand out as the emergency problems of the day."[32] Maintaining the schools continued to plague the administration of the one-time Cheney Normal School student.

In January 1935, schools across the state struggled to remain open; eighty-seven faced closure by March. In addressing the legislature then, Martin sought $26 million in funding, and sounding very much the champion of teachers, said:

> Children are born and grow up in times of depression. We cannot put them into cold storage until better days. They have only one chance for childhood, one chance for education, and these opportunities cannot be postponed. Some material things can wait, if necessary, but not our children. . . .
>
> We should make a definite stipulation for a reasonable restoration in the compensation for teachers, with the first increases being for the teachers in the lower brackets. Our teachers need something more substantial than merely the praise of being members of a noble profession, and it is regrettable that the pay for teaching our children is less than that which prevails in the commercial and business fields.[33]

By August 1932, King County neared its constitutional debt limit, and banks sometimes refused to cash county warrants issued for relief payments.[34] Citizens could not pay their taxes, so Seattle teachers not only had difficulty cashing warrants, they also saw their salaries reduced.

During that summer of 1932, the Seattle School District made its first Depression decade across-the-board salary cut of 6.25 percent. A second cut of 2.5 percent came in 1934. Earlier, because of uncollected back taxes and possible reduction of future revenue, the board had eliminated sick leave payments and reduced materials and supplies. The Seattle district, long competitive and attractive from a salary standpoint, declined in national ranking; Municipal League figures show the average Seattle teacher salary dropping from $2,215 in 1931 to $1,901 in 1933 and declining further to $1,685 in 1935. By the 1937–38 school year it had climbed back to $2,111.[35] Given the widespread unemployment, however, any teacher salary was truly considered handsome.

Some random examples illustrate the reversal of fortune. One high school teacher from Illinois had taught in Seattle since 1921; she received an annual salary of $2,600 in 1931; after cuts in 1932 and 1934 she received $2,145. A longtime grade teacher, Minnie Maloney, had come to Seattle in 1902 after six years teaching in her native Minnesota and three in Spokane. By 1922 her annual salary had reached $1,950 and in 1930 stood at $2,200. After sustaining the two salary cuts, she earned $1,915 in 1935, the year before she retired. Lacking much in the way of a retirement program, she had the memory of her travels during a 1931 spring semester sabbatical leave to console her.[36]

Borghilde Olsby, a North Dakota native with twelve years of experience there and in eastern Washington, started at Dunlap Elementary in the city's south end in February, 1931, at an annual salary of $1,500. After two cuts she received $1,425. She transferred to John Hay Elementary on Queen Anne Hill in 1935; three years later, following a slight upturn in the economy, her salary was $2,300. A third salary cut, in 1939–40, reduced that to $2,231; during the war her fortunes began to improve, and she reached the maximum of $2,900 before she died in January 1948.[37]

Faced with a legal mandate to balance the district's budget, the board instituted a 1939 salary cut of 4.5 percent. Revenue deficiencies "particularly in state apportionments [had] made a reduction inevitable." The legislature's appropriation did not provide the full twenty-five cents per day per pupil to which local districts were entitled.[38]

By the time the third salary cut came, the legislature had set a minimum teachers salary of $1,200. One teacher hired as a cadet in 1938 recalled those difficult days:

> The first year that I taught, the money wasn't coming in . . . so they were going to have to cut the teachers' salaries in the middle of the year. . . . I came in at $1200 and that was a state law, a minimum salary, so they couldn't cut my salary—but all the other teachers had to take a cut. . . . The teachers felt badly about it, but at the same time realized there was no other way to do it.

There were not many teaching jobs in Seattle during the Depression. Another cadet, hired in 1935, later observed that the cadet program provided many of the few new hires.[39]

Two years into his administration, Superintendent McClure sent out Christmas greetings that put the best light possible on things just six months before the first salary cuts came:

Seldom has there been a year when there has been so much opportunity to bring joy into the lives of children as we have in this testing time of 1931–32.

To the Seattle Grade Teachers' Club and its members, who know how to give so richly of their sustenance and of themselves, I wish the joyous Christmas of those who share much, and the confident New Year of those who follow the gleam.[40]

The new year of 1932 did not gleam too brightly, and as the Depression deepened, classrooms reflected the plight of unemployed parents. An early response came from the city's Parent Teacher Association, which had formed its Child Welfare Board in September 1931, "at a time when no organized relief was available and it was apparent that many hundreds of children would require food, clothing and carfare." Citywide PTA resources went to children in those areas that could not care for their own. School faculty contributions and district lunchroom surpluses provided free lunches, and the Child Welfare Board became a clearing-house for used clothing.[41]

Amid unprecedented unemployment, people coped as best they could. The economy hit bottom in spring of 1933, but even after Northwest lumber production began to show improvement, unemployment in Seattle still hovered near 20 percent and would increase further in 1935.[42] Teachers in the city's working-class neighborhoods saw signs of despair among their students. A first-grade teacher recalled that

> At Concord School when things were so difficult for people and children were not having enough to eat—and they suffered—the children in our district suffered a lot. . . . They closed school an hour earlier for a while, so the children could go home and rest and then they provided food for some children.
>
> I had . . . [pupils whose] parents . . . didn't have *anything*—nothing. Those poor children, you just knew they didn't have enough energy to be alert all the time. The [school district] didn't do free lunches at that time, but *our* school did. We had a PTA and the PTA helped children like that.[43]

Subsidized lunch programs, common by the end of the century, were beyond imagining in the early 1930s. There were, however, some excep-

tions. Thelma Chisholm recounted her first year as a history teacher at
Queen Anne High School:

> It was [near] the end of the depression—well *still* the depression, 1937—
> we had midmorning milk at the high school level for some of the students
> who needed it. Always, the time that I was there, we had what were called
> lunch tickets that we could give to children who couldn't afford to buy a
> lunch.[44]

By the end of the decade, Thelma Chisholm had been named girls
adviser at Queen Anne, a position from which she saw dramatic changes
in school and community during the coming war.

The few new teachers who moved into the Seattle district during the
1930s came in order to be part of a system that still enjoyed a fine reputation. Although by the end of the decade the British conductor Sir
Thomas Beecham would deride Seattle as an "aesthetic dustbin," the
Ladies Musical Club and the symphony had continued to offer music in
the city. Live theater flourished under the direction of Florence and Burton James at the Seattle Repertory Playhouse. On the visual arts front,
Nellie Cornish managed somehow to keep her school afloat. A $250,000
donation enabled construction of the Seattle Art Museum in Volunteer
Park; when it opened in 1933, the collection donated by Richard Fuller
put it in the front rank of Asian art repositories. Seattle remained a good
place for teachers to work and to live, despite salary deficiencies and
retrenchments.[45]

Those who did find work in Seattle's grade schools during the Depression decade were older on average than their counterparts of the 1920s.
Of those sampled, 43 percent were between twenty-six and thirty years
old (up from 32 percent),and a whopping 48 percent were between thirty-
one and thirty-five (up from 9 percent). Eighty-seven percent applied from
within Washington, and the state's own normal schools had trained 43
percent of that number. Twenty-two percent already held bachelor's
degrees, and 74 percent would earn one during their careers. They were
more experienced, 78 percent having taught more than six years compared
with 33 percent a decade earlier, but the lengths of their tenures did not
differ markedly from before. None taught beyond the age of seventy, a

result of mandatory retirement laws if not testimony to improving levels of retirement benefits that came about during the 1960s.[46]

High school teachers hired in the thirties were also older than those hired in the twenties—only 47 percent were under thirty years of age, compared with 85 percent earlier. They also had more years of experience to their credit—59 percent had taught six years or more, compared to 24 percent of those who applied during the twenties. Virtually the same number had graduated from Seattle high schools, and 76 percent held degrees from the University of Washington. More of them would earn master's degrees—29 percent. The tenures of the later group did not run as long as those of their predecessors; only 24 percent taught more than thirty years (39 percent of those hired earlier had). More of the Depression-era group resigned to pursue other work, an indication perhaps of greater opportunities that opened for capable women during World War II. Fewer resigned to be married. Of those who taught until retirement, half were between sixty and sixty-five and half older than that. None taught beyond age seventy.

One of very few new teachers hired in 1930, Alma Johns came from Fairibault, Minnesota, after eleven years as a kindergarten teacher in the Midwest. Her starting salary of $1,500 had dipped to $1,425 before she resigned to be married in June of 1935.[47]

Those who married may have fared worse financially during the Depression than those who remained single and at least kept their jobs. Iva Shepardson, for example, had a normal school degree from Cheney and came to Seattle from Astoria, Oregon, in 1926 to teach sixth grade at Youngstown School. When she resigned to be married in June 1928, she made it known that she wanted to continue as a substitute. By August 1932 her situation had become so serious that she made formal application for substitute teaching, noting that her "husband has not been employed for several months." A severe shortage of teachers during World War II forced the district to hire married teachers, and in February 1944 Iva Shepardson Trenholme returned to the teaching corps, starting at Gatewood School in West Seattle at a salary of $1,920. Seattle salaries slowly improved, and by the time she retired from Gatewood in 1962, hers had reached $5,800.[48]

The school district tried to accommodate its former teachers; in September 1935, the board elected a large number of women to the substitute ranks. Superintendent McClure explained that "the economic status of each individual had been investigated and preference given to those in greatest economic need, other conditions being equal, in accordance with the policy of the Board, compensation to be $5 per day of service."[49]

The case of Marion Coyle further underscores the predicament of those who married; she, too, was among the few hired in 1930. Born in Minnesota, she had moved west with her family to Valley City, North Dakota; she completed the two-year course at Valley City State Teachers College in 1926. By the time she came to Seattle, she had taught public school music for eight years and completed a summer term at the University of Washington. Her initial Seattle salary was $1,500, and she sustained the first two salary reductions. While teaching at Emerson School in south Seattle, she completed her B.A. in music. She married Fred Smith in June 1935 and tendered her resignation. Four years later, the couple's economic circumstances critical, she substituted for a semester at Columbia School. One of the first to return to emergency service, she finished her career as music teacher at University Heights. Her salary had reached $11,350 by the time she retired in January 1969 at the age of sixty-eight.[50]

The interwar period was a banner time for the woman elementary principal in Seattle. Although men always outnumbered women in the principals' offices, the gap narrowed during the 1920s. In 1919, the ratio was forty-six men to nineteen women; in 1930, forty-three men to thirty-four women; but by 1940 men again greatly outnumbered women—forty-nine to twenty-two.[51] The women principals of the twenties and thirties were benevolent autocrats who left indelible marks on the community. They set the tone in their buildings, most ruled with authoritarian methods, and they are remembered by their students as virtually "God incarnate." Parents appreciated them and supported their authority. During the 1930s, however, these remarkable women began to reach retirement age.

The departure of such a model principal as Emma D. Larrabee signaled the end of an era in Seattle. She had come from New England in 1911 to teach fifth grade at Green Lake Elementary School. In 1914, the district sent her to a newly opened annex a few blocks south in the Wallingford district and a year later named her principal of what had become McDonald School. While on a health-related leave of absence for the 1940–41 school year, she died. Emma Larrabee considered the principalship "a position of supreme responsibility" and presided over McDonald School with a quiet, unassuming personality. But, in the rather flowery words of Worth McClure, her influence "extended itself without seeming effort and [her] sweetness of life was a benediction to those associated with her." The superintendent noted her high standards and lauded her school's contributions in the community as "an enduring monument to the woman under whose influence it fell during its formative years and under whose leadership it has served for more than a quarter of a century."[52] His commendation of Emma Larrabee could apply to any number of her fellow principals.

The board had earlier voiced concern over an aging teaching corps and in 1938 brought compulsory retirement to the forefront of issues for teachers. In June 1939, after an amount of public input highly unusual for the time, the board made age-related policy decisions. Beginning that September, all teachers sixty-five or older would be required to take a physical examination. Further, all "who will become 71 or more years of age prior to September 1, 1940," must retire in June 1941. Given the dismal state of the retirement system—a meager $40 per month—older teachers received news of the policy change with trepidation.[53]

Both federal and state governments had provided some relief for the schools as the Depression worsened, but in 1939 the economic situation deteriorated nationally with the so-called Roosevelt Recession, and the Works Progress Administration reduced its projects in Washington by 60 percent. Cutbacks in federal assistance contributed to the need for the 1939 salary cuts for teachers.[54]

The experience of Gertrude Tormey, a high school English teacher who started with the district in 1928 at $1,800, illustrates the teachers' dilemma. Her salary had reached $2,100, dropped in 1932 and again in 1934, crept up to $2,700 in time for the cuts of 1939–40, and returned at last to $2,700 until 1946, when it advanced to $3,400.[55]

The Depression wrought changes in the school district beyond the financial. Seattle's population, 368,302 in 1940, had remained stable and homogeneous for twenty years. In the midthirties, refugees from the Dust Bowl arrived and enrolled their children in school. A 1937 survey of new students in the city's high schools indicated "a particularly striking influx from the 'dust bowl.'"[56] The face of the district began to change with the start of war mobilization.

Enlarging the navy, strengthening the air forces, and launching the Lend-Lease program to bolster Great Britain put the nation on a wartime footing. Mobilization had a positive effect on the state's economy, and population growth accompanied economic growth. The Boeing Airplane Company's payroll grew from a mere 4,000 in 1939 to 10,000 in mid-1941 and 30,000 by the end of that year. Washington State soon ranked as one of the nation's largest recipients of defense contracts. The flood of workers coming to defense-based industries again brought financial and logistical problems to the Seattle schools as it had in World War I. Social dislocation of unprecedented scope came too.

Throughout the Depression and the early years of World War II, Seattle teachers maintained district standards and stability in their classrooms. After Japan's 1937 invasion of China, they tracked the drive into southeast Asia. During the Munich Crisis in 1938, they brought radios to allow students to hear "the history makers as their voices came into classrooms," and they followed Nazi Germany's conquest of western Europe.[57] But the December 7, 1941, attack on Pearl Harbor rocked the nation, the city, and the Seattle schools, and nothing could have prepared them for its aftermath.

By nightfall of that awful Sunday, officials had announced a total blackout for the next night, and rumors flew, fueled by fear and anger. Monday's declaration of war with Japan and the broadcast of Franklin Roosevelt's "Day of Infamy" speech brought the war home: students in one grade school listened to the president and never forgot the tears in the eyes of a disciplined, austere homeroom teacher who had already taught through one world war. That same morning administrators and principals began emergency planning. That night, rioters protesting light shining from inside stores milled through downtown Seattle, smashing windows before being dispersed by police and firemen.[58] The first air raid drills took place in schools that Friday, December 12.[59]

The war left no civilian life untouched, but it totally altered the lives of Seattle's large Japanese-American population, which received treatment unprecedented, unexpected, and undeserved by citizens of the United States. Within hours of the attack on Pearl Harbor, the FBI had detained some community leaders, and the president's Executive Order 9066 issued on February 19, 1942, placed all Nikkei under the military control of the

Western Defense Command. Deprived of their legal rights and much of their property, by late spring most had been uprooted from their homes and sent to relocation camps in such interior locations as Minidoka in southern Idaho.

While every school principal stressed the need to remain calm, at Bailey Gatzert School, with a predominantly Nikkei student body, the principal Ada J. Mahon told pupils on December 8 to remember that "you were American citizens last Friday; you are American citizens today. You were friends last Friday; you are friends today."[60] The same solemn urgency permeated Washington School, where the seventh-grade English teacher Ella Evanson later recalled, "We had a good mixture of white, Oriental and black children. It was an interesting school." The principal Arthur Sears called a schoolwide assembly on December 8, and Miss Evanson charged her students to write essays on his message. The following excerpts from three of the essays reflect the atmosphere that Sears and his teachers had established.

> Mr. Sears said that no matter what race or color you are that you are all American citizens and that even if your parents came from a country that are fighting against us that we had nothing to do with it.
>
> Mr. Sears said that we should not fight each other; . . . we are all citizens of America and citizens should not fight but be friends and help make America a strong nation.
>
> Mr. Sears said that people said to him that they thought he would have trouble with the children of Washington School because of the many different races but Mr. Sears said that he trusted us and knew that we would not be intolerant.[61]

The immediate response in schools throughout the city differed little. The Japanese-American secretary at Whittier Elementary in the Ballard area recalled that the principal Guy Loman, whom she considered very fair and evenhanded, set the tone. The day after Pearl Harbor "went on like any other day; nothing was said; their behavior toward me didn't change . . . maybe some of the teachers didn't even know I was Japanese American, it didn't matter to them."[62]

The mayor called for tolerance, and, on the whole, citizens did display it, but by February 1942, a committee of three mothers at Gatewood School in West Seattle had embarked on a successful campaign to rid the schools of their Nikkei clerical employees. Some Seattle teachers may have shared such racial antagonism, which gripped the entire West Coast periodically throughout the twentieth century, but the records are silent.

World War II became strikingly real at Highland Park School when pupils returned from Christmas vacation in January 1942, to find army trucks parked all around the building, filled with soldiers waiting for transport to Alaska. Lacking permanent barracks, the army billeted them in the school, where "they spent the night lying like cord wood in the halls on the floor." They spent daytime hours sitting in their trucks. The reading teacher Margaret Houston recalled that this arrangement lasted several days, and though "the neighbors felt so sorry for these poor guys sitting out there . . . it was very exciting for the children." Other schools might not have had soldiers sleeping in their corridors, but crowding and intensified wartime scheduling were common. Florence Byers taught oversized classes at John Muir; her room had two doors, and at the end of each class "forty kids went out the back and forty kids came in the front [and teachers] had no study period—no free period."[63]

Early in the war when rationing went into effect, first of sugar and then other commodities, grade schools served as neighborhood headquarters for issuing ration books. Grade teachers volunteered hundreds of hours to processing and issuing books to parents of their pupils.[64] Ration books that survive bear the unmistakable handwriting of women from the interwar cohort of Seattle grade teachers.

With a severe labor shortage in the Puget Sound region, Seattle's women teachers found themselves moonlighting in a variety of jobs. Any number spent their wartime summer vacations doing sundry jobs at the Boeing plant. Many from Queen Anne High School responded to a desperate call for postal workers; they worked after school, from four until ten o'clock or on weekends at the main postal terminal for eighty-five cents an hour. Civil Defense relied heavily on the schools' physical education faculty to teach its first-aid classes.[65]

That severe labor shortage caused the school district to tap a source heretofore shunned—the married woman—and in 1943 it began to hire married teachers on an emergency service basis. Many of the women who had resigned during the twenties and thirties returned to teach. Sixteen percent of the married grade teachers hired in the 1920s returned, and of that number a third taught for an additional twenty years or more. A fourth of those married high school teachers from the 1920s also returned, and nearly half taught for an additional twenty years or longer. Thirty-five percent of the sample hired during the Depression decade had resigned to be married, and a fourth of their number returned to teach during the war. The school district finally abolished the marriage ban permanently in 1948.[66]

Some unique opportunities to aid the war effort presented themselves. Sylvia Vopni, herself a Queen Anne graduate who held a doctorate, taught advanced math and chemistry at her alma mater. Although the school board denied the navy's request to grant her "a leave of absence for the duration of the war," she did extensive classified work on sonar detection devices that took her away from the school for weeks at a time. Frankie Close Schmitz had taught retail selling in the high schools since that program's inception in the early twenties and also had experience in general personnel management. In 1943, she agreed to make a study of the training program for women employees at the Puget Sound Naval Shipyard in Bremerton and to recommend ways to improve it.[67]

In the high schools, teachers helped young men prepare to take exams for officer candidate school or placement in the so-called V-2 training programs on the state's college campuses, and they corresponded with many who had been drafted, some before they had graduated. As Queen Anne's Thelma Chisholm recalled, "We kept in touch with a lot of the boys. . . . I think we lost almost a hundred killed."[68]

Teachers were caught up in civil defense and war-related work; support for the war effort was virtually unqualified, even as life on the home front grew increasingly challenging. Sheer numbers of people made even the routine of shopping or going to and from work difficult. Waiting in lines became a way of life. More than 500,000 people poured into the state during the war, and many rural and small-town Washingtonians gravitated to more lucrative jobs in Seattle.

One of the worst wartime housing shortages in the nation plagued Seattle; construction could not keep up with the demand. The Seattle Housing Authority built its Shearwater and Highpoint housing projects to accommodate newcomers. High Point School opened under somewhat rugged conditions for the women who taught there—in a series of three duplex houses that the district moved onto a barren terraced hillside in West Seattle.[69]

Like other Seattleites, women teachers suffered the uncertainty and inconvenience of wartime; they also bought their share of Victory Bonds and entered military service themselves. Programs such as physical therapy training at Fitzsimmons Army Hospital near Denver attracted them, and, after the war ended, others served with army library programs in Korea and in Occupied Japan.

In the spring of 1943, with victory by no means certain, Lois Potter applied for officer training in the Coast Guard and reported to New London, Connecticut, that September. Born in Northport, Washington, in 1903, she had come from Cheney Normal School to the Seattle district in 1925 to teach sixth grade at Lafayette School. Five years later she completed a bachelor's degree at the University; on sabbatical leave during fall semester of 1938, she traveled throughout the world. After her two-year military stint, she returned to serve as an academic counselor at Pacific School, which in 1940 had become a Prevocational Center for developmentally handicapped pupils. She finished out her career there, writing on her retirement in 1956 that "it has been a privilege to teach in the Seattle Schools for thirty years. . . . No assignment has been more interesting than the past ten years at Pacific School. . . . I shall always remember these years with pleasure and satisfaction."[70]

To former students of Tennie Coffey it came as no surprise that she had gone on to serve eighteen months in the Women's Army Corps after their time with her in third grade at Bryant Elementary School. They remembered her as a good teacher who exuded efficiency and certainty; everything was clear cut with her, "You were right or you were wrong."[71] An Iowa native, Coffey was another of the lucky few hired in 1930, and had most recently taught in Aberdeen in coastal Grays Harbor County. She started in Seattle at a salary of $1,500, endured the pay cuts of the Depression, and earned $2,425 before going on military leave in 1944. She returned for fall semester 1945 at Bryant, where she continued to teach until her death on September 4, 1960, at the age of fifty-six.[72] A career of thirty years or more in one school was common for the inter-war cohort.

During World War II, many of the women hired by Frank Cooper began to retire. Their careers had lent stability and continuity to their schools, none more so than that of Zula Smith. Born in 1876, the year the nation celebrated its centennial and Rutherford B. Hayes ran for president, Zula Smith completed the normal course at Huron State College in South Dakota. After teaching fourteen years in her hometown, she came to Seattle in 1910—perhaps after attending the AYP. For the next thirty-two years she taught sixth grade at T. T. Minor School, retiring in June of 1942 at the age of sixty-six. Her starting salary appears to have been $930, it increased to $1,950 by 1922; she retired at $2,200 after forty-six years in the classroom.[73]

Another loosening of the bond with Cooper came when Myrtle Whitham retired in 1943. Born just ten years after the Civil War ended, she had graduated from Plattesville State Normal School and moved to the Puget Sound area from Wisconsin by way of teaching jobs in Michigan and Iowa. Her Seattle career began at Brighton School in 1908; she taught at West Woodland School from 1929 until her retirement. The veteran fourth-grade teacher responded to the wartime shortage, and her name went on the district substitute list in September 1945, when she was seventy-one years old.[74]

Wartime shortages and overcrowding gave way to unprecedented changes in society and the public schools. Although the Second World War had been less divisive than the First, the onset of the cold war again brought the specter of communism to the fore. In the postwar years anti-Communist crusades of the House Un-American Activities Committee and Senator Joseph McCarthy riveted attention on loyalty and patriotism. Seattle teaching contracts now contained a loyalty oath, and scattered throughout the archival record are shreds of evidence that some teachers were under police scrutiny. The superintendent received accusing letters; one in 1948 proclaimed: "There are Communistic teachers in Lincoln High. They voice their views and try to enforce them, and I, as a Christian, thought that this should be reported."[75]

The obsession with communism reached into public school curricula in the aftermath of the 1957 Russian Sputnik launching, and anxiety grew amidst the controversy created by Rudolph Flesch's book *Why Johnny Can't Read.*

Traditional education and the technology gap still demanded the attention of the district and its teachers as the social revolution of the 1960s got under way. In Seattle the issue of racial desegregation remained on the outermost periphery of awareness in the first years after the U.S. Supreme Court's ruling in *Brown v. Board of Education.*

The city's minuscule African-American population had grown considerably during the war; by 1957 its children constituted 5.7 percent of the school enrollment. Ten years later their numbers stood at 11 percent. Seattle did not maintain an officially segregated school system, but as the integration movement came to encompass de facto as well as de jure segregation, the school district instituted compensatory and other programs that broke new ground in equal educational opportunity—honest attempts to deal with a growing and bewildering problem. In 1963, the school board created the Voluntary Racial Transfer Program that ultimately saw some 1,400 African-American students from Central Area schools enroll elsewhere in the city. The board voted to accept mandatory two-way assignment of students in 1968 and finally implemented it in 1972.[76]

A number of the interwar cohort of women teachers continued teaching through these changes. Those who did so saw two more changes in the superintendent's office. Worth McClure had been succeeded in 1945 by Samuel Fleming, who had headed the vocational education program before becoming assistant superintendent. When Fleming retired in 1956, after forty-eight years with the district, the board made no search for a successor; its members were "quite universally agreed" that Ernest Campbell would succeed him.[77]

Campbell, a graduate of West Seattle High School and the University of Washington, had joined the district in 1936. When he stepped down in 1965, the school board broke a precedent in appointing his successor. It hired Forbes Bottomly from Colorado's Jefferson County system—the first superintendent from outside the district since Frank Cooper came in 1901. The state legislature passed the Professional Negotiations Act in 1965; collective bargaining and desegregation stamped the tumultuous years of Bottomly's tenure.

Those two factors also imprinted the last years of teaching for the inter-war teacher cohort. Those women had seen the city grow and change enormously. In the era when teaching was virtually the only profession open to women, Seattle's teachers were crème de la crème. Through their students, they contributed enormously to making their city the attractive and livable place that it remained. Through postwar decades of growth and change, the city remained firmly in the hands of men and women who had attended Seattle's public schools in the interwar years.

3 / Quality of Life

Home, School, Transportation

Teachers frequently requested transfers to schools "nearer home" in the early twentieth century. Much in their lives was determined by the school district, including where they lived, where they taught, and how they traveled between home and school. In hilly hourglass-shaped Seattle, the interwar cohort of teachers relied on the predominantly north-south streetcar system to commute to work. By World War II, many teachers owned automobiles; gasoline rationing for them and an overcrowded public transit system for the others again prompted requests for assignments closer to their residences. Some of the schools themselves left much to be desired. Budget cuts in the early twenties slowed new construction and physical plant updates, and Depression austerity followed by wartime overcrowding kept amenities low on the district's priority list.

In the fall of 1920, the *Seattle Times* welcomed new teachers to the city and sent a questionnaire to help them in "making their living arrangements and in forming their social and community relationships." It asked for their teaching assignment, their normal school or college, their club, church, and sorority affiliations; when they expected to arrive; and whether they had friends in the city. More to the point, it asked, "How do you wish to live in Seattle?" and gave choices for a prospective boarder—private home, apartment, or hotel. A preference to "keep house" presented the choice of apartment or house; a respondent with extended responsibilities could also indicate that she "wish[ed] accommodations for others in

[her] family." The *Times* had run an advertisement for available living accommodations and investigated the responses "as far as possible." Such groups as PTAs, business clubs, churches, the YWCA, and the Educational Committee of the chamber of commerce joined the newspaper in hosting a Labor Day reception for the new teachers, making their welcome a broadly based community effort.[1]

Three weeks later, the chamber of commerce and the commercial club honored the incoming teaching corps at a dinner preceded by "automobile rides about the city . . . [which originated] on the Central School Grounds where citizens met the new-comers in their machines." The first after-dinner speaker gave a simple, brief message: "You are the architects of our children's future. We want you therefore to be in sympathy with the ideas and ideals of Seattle."[2] Within two years, many of the same people joined in the drive to reduce teachers' salaries.

When Superintendent Julia Kennedy had driven her buggy on her rounds of the city's three schools, single women in Seattle had few residential options. There had been apartment hotels as early as the 1870s, which, with boarding houses, had been the residence of choice for single adults. Boarding houses provided a mixed gender living environment.[3] When Trella Logan came to teach at Mercer School in 1902, she lived in a boarding house on Sixth Avenue, just north of downtown.

In answer to an obvious need, the Sarah B. Yesler Women's Hotel had opened in 1891 at the intersection of Queen Anne Avenue and Denny Way. It was designed for women "coming to the city on business or pleasure, and for the business women of our city," whose success "involves tact, rapid movement, and faithfulness to detail." For a weekly cost of four or five dollars, the hotel "offered spacious quarters . . . a pleasant dining room with good food . . . a sewing room with a modern sewing machine, and large parlors . . . for visiting and recreation."[4] Teachers assigned to Denny or Warren Avenue schools a few blocks away may have lived for a while at the Sarah B. Yesler Hotel.

Seattle has traditionally been a city of homeowners, and in 1913, the school board made clear its preference that teachers live in those private homes. Around 1910, countless advertisements proclaiming "Boarders Wanted" and "Rooms for Rent" appeared in the city's newspapers, and many "specified that they were looking for 'young ladies,' 'gentlemen,' or 'refined' boarders."[5] No boarders were more refined than Seattle's teachers, and they continued to board in private homes for decades.

The Alaska Yukon Pacific Exposition (AYP) in 1909 spurred hotel building, and the residential hotel remained a preference for many teachers well into the interwar years. Even before the AYP, Seattle had acquired a number of impressive hotels, including the Lincoln at Fourth Avenue and Madison Street, two blocks away from Central School. The Lincoln accommodated a "middle class seeking gentility." The Sorrento, five blocks farther up First Hill on Madison, catered to a more up-scale clientele in an elegant building with a view dining room.[6] Teachers lived in both places.

Adelaide Pollock, principal of West Queen Anne School, lived at the Lincoln early in the century but moved to Queen Anne Hill by 1910. Josephine Gannon lived at the Lincoln in 1915; she taught seventh grade at Seward and Pacific schools before transferring to McGilvra to teach until she retired in 1940. Lila Delano, teacher of art and design at Franklin High School, lived at the Lincoln Hotel in 1918, and among the grade teachers living there then were Hester Attebury and Mabel Bigelow, who continued to teach first and second grades at Pacific School into the late twenties. Elizabeth Willcox, who lived at the Sorrento that year, taught algebra and geometry throughout the interwar years at Lincoln and Roosevelt high schools. First Hill remained a district of residential hotels, and the residential hotel remained a favorite home for many school women through the interwar years. Half of the fourteen women who taught at blue-collar Emerson School in the city's far south end in 1919 lived in residential hotels, and most of them continued teaching in Seattle throughout the next two decades. Four of the Emerson teachers lived at the Glencairn on First Hill.[7]

Among other hotels that teachers chose were the Otis on First Hill, the Wintonia on Minor Avenue, and the Assembly, four blocks up Madison from the Lincoln. The Savoy, on Second Avenue at University Street, proved a popular early downtown location for teachers. Near Pioneer Square at Third Avenue and Yesler, the Frye Hotel, Seattle's grandest when built in 1911, continued to bid for teacher patronage through the 1930s. These were joined later by such as the Vance, the Waldorf, and the New Richmond. The latter two gave special rates to teachers and in 1928 advertised that grade teachers had, for several years, "lived in these two fine homelike fireproof hotels, returning year after year." The 1930 census confirms that Seattle had more full-time hotel guest rooms, per capita, than any other city of its size,[8] and its teachers occupied many of them.

The residential hotel offered the anonymity some sought, even as it provided social opportunities and friendships. The atmosphere there was casual and friendly. Managers often knew the residents by name and knew "their individual needs and peculiarities." Life sometimes could mirror that in a small town, but without the intrusiveness that a young woman might have fled.[9]

The magnet of economy brought many to hotel living. A young woman accustomed to middle-class standards in her parents' home could replicate them more affordably in a hotel than she could in furnishing a separate household. Because managers negotiated monthly rents on an individual basis and seldom advertised them, it is difficult to gauge the cost for a teacher. In 1910, the Hotel Rhein in downtown Seattle did advertise rates of three to five dollars a week, with "special monthly rates." The Clark Hotel, long a favorite among teachers, publicized its location in the heart of the "Business and Theater District" and touted amenities such as electric lights, hot and cold water, steam heat, and a telephone in every room. In 1914, a room at the Clark on the European plan rented for a dollar a day "and up;" a room with bath started at a dollar and a half. One estimate suggests that monthly rent could be as low as half the weekly charge. A member of the interwar cohort recalled, "Women teachers often . . . [roomed] together to cut down on the costs." By sharing hotel accommodations, they lived more cheaply than they could by boarding in a private home. In Seattle, as in Chicago, three teachers in the midtwenties who "had been paying $6 or more per week for rooms with individual families" found that "by pooling their rent money for a large room in an elegant midpriced hotel, they each saved a dollar a week and lived far more conveniently and convivially."[10]

The residential hotel provided better plumbing and heating than most private homes on into the twenties. In 1910, most hotel rooms included a sink with hot and cold water and a shared bath down the corridor; by the midtwenties, a mid-priced residential hotel typically offered a suite of two rooms, and by 1930, a separate bath.[11]

Escape from housekeeping chores held great appeal. A 1927 survey found that 14 percent of the residents in one of Seattle's larger hotels taught in the city's schools. One, a ten-year hotel dweller, made the teachers' case for the hotel as refuge: "When a woman has taught all day and disciplined forty-odd lively children she wants to go home to a room or apartment far above the street level, where there's lots of heat and hot water and no noise." A colleague found obvious advantages over living in a private home:

In the hotel I can entertain my friends without feeling that they are not wanted. I do not have to take care of the room. I have four towels each day, fresh sheets several times a week, hot water at any hour, lots of light and heat and a private bath. In the hotel are a restaurant, laundry, dry cleaning establishment, bootblack and many mail deliveries a day. The management does not object to the use of electrical appliances so I have a grill, iron and percolator.[12]

In its residential hotels in the 1920s, teachers mingled with a cross-section of Seattle's other professional women, including department store buyers, business executives, writers, librarians, social workers, and politicians.[13]

Social life could be what one made of it. Bridge foursomes could easily materialize, and weekend activities with fellow hotel dwellers led to lifelong friendships. The Chargois sisters came to Seattle from Ritzville in eastern Washington to teach in the midtwenties. "Oh it was fun! Living in those small residential hotels was fun," recalled Doris Chargois. She and Mildred lived at the Mission Inn, a small three-story hotel on Capitol Hill where

The dining room would be cleared once a month, at least. . . . a young couple with a little kid operated it—and about once a month they'd clear out the dining room after dinner, have an orchestra . . . [or] maybe just someone with a piano, but have some music, and dance.[14]

The teachers' record for residential hotel living may belong to Harriet Pennington, who came to Seattle during World War I and taught first grade at Washington School until she retired in 1938. She had lived in hotels since 1908, while teaching in various parts of the country. Hotel guests included many men, and she reportedly had found "the free and easy life" surprising and shocking at first. But soon she "enjoyed the ease of making acquaintances and the numerous social contacts, . . . [and] in company with her roommate, another teacher, Miss Pennington had an exceptionally good time." In 1920 she lived at the Hotel Clark, and by 1930 she had moved to the venerable Assembly Hotel on Madison.[15]

Excessive concern for safety did not define interwar Seattle. Gladys Charles, a teacher new to the city in the midthirties, lived downtown and recalled, "I walked all over this city, sometimes at night—I went places, and you never had a fear in the world. There was no reason to—it was a safe, comfortable city to live in." Even early in the century, as Roger Sale points out, around Skid Road near the waterfront,

> The residential nature of this area south of Yesler Way probably meant that it was not as wild and dangerous as many who lived elsewhere in the city thought. Single women who were not prostitutes did not walk the streets here, but this is not to say they could not have done so.[16]

Security provisions and fireproof construction would have mitigated the fears of those less sanguine than Gladys Charles.

By the 1920s, another type of multiunit building, the apartment hotel, presented the greatest competition for the mid-priced residential hotel. It had been available in Seattle for decades, but, with the AYP, had moved up the social ladder. Efficiency units, which included a private buffet kitchen, offered tenants the option of cooking their own meals or eating in the public dining room. In 1925 the Claremont Apartment Hotel was built in the heart of downtown at Fourth and Virginia, and it attracted teachers. In the early thirties, Anna Pelton, who presided over classes held in conjunction with the Children's Orthopedic Hospital, lived at the Claremont, which advertised "attractive weekly and month rates on all single rooms and apartments."[17] Increasingly popular, apartment hotels heralded a transition to conventional apartment buildings that already clustered on Queen Anne Hill, Capitol Hill, and in the Wallingford and University districts. All four areas became residential enclaves for teachers during the interwar decades.

In her 1910 move to the top of Queen Anne Hill near the school she headed, Adelaide Pollock relocated slightly ahead of the hill's apartment-building boom. Seattle's first apartment buildings had appeared before 1900, "generally along street car lines and near neighborhood commercial areas." Many apartments were built on Queen Anne between 1900 and 1910. In 1907 two elegant ones went up on the hill's lower south slope—the Kinnear Apartments and the Chelsea Apartment Hotel. More buildings noted for "their aesthetic contribution" to the south slope came before World War I, and in the 1920s intense apartment development on the hill continued.[18]

Queen Anne was always a prime residential choice. Letha McClure, the school district's longtime director of music, lived at the Kinnear Apartments in 1915. L. Maxine Kelly, principal of Interbay School at the foot of the hill to the west, had lived in a new building at 326 Queen Anne Avenue since 1910 and would stay there until 1951.[19]

In the memories of Queen Anne High School graduates, every teacher at the school lived in an apartment on or near the hill. Although that perception may be off the mark even for the 1930s, nine of the twenty-one women on the Queen Anne faculty in 1919 did live there. The hill's grade teachers, too, opted for apartment living close to their assignments. The principal Elizabeth Tharp of Frantz Coe School lived at the Assembly Hotel on Madison, but one-fourth of her teachers lived on the hill. Five of John Hay School's twelve teachers were Queen Anne dwellers in 1919. Children often knew where their teachers lived, and a pupil from the thirties recalled that when they walked by one teacher's apartment "we were very aware that she was up on the third floor."[20] Teachers who lived on the hill taught in schools all over the city and relied on public transportation. With streetcar travel usually requiring at least one transfer, teachers obviously found Queen Anne apartments attractive and affordable.

As Seattle had expanded, single-family homes began to appear on Capitol Hill, and apartment buildings, too, rose on the slope that adjoined First Hill on the northeast. With an upper-middle-class neighborhood developing near Volunteer Park, some Capitol Hill apartment buildings offered living on a fairly genteel scale. One of the earliest, built in 1911, was the Gables which began as a residential hotel. There seems to have been some conscious effort to mingle multiunit structures, such as the Phoenix built in 1924, with single-family homes on Capitol Hill. The builder of the

Phoenix lived next door to it, and "clearly believed that single-family homes and multifamily buildings could harmoniously co-exist."[21] Ready access to streetcar lines cemented the appeal for the multitude of teachers who lived on Capitol Hill between the two world wars.

Since 1895, a streetcar bridge had allowed university students to reach the campus from downtown across the confluence of Lake Union and Portage Bay. But before the Montlake Bridge opened to automobiles and streetcars in 1925, many teachers in the schools in the city's north end chose to live north of Lake Union and the ship canal. Twenty of the twenty-five women teaching at University Heights School in 1919 lived north of the waterways, as did four of Bryant School's five women. All fourteen women teaching at Ravenna in 1919 lived in or near that growing area, which had only recently acquired reliable, if not very convenient, streetcar service.

The University District had been home to any number of teachers while they attended the university, and, geography aside, they often chose to remain near the campus because of its cultural and sporting events. Many moved into private homes as boarders after leaving the ubiquitous student rooming houses, and after World War I, in great numbers they moved into new apartment buildings that went up west of the campus and north to Ravenna Park. Brick structures such as the Campus, the Stanford, the Wellesley, the Varsity Arms, and the Canterbury garden bungalows lined Brooklyn Avenue. Malloy Manor and the Malloy Apartments, built in 1923, remained teacher favorites in the district for decades. In the early thirties, Malloy Manor, a block from the campus, advertised one- to five-room apartments that rented by the day, week, or month, and it boasted a dining room, beauty parlor, and seventy-five-car garage.[22]

Before the Fremont Bridge opened in 1916, streetcars brought teachers who lived downtown and on Queen Anne Hill over a trestle across the ship canal to reach such schools as B. F. Day, McDonald, Interlake, and Latona. But many teachers chose to live in the growing Wallingford neighborhood north of the canal. Both apartment houses and bungalow courts had appeared early in the century, and by the First World War they dotted the area. A postwar apartment boom produced some fine buildings; in 1923 the Hawthorne on Fremont Avenue joined the Linden Court bungalows built earlier on Linden Avenue.[23] One of the city's few east-west streetcar lines ran through Wallingford along Forty-fifth Street; hence, apartments in the area also attracted teachers bound for schools in Ballard.

In 1919, twelve of B. F. Day's teachers lived north of the ship canal, and eleven of Latona's eighteen did as well. Only the principal Emma Larrabee, who lived at the Wintonia Hotel on First Hill, and two other McDonald teachers did not live in Wallingford or its adjacent neighborhoods. Harriet Farrell, who taught sixth grade at Interlake beginning in 1926, epitomizes both the stability and tenure of those who lived near their work; when she retired in 1969, she still lived on Wallingford Avenue, six blocks south of the school where she taught for forty-three years.[24]

Very few of the women teaching in the city's south end, at such predominantly blue-collar schools as Brighton, Columbia (City), Concord, Dunlap, Hawthorne, South Park, and Van Asselt, chose to live near the schools where they taught. This was true when many of the interwar cohort began their careers in those schools, and it held true throughout the next three decades: in 1910, only 28 percent of the women teaching there lived south of First Hill; in 1915 and 1919, fewer than a fourth did. Even the long-established Columbia City neighborhood, with a greater percentage of its teachers living nearby than most south-end schools, offered little attractive housing. In 1910, five of Columbia's nine teachers lived in the same block, three at the same address; the others had downtown or First Hill addresses. None of the teachers at Van Asselt, South Seattle, Hawthorne, or Dunlap lived anywhere near those neighborhoods.[25]

After its annexation to the city in 1908, West Seattle remained something of an entity apart, on occasion, over the years, even threatening to declare independence and secede. Teachers living centrally or in the north end of town reached West Seattle by way of streetcar after transferring in Pioneer Square. They traveled over an elevated wooden trestle above Spokane Street, and most had to transfer again to reach their schools. Given the difficulty of commuting, teachers often chose to reside in the neighborhood. More than half of the teachers at West Seattle School lived nearby in 1910, as did two of the five at Youngstown. Both women teaching at Alki School that year lived at Alki Point. By the time West Seattle School had been renamed Lafayette during World War I, 39 percent of the teachers in those three schools lived in that area.[26]

The vast majority of the interwar cohort lived in multiple-unit buildings. Others continued to live in their families' homes for varying lengths of time as they taught. A few bought property in the city in partnership with parents and other family members, but until New Deal housing initiatives bore fruit after World War II, not many women teachers owned their own homes.

Mary Louise Sawhill remained in the family home longer than most. In the spring of 1998, the retired Madison Junior High School Latin teacher still lived in the Montlake area house where her family had lived when she graduated from Broadway High School in 1921. In the case of Eunice Copeland, the 1895 graduate of Seattle High School stayed in her parents' home on Terry Avenue only until 1901. She moved up to Capitol Hill that year, closer to her assignment at T. T. Minor School. By 1910 her sister, Fanny, had begun teaching, and the two women shared quarters on Capitol Hill. They lived together the rest of their lives, most of their later years in the Montlake area while Eunice served as principal at Fairview and Fanny taught at Bryant.[27]

In 1934, a young teacher and her mother built a house in West Seattle. On graduating from San Diego State College in 1931, Margaret Houston had come north to teach as a cadet at Fauntleroy School. Her recently widowed mother came from California with her. Sixty-seven years later, Miss Houston chuckled when she recalled, "Oh Yes! she wouldn't let her chick go off—she was with me until she died" in 1959. They first lived in a small apartment one block from Fauntleroy but "got tired of paying rent." After she had transferred to Highland Park School, with proceeds from selling their house in San Diego and "a little money from selling some stock," they bought two lots near the southern city limits from a developer for $75 a lot.

When we got there it was so thickly timbered that the only thing we could do was to hire somebody to come in and cut down and haul off the trees and bushes. . . . A little ways [in] they found that clear across both lots there was a huge downed log—cut at the first cutting of the original timber and left there to rot. We couldn't even see it when we bought the place. So we had a job getting rid of all that and all the stumps—the first cutting stumps were still there—big tall ones, ten feet high, . . . that was interesting. We built a little double garage and moved into that and turned it eventually into a house.[28]

They stayed there until Margaret transferred to Seward in 1944, then bought another house together in north Seattle.

Mary and Effie Aiken, too, owned a home. The sisters had come to Seattle together in 1906 from Pennsylvania, both graduates of Slippery Rock State Normal School. Mary had nine years of experience in Pennsylvania; Effie, fourteen years her junior, had none. They lived together on Capitol Hill while teaching in schools citywide. In 1919, both transferred to Highland Park and stayed there until they retired—Mary in 1933 and Effie in 1950. At some point before 1926, they acquired property and built a house; according to the *Seattle Grade Club Magazine*, in May that year they hosted "a lovely luncheon at their home at Three Tree Point."[29]

Ravenna School opened in 1911, when that area north of the university was still heavily wooded and difficult to reach. In looking back, one pupil whose eight years at Ravenna began in 1918, said, "I don't think anybody lived close enough to walk—but they'd get off down at Cowan Park and take the jitney bus." From the end of streetcar lines near the campus, the seven-passenger jitney ran twelve blocks north and east to reach the school. Later, a Ravenna streetcar began operating and took teachers and students within three blocks of their destination.[30]

Pearl Dartt taught at Ravenna from its opening until she retired in 1935 and never worried about streetcars and jitneys. She owned her own home seven blocks from the school, well within walking distance. She lived in what a student described as "a Hansel and Gretel house" throughout her career.[31]

Homeownership remained beyond the means of most teachers and sufficiently rare that it merited coverage in the *Grade Club Magazine*. In February 1922, an item reported that Adelle Wheeler and May Hurd, both teachers at Wallingford's Interlake School, had "purchased a dear, little, bungalow home" near the school with a view of the Olympic Mountains. When Adelle Wheeler started her Seattle career at Latona in 1902, she lived in a downtown flat but soon moved north of Lake Union. On transferring to Interlake, she moved to the same University District address as May Hurd, who then taught at University Heights. Miss Hurd transferred to Interlake in 1921, and the following year they bought the bungalow. Miss Wheeler transferred again, to Montlake School, from which she retired in 1933. May Hurd moved with Interlake seventh- and eighth-graders to Hamilton Junior High when it opened in 1927, teaching English and social studies. She finished her career in West Seattle at Madison Junior High in 1947, retiring at the age of seventy.[32]

Two other Seattle grade teachers joined the ranks of homeowners in March 1922. The careers of two longtime friends, Myrtle Kiger and Grace McCauley, testify to the enduring influence of Frank Cooper's Seattle Way and the stability of the interwar decades. Cooper hired the experienced Myrtle Kiger from West Virginia in 1902. In 1904 he hired Grace McCauley, who was just two years out of Mansfield Normal School in Pennsylvania but had already taught several years in her home state. After two years teaching at J. B. Allen School, Miss McCauley transferred to Cascade School to be nearer where she lived on Capitol Hill. The two women met at Cascade, where Miss Kiger spent her entire Seattle career. By 1918 they and several other teachers lived at the Sherwood on Capitol Hill, but four years later the *Grade Club Magazine* announced that the two Cascade teachers would "move out to their new home at Morningside Heights."[33]

"Out to their new home" was the operative phrase. From Capitol Hill, Cascade was a short streetcar trip involving one transfer; from the new house ten blocks north of the city limits, travel to school surely required them to own an automobile. Myrtle Kiger and Grace McCauley remained in that house the rest of their lives; both retired in 1940. Their letters of resignation elicited this response from Frank Willard, the assistant superintendent whose Seattle career began, like theirs, in Frank Cooper's first decade:

> What I would say to one of you I would say to both, since you have been and always will be associated in my mind as a part of that splendid group that for so many years . . . made the Cascade School a real center of good will and efficiency expressed in fine teamwork. . . . I am glad that you can look back upon an experience that must be so filled with satisfaction . . . [and] that you are looking now to other interesting things which you can enjoy free from the strain that is ever present in the classroom.

The two women had for nearly four decades taught in the same working-class school and consistently earned superior evaluations. Miss Kiger died in 1960 at the age of seventy-eight, and her 1931 evaluation would have served as a fitting epitaph for both: "She is ideal in treatment of children and is highly regarded by all."[34]

Whether as sisters living together, daughters living with parents, friends from normal school or college sharing an apartment, or new colleagues within the teacher corps, most of the interwar cohort did share quarters. It is impossible to know the nature of the latter relationships, some of which, by the end of the twentieth century, would no doubt be seen as lesbian. At midcentury no one considered such partnerships anything other than the height of devoted friendship. Economic factors may well have accounted for more shared accommodations than did sexual orientation.

The anonymity and sophistication of a city did provide "homosexual women . . . more opportunities to live the lives they wanted," and statistical probability dictates that some teachers moved to Seattle for that reason. It has been argued that during the twenties the new psychology of sexuality "made close relationships between women suspect," but evidence of that suspicion in Seattle is hard to find. When given the chance, few interviewees addressed sexual orientation. Speaking of teachers in Queen Anne schools who lived together, one former student recalled, "We were happy that [they] lived together . . . we were . . . totally unaware of homosexuality—they were just good friends." The occasional clandestine marriage, not sexual orientation, provided grist for Seattle's rumor mills in the twenties and thirties.[35]

If Grace McCauley and Myrtle Kiger did indeed own an automobile in 1922, they stood in the vanguard of teachers behind the wheel. In the first decade of the century, few women drove. Invention of the self-starter in 1911 eliminated need for the odious and dangerous hand crank, and the number of women who took to the road slowly increased. World War I proved a catalyst; indeed, "wartime service had publicized and legitimized driving for women in general." Those who served in the women's motor service, both at home and in France, continued to drive after 1918, and those who came of age during the war would drive with a skill and confidence their mothers had never had.[36]

Cost presented the greatest obstacle to a teacher wishing to own a car. In 1921, *Motor* magazine estimated that a city dweller owning a car valued at $600 would need at least a $2,800 annual income; three years later, the National Automobile Chamber of Commerce speculated that people earning less than $1,500 were still "unsupplied with motor transportation."[37] Most Seattle teachers' salaries did not even approach $2,800 in the twenties; little wonder few owned automobiles.

The desire for a car fueled what became the time-honored American practice of buying on credit. By 1921, about half of all automobiles were being sold "on some form of deferred payment system," and the next year the number rose to 73 percent. By the midtwenties, "the market for both new and used cars was being maintained primarily by installment sales."[38] Buying on time made car ownership possible for the teacher who wanted to drive and had no reservations about going into debt.

Price had always been the greatest attraction of the Model T Ford, and Seattle's Ford dealers advertised regularly in the *Seattle Grade Club Magazine*. The growth of the used car market made buying a car even less expensive, and the number of teachers "motoring" while on summer vacation increased. The automobile itself became more attractive. By the end of the twenties, operator friendly transmissions, low-pressure balloon tires, and closed body construction, together with color options beyond black, attracted more women to car ownership. In 1927, *Motor* magazine observed, "The automotive business has almost over night become a feminine business with a feminine market."[39]

Seattle automobile dealers saw market potential among teachers. In 1931, one dealer advertised that he loaned "Private Money . . . to Teachers on Their Automobiles!" Another touted his agency as "The Ideal Place for the Woman Buyer to Select a Fine Guaranteed Model A Ford" and assured teachers they needed no mechanical knowledge to buy a used car under his plan.[40]

Teachers, with their comparatively stable incomes, remained the target of auto dealers throughout the Depression. As school ended in 1934, a Chevrolet dealer proclaimed that "assurance of a real vacation is yours in a new Chevrolet '6.'" He offered a "FREE Demonstration Ride at your own convenience, absolutely without obligation," and "Special Easy Terms for Teachers!" At least two teachers responded to such persuasion.

At the end of the year, Cora and Evelyn Anderson "appeared at a party, the proud possessors of a new 'Chevy.'" The Anderson sisters taught first grade at Magnolia and Adams schools. A number of teachers reported driving throughout the West that summer.[41] Even with greater opportunity and inducement to buy, car-owning teachers were a minority during the interwar years. It appears that more cars were owned by principals and supervisors of both sexes.

The district opened new schools to accommodate residential development in northeast Seattle, but the jitney experience of Ravenna teachers suggests that the streetcar system did not keep pace. When school opened in 1924, Superintendent Cole reported a "lack of transportation facilities for teachers at the Laurelhurst school," a portable school in an area especially difficult to reach. The board authorized giving Dora Herren, the head teacher, or principal, "$10 per month as auto allowance for providing transportation for herself and another one of the teachers."[42]

Teachers who drove to school are memorable for that fact. Former pupils recall that few Laurelhurst teachers drove until late in the 1930s, and those who did stood out. In 1931 Marion German joined the faculty; the young woman just out of Bellingham Normal School is remembered as "a real treasure because she drove this big car that [all the boys] loved—sort of a touring car." At the south end of the city, more teachers at Emerson began driving during the thirties, thus avoiding a multitransfer forty-five-minute streetcar trip from downtown. Emerson's manual training teacher utilized cars parked at the school as teaching devices; he had his students crawl underneath to inspect and evaluate their frames.[43]

As the number of teachers who drove grew, carpooling proved a real boon to downtown and First Hill dwellers who taught in the far south end and in West Seattle. When Gladys Charles Perry began her teaching career in 1935 at Concord Elementary, she lived downtown and "traveled back and forth by streetcar. . . . it was a long way, indeed it was." She recalled that a fellow teacher, Mary Luch,

drove to Concord and she picked up teachers and they paid her then for going in her car. Once in a while I would come home with her—she didn't pick me up in the morning, but if she had room in her car she would bring me down town because she had to go through town.[44]

Mary Luch had been with the district since 1927 and shared a large First Hill apartment with her sister, Sara, and two other teachers. That location had not presented transportation problems for Sara in 1934 when she began teaching at Ravenna, which had secured good streetcar service by then. But when she transferred to Madison Junior High School in West Seattle, she carpooled with May Phillips, Madison's music teacher. Phillips's own move to West Seattle forced Sara to revert first to streetcars and then in 1940, buses. She had learned to drive but did not acquire her own car until her brother entered the service in World War II and sold her his.[45]

In the era of standard, or stick, shifts, Seattle's hilly terrain intimidated more than a few drivers but did not stall the growth of their numbers. By the midtwenties traffic in the city presented a safety problem so serious that Mayor Bertha Landes considered it a major concern. The traffic death of one teacher and serious injuries to others in the spring of 1925 while she served on the city council no doubt heightened the mayor's awareness. Margaret Moran, fifth-grade teacher at J. B. Allen School, was struck by a car and killed on March 7. McDonald School's Fannie Belden had survived a pedestrian-auto mishap early in the school year, but the lingering effect of injuries caused her to miss another two weeks of school later in March. Ada McCullough lived on Capitol Hill and taught at Webster Elementary in north Ballard that year; one afternoon she "had an accident while driving home in her car." Her injuries kept her from the classroom for a week; a fellow teacher riding with her was thrown out of the car. Injuries sustained in an auto accident by Florence Dahl, first-grade teacher at Interlake School, forced her "long absence from school."[46]

Mary McConnel's auto ownership proved more positive than some. As president of the state organization of grade teachers, Miss McConnel attended a convention in Spokane in April. Washington's Good Roads Association had long lobbied for cross-state highways, but by 1925 the only road built through the Cascade mountains was at Snoqualmie Pass. Vacationing teachers made good use of that route, but with the pass still under several feet of snow in April, Miss McConnel made a much longer, more indirect trip. She drove an additional three hundred miles via Portland and along the Old Columbia River Highway, through Pendleton, Oregon, to reach Spokane. Taking at least two days to return, she drove south to cross the Columbia on the newly completed Bridge of the Gods at Cascade Locks, then downriver to Portland and on home to Seattle.[47]

Until replaced by buses and trackless trolleys in 1940, the venerable streetcars in Seattle transported most teachers to work and home again. Those teaching in the industrial south end or in West Seattle continued to transfer on First Avenue. After riding a car in from the north end of town or the apartment enclaves on the surrounding hills, they might wait in Pioneer Square, under the pergola, an "ornate iron enclosure with a roof against the rain." Teachers bound for schools in the Rainier Valley or the far southeast corner of the city transferred on Fourth Avenue, then, if headed for Emerson School, switched to the Renton car at the Prentice Street turnaround.[48]

Streetcar travel was not hazard free; some spectacular accidents probably gave teachers pause. A streetcar inbound from West Seattle overturned one morning in January 1937, near the spot where another had jumped the tracks on the trestle and fallen to the street below in April 1928. Teachers could have been aboard when the Summit Avenue and Capitol Hill cars collided in November 1924, and teachers bound for South Park School regularly rode both the West Queen Anne and South Park cars, which had collided earlier that year.[49]

The school district usually accommodated requests for changes in assignment, and transportation continued as a factor in those requests beyond World War II. Edith Davidson, who started as a cadet from Cheney Normal School in 1927, taught at Seward, the demonstration school, throughout the war. In March 1946, saying "I do not wish to remain in demonstration work," she requested a transfer, and added, "I would appreciate a place relatively close or convenient for city bus transportation as I do not have a car."[50] Assignment to Leschi the following year gave her the choice of two bus routes. In 1948 she transferred to school district headquarters and served as head of audiovisual services until her retirement in March 1966.

By the time Edith Davidson Lind retired, none of Seattle's school buildings lacked basic amenities. All may not have reflected state-of-the-art design and mechanics, but remodeling projects had updated electrical and plumbing systems in all the schools. Over the long span of their careers, not all in the interwar cohort enjoyed building facilities of comparable quality. Many who came early in the century taught in fairly primitive circumstances. Although not a matter of record, along with its accessibility, a school's physical state could well have figured in a teacher's desire for a building transfer.

School architecture and building maintenance probably enhanced the appeal of Frank Cooper's new system in Seattle. Even Seattle's less comfortable buildings would have been a vast improvement over the sort of one-room rural school in eastern Washington where many began teaching. The school district's faithful, hardworking corps of custodians would have brought joy to any young woman just out of normal school, who was often expected to clean her rural school house and stoke its woodburning stove. Rural grade teachers knew that urban districts west of the Cascades paid better salaries, and word of new school construction in those districts spread quickly.[51]

Building many neighborhood grade schools in the growing city had been a hallmark of Cooper's early years. The architectural historian Jeffrey Ochsner finds that same pattern in the late nineteenth century as well. He contends, "In many ways, the 1880s and 1890s were the defining decades for the character of urban Seattle" and for its school architecture. Many schools built in those decades fall in the eight-room "two-story wooden box" category; but by 1890, well-designed brick structures had joined the mix.[52]

Other frame buildings in the district did not resemble wooden boxes. The district was "particularly proud of" Denny School, completed in August 1884. Described as Italianate and "handsome in the extreme," it was a rectangular building containing six first-floor classrooms; the second floor housed five classrooms along with a library and the principal's office.[53] After additions in 1891, Denny School was indeed a handsome, imposing structure atop the hill of the same name; it remained a desirable teaching assignment well into the next century.

Whitworth School opened in 1908 in far southeast Seattle's recently annexed Hillman City. Three women who taught into the late 1930s served on its original faculty. The year before construction of the new brick building, one of the three—Nell Hart—shared a wooden portable with another, teaching in half-day sessions. Miss Hart retired in 1940, from Laurelhurst;

her two 1908 teaching colleagues, Gertrude Gayton and Edith Gourlay, retired in 1938, as did Whitworth's original principal, Emma C. Hart.[54]

Others of the interwar cohort whose tenures began before World War I taught in physical plants that ranged from good to barely acceptable. Building conditions were an ongoing concern. At one of its earliest meetings, February 25, 1913, the Grade Teachers' Club appointed a committee "to investigate heating conditions in all Grade Buildings." When the committee chair Elsie Judd, who still taught fourth grade at T. T. Minor School in 1941, reported back in October, it was decided "that each teacher keep a record of the temperature in her school room at short intervals for several days" and send the data to Miss Judd. The club also had a committee on ventilation.[55]

Inadequate or nonexistent plumbing plagued teachers for years. Hot water did not reach all buildings until long after World War I; in June 1919, the school board began to ponder the cost "of installing hot water service in all of our schools." But budget cuts in the early twenties barely allowed for basics, let alone physical luxuries. In 1924, the PTA of Webster School continued to petition the school board to bring hot water into that north Ballard building.[56]

With or without hot water, separate restroom facilities for teachers were not standard. The 1911 faculty of Columbia School (later renamed Lowell) on Capitol Hill did not enjoy such convenience. When the board learned that a storeroom in the building was "the only one available for a rest room [it] recommended that a sink be installed in said room." Nina O. Buchanan taught first grade in a portable there that year; the inadequate facilities undoubtedly influenced her turn to political and professional activism, which culminated in her 1935 election as King County superintendent of schools.[57]

In 1914, the board requested a "list of all schools where no separate teachers' toilets are provided"; a year later the assistant superintendent Almina George brought yet another report to the board on the state of restrooms. The board finally authorized installation of plumbing at Wallingford's Interlake School in February 1915. Two other schools, Interbay and South Seattle, had totally inadequate toilet facilities; in 1917, the board recommended the same solution for South that it had for Interbay the year before—"rearrangement of recess periods, so as to make the present equipment ample for the needs of the school."[58]

Teachers in some high schools fared little better. In Ballard High School in 1911, a partition was installed in a classroom "to be used as a teachers' rest room." The cost of $120 to "install plumbing for toilet and wash basin" deferred completion until 1922.[59]

Rodent infestation posed another challenge to the interwar cohort throughout their careers. In the winter of 1915, the district's medical inspector briefed principals on "the importance of trapping all rats that may appear in school buildings." The *Seattle Times* deemed it worth editorial comment in the spring of 1939 when a rat darted from a portable and bit an eight-year-old boy: "Seattle's school buildings are not overrun with rats. But there are enough of them, particularly around the portable buildings." By then, the Depression had halted building construction, and in the late thirties an estimated 14,000 Seattle pupils and their teachers spent their days in overcrowded portable classrooms "with poor heating and ventilation facilities."[60] Little wonder that the desire to get out of a portable appeared on requests for building transfers.

Oddly enough, insufficient school lighting persisted in a city renowned for electricity and considered a bastion of municipal utility ownership. The school district hired its first electrician in 1911 and for the next decade undertook to improve lighting in all its buildings. Early progress was piecemeal at best; even schools that had electric lights did not, or could not, use them regularly. In 1915, the school district medical inspector supported principals' requests "for electric lighting of the building on dark days, [and] that certain dark green walls be calsomined a lighter color." The board asked for a report from principals "on the loss of time and interference with regular school work due to lack of light on cloudy days during the winter months."[61]

Accordingly, Queen Anne High School reported that it was "equipped with lights, which are resorted to on dark days," as did Maple School on Beacon Hill. At Adams School in Ballard, "Work suffer[ed] greatly on dark days, from November until the middle of January, on account of deficient light . . . especially true on north side," and its principal was "fully satisfied that much of eye-strain among pupils and teachers has had a beginning at the school." Anna B. Kane reported that eleven rooms at Colman had to alter schedules on dark days; in one month a room that had lights "made use of these all of one day and part of fourteen days." At Latona School, where the "greatest per cent of absence due to headaches comes on dark days," pupils had "great difficulty in seeing [the] blackboard during first hour in morning and last in afternoon." Most principals agreed in some way that "electric lights would be a great saving on eyes." Only the redoubtable Bella Perry, at Hawthorne School, found "Rooms sufficiently lighted."[62]

Other women principals weighed in on the side of improving the lot of their pupils. West Queen Anne's Adelaide Pollock found the school "too dark to permit work after four," and Emma Larrabee reported that at McDonald it was "frequently too dark to permit use of books." Main Street School had four rooms with electric lights, but Principal Ada J. Mahon stressed that "first grade needs lights very badly." Elizabeth Tharp, at Coe School, reported "irregular" work on dark days, and in one parting thought said, "If we are planning for children, we need lights here."[63]

A year after receiving the principals' report, the board still doled out additional lighting in parsimonious fashion; it authorized lights at Green Lake and Minor schools "in such rooms as in the judgment of the Superintendent seems necessary." New grade buildings, however, came routinely to include electric lights and, after 1917, even "electrical outlets for stereopticon and moving picture machines in meeting-rooms." But as late as 1921, teachers in portables did not enjoy the benefits of electricity.[64]

Perhaps it could be labeled a tradeoff, but when the board voted to install lights for Elizabeth Tharp at Coe, it denied the PTA's request for a toilet in the girls restroom. Deeming the "toilet installed in the Teachers' Rest Room . . . sufficient equipment in this line for this school,"[65] the board no doubt cemented the activist resolve of Nina Buchanan, who was then teaching first grade at Coe.

The dedicated women who would teach in Seattle for decades enjoyed few creature comforts in their buildings, but the lack of telephones came closer to causing mutiny than plumbing and lighting. When the telephone company raised its rates in November 1911, the board ordered all phones removed from the schools. Despite teachers' protests and those of Frank Cooper, for several years the district's Central Office communicated with schools "by postcard or courier." Phone service returned to the high schools fairly soon, but not until 1918 did the board authorize *pay* phones "in all the grade schools and all phones now installed in the grade schools to be replaced with pay phones." A year later high school teachers joined with grade colleagues to resolve "That all Seattle schools be provided with business telephone service available to teachers without charge."[66]

The board's response to grade teachers' request for free phone service can only be described as patronizing and insulting. It instructed Cooper "to prepare rules under which such phones might be used without interfering with school work." Telephones eventually returned to all schools, but as late as 1939 a building would have "one phone that the secretary would pass back and forth," and school phone numbers were not available to parents.[67]

School district decisions and teaching assignments often dictated the quality and direction of teachers' lives; nothing illustrates this better than the saga of Denny School. In the midtwenties, city engineering plans and school district policy converged in an "only in Seattle" scenario that severely affected the lives of its teachers: demolition of the magnificent old school that stood not far from a future city landmark—the Space Needle. A succession of regrades had altered the school's neighborhood, and by 1927 declining enrollment had reduced the faculty from twenty-one to a mere five. Once a plum teaching assignment, Denny School, now minus one wing, stood atop an ever-shrinking piece of land. From 1926 to 1928, its dwindling corps of teachers arrived at their streetcar stops, walked two blocks or so, and climbed a makeshift wooden ramp and flight of stairs to reach what was left of a school marooned forty feet in the air.[68]

Mary Allen scaled the ramp and stairs to her first-grade classroom in 1927, after exiting the North Queen Anne streetcar at Denny Way and Fifth Avenue. A 1906 graduate of Ypsilanti Normal College, the Michigan native had taught in her home state and a year in Port Angeles, Washington, before moving to Seattle where in 1918 she began teaching third grade at South Park School in the heart of an industrial area adjacent to what became Boeing Field. After four years of arduous streetcar commuting from her family's Queen Anne home, she requested a transfer to "be nearer home" and was assigned to Denny School. After Denny's closure, she taught at Ross School, north of the ship canal, until she resigned on October 14, 1939. Her twenty-one years with the Seattle district had been

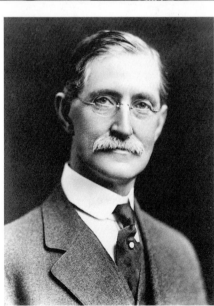

Frank B. Cooper, the "teachers' superintendent," arrived in Seattle in 1901. He developed an urban school system that attracted experienced women teachers for careers of long tenure, including many who taught at Broadway High School *(above,)* which opened in 1902. Seattle Public Schools Archives.

Noontime in the teachers lunchroom at Warren Avenue School, 1905. Five of that year's faculty taught well past World War I, including the principal, Emma C. Hart, who retired in 1938. Washington State Historical Society, Asahel Curtis 6179.

(Facing page, top) Seattle teachers depended on streetcars for transportation until 1940. Pioneer Square, its pergola a shelter from the rain, was a key transfer point. Teachers living in hotels on First Hill and bound for schools in West Seattle or the industrial area could have been among those shown here, ca. 1914. Museum of History and Industry, 83.10.9094.

(Facing page, bottom) The Hotel Otis, ca. 1915. The new brick addition enhanced the First Hill hotel where teachers had lived since early in the century. Washington State Historical Society, Asahel Curtis 10626.

(Facing page, top) This 1914 classroom, typical of those throughout the interwar years, shows thirty-nine children intent on their science project involving frogs and tadpoles. Before World War I, classes ranged upward from an average of thirty-eight pupils. Washington State Historical Society, Asahel Curtis 6191.

(Facing page, bottom) Many of the interwar cohort taught in portable classrooms reminiscent of the one-room rural schools they had forsaken earlier. This grade school sewing class, ca. 1916, occupied a portable with an unfinished interior and no electric lights. Washington State Historical Society, Asahel Curtis 6111.

In 1937 a portable on the grounds of McGilvra School accommodated an overflow enrollment. A woodstove still provided heat, but portables had acquired electric lights by then. Museum of History and Industry, PI 25607.

Winona Bailey and Lulie Nettleton, seated side by side on the summit of Mount Olympus in 1913. Both women—Queen Anne High School Latin teacher and legendary grade school principal—had joined the Mountaineers in 1907. Special Collections, University of Washington Libraries, Mountaineers Collection, 18159.

Janet Dewhurst, ca. 1920. A 1918 graduate of Broadway High School, she began teaching in Seattle as a cadet. Active in professional affairs and a champion of teacher interests, she retired in 1964 from the principalship of Leschi School. Seattle Public Schools Archives.

Amelia Telban, ready for normal school in 1925. Seattle selected her as a cadet teacher from among the top of her class at Ellensburg two years later. Photo courtesy of Ethel Telban.

(Below, left) Margaret Houston as a teacher in the district's cadet program in 1931. She retired in 1968, having become a principal—"A gem! A really strong woman who backed her teachers 150 percent." Seattle Public Schools Archives.

(Below, right) Ruth Fulton Isaacs began her long career as an English teacher at Garfield High School in 1926. She gained national prominence in 1950 with the first ever foreign exchange of American students and teachers, which she arranged between Garfield and the Oberschule for girls in Braunschweig, Germany. Seattle Public Schools Archives.

The demonstration school provided teaching examples from the Seattle Way for the benefit of local teachers and many others drawn from cities nationwide. Here, ca. 1929, a master teacher moves among her pupils as visitors observe from the back of the room. Seattle Public Schools Archives, 273–19.

(Facing page, top) The interwar cohort stressed courtesy, kindness, and respect. The Arthurian motif of chivalry permeated Jesse Lockwood's John Muir School. At an assembly in 1920, pupils dramatized the exploits of Sir Galahad. Seattle Public Schools Archives, 256–21.

(Facing page, bottom) "Learning-by-doing" marked the Seattle Way, and the weekly bank day taught the habit of thrift. Longfellow School pupils line up to make their deposits, which in the Depression year of 1935 ranged from ten cents to several dollars. Seattle Public Schools Archives, 092–6.

Longfellow School Seattle Washington
School Savings Bank Day April 9th 1935

Denny School, once the crown jewel of Seattle buildings and a plum teaching assignment, is shown here in 1928, just prior to demolition in the final regrade of Denny Hill. Teachers endured great inconvenience and found the school difficult to reach as the hill was sluiced into the bay. Seattle Public Schools Archives, 6.

(Facing page, top) On a rainy day in 1921, the entire student body of the old Main Street School, protected by coats and umbrellas and led by Principal Ada J. Mahon, walked some eight blocks to their large and airy new building—Bailey Gatzert School. Museum of History and Industry, 83.10.2409.1.

(Facing page, bottom) A group of Bailey Gatzert School pupils, possibly members of the Good Citizenship Club, assembled with teachers in January 1937. Back row, left to right: secretary, K. Ichihara, Principal Ada J. Mahon, and faculty members Mary Brewer, Millie Bethke, Nell Phalon, Mary Fassold, Lorna Lowry, Ava Chambers, and Marie deGallier. Seattle Public Schools Archives, 226–4.

Constance Harding and her sixth-grade class at polyglot Interbay School, ca. 1932. The pupils remembered her as a strict disciplinarian. Photo courtesy of Dorothy Raymond.

(Facing page, top) Interbay School's 1932 graduating eighth-graders. L. Maxine Kelly, its longtime principal, stands on the far right in the second row, and the veteran teacher Ella Harper is third from left in the back row. Photo courtesy of James and Evelyn Tracy.

(Facing page, bottom) Anna B. Kane served as principal of Colman School from 1912 until retiring in 1940. Here she stands with its eighth-grade class in January 1935. Seattle Public Schools Archives, 212–13.

The annual Teachers Institute, a one-time gathering of the entire corps, officially launched the school year and provided the opportunity to renew longtime friendships. The 1935 event, shown here, was held in Meany Hall on the University of Washington campus. Museum of History and Industry, PI 25774.

When commodities rationing was imposed early in World War II, grade schools became headquarters for issuing ration books to neighborhood residents. Grade teachers volunteered countless hours to processing and issuing the books, as shown here in one school auditorium. Museum of History and Industry, PI 28104.

Seattle teachers filled various roles for the military during World War II. The reading teacher Amelia Telban *(back row center)* served army libraries in Japan and Korea after the conflict. Photo courtesy of Ethel Telban.

The onset of World War II added air raid drills to the teachers' school routine. Here pupils have "hit the deck" in 1942. Seattle Public Schools Archives, 273–61.

typical—she continued to live in the family home listed on her employment application, and she relied heavily on the streetcar system.[69]

All of Denny School's four other teachers lived in apartments on Capitol Hill when they were reassigned for the 1928–29 school year. At Denny since 1923, Iva Dresser had come to Seattle during World War I to teach fourth grade at Horace Mann, not far via streetcar from where she lived. Her reassignment to Magnolia School meant a long and difficult crosstown commute. After a year, she taught at schools closer in, until she retired after World War II; she continued to live within a few blocks of her original 1918 address.[70]

Minnie Castonia came to Seattle in 1919, having taught in her home state, Michigan, for ten years. She was assigned to the fifth-grade classroom in Denny School, and when the school closed nine years later, she fared better than others. She went to Pacific School, near First Hill, then moved in 1940 to Cascade, just north of downtown; she retired in 1952. Throughout, she remained in her original First Hill apartment on Summit Avenue.[71]

Both Helen Finch and Alice Hargraves moved from Capitol Hill when Denny closed. Miss Finch, too, had begun teaching in Seattle during the First World War. In 1928, reassigned to Alki School, she did not wait to experience the long multitransfer trip by streetcar over the elevated Spokane Street trestle; she moved that summer to an apartment in West Seattle, where she remained until she retired in 1940.[72]

Alice Hargraves had taught at Denny since arriving in Seattle in 1913, a thirty-six-year-old native of Winnebago, Minnesota, and a veteran teacher of small-town Minnesota schools. The Seattle Way or urban anonymity may have drawn her west; perhaps the mild climate in the Northwest attracted her; she may even have attended the 1909 AYP Exposition. Whatever her reasons for coming, she took over Denny School's first-grade classroom in the fall of 1913. When the Denny closure sent her to McDonald School, just south of Green Lake, she moved to the University District. Even when reassigned to Webster School in Ballard, she kept her apartment two blocks from the university campus and lived there beyond her retirement in 1938.[73]

The case of Denny School's last teachers may be an extreme example of school assignments changing the lives of teachers, but reassignment in succeeding decades continued to affect living patterns, and requests for transfers to buildings nearer home continued. Seattle annexed a large area north of the city in 1943, bringing schools there into the Seattle district; some teachers moved to the suburbs after World War II. Although automobile ownership became the norm, many teachers continued to rely on public transportation and to live in their longtime residences. Those well-established patterns may have evoked the rather sentimental thoughts expressed by an anonymous poet in the *Grade Club Magazine* in 1931:

> I would not change with anyone
> Although my room is mean,
> It looks upon an apple tree
> And dainty plot of green.
> A baby plays there in the sun,
> White clothes wave on the line.
> These things belong to other folks
> But still . . .
> The view is mine.[74]

4 / Perpetuating the Seattle Way

Cadets and a Demonstration School

Young women who entered the Seattle system as cadet teachers received a year-long indoctrination in the Seattle Way during their first year of teaching. For other teachers new to the district, a demonstration school provided the way to imbue them, too, with Seattle's philosophy and priorities. Both were part of Frank Cooper's legacy, perpetuated by his disciples—longtime administrators and veteran teachers. Cadets of the 1930s knew about Cooper, his policies, and his procedures. Although they came long after his tenure, they definitely understood his heritage. The demonstration school, for example, "was the kind of school that he wanted. Cooper was very liberal in the things that he believed, but he was very dogmatic about how you would apply this"; the practices that he initiated endured into the 1940s.[1] The cadet program too, from its inception in 1917 until it ended during World War II, was maintained to Cooper's high standards. Many postwar leaders in the school district and in the Washington Education Association began their careers as cadets in Seattle.

Less than a month after the United States entered World War I, with the wartime economy sure to produce a teacher shortage, Cooper presented his plan to employ as "novitiate teachers" graduates from the state's "accredited higher institutions of learning." At its May 23, 1917, meeting, the school board's two most liberal members, Robert Winsor and Anna Louise Strong, moved and seconded the plan that the board adopted "in principle."[2] That

September, the board approved the hiring of ten of the first cadets at an annual salary of $720. Two of that group continued teaching beyond the interwar years and lent great stability to the teacher corps. Mary W. Coughlin taught first and second grades at Interbay until the school closed in 1935; she then moved to Warren Avenue School, where she remained until retirement. Inga Olson began her career at and retired from Ballard's Webster Elementary, where she taught fourth- through sixth-grade academic subjects.[3]

In 1918 the board approved creation of a supervisory position that became an administrative steppingstone for women. The first to be selected as "head teachers to supervise work of novitiate teachers, with an additional salary of $10 per month," were Ida Vetting and Maude Moore, whose annual salary leaped to $1,420. By 1922, Maude Moore no longer taught in Seattle. In the midtwenties Ida Vetting went from cadet supervisor to the ranks of grade school principals. She began at Columbia School and by 1929 presided at Summit, the district's recently established demonstration school. When that program moved to Seward School, she moved with it and continued as principal there through World War II.[4]

Seattle selected its cadets from lists of promising graduates submitted by Washington's three normal schools. Most teachers in the school district had followed the time-honored pattern of rural or small-town teaching to gain experience necessary for acceptance in Seattle. Those chosen for the cadet program were exceptional, and long after they retired, former cadets were proud to have qualified. Cadet letters of recommendation provide clues to what, in addition to teaching ability, the normal schools deemed important to the Seattle School District. One Ellensburg candidate came recommended as "a beautiful girl, refined, neat and well dressed. Her voice is well modulated and her English is excellent. She has considerable social poise." On the other hand, Bellingham Normal shared a word of caution, "You will be justified in investigating Miss M—— more carefully, since her teaching may be over-estimated on account of her attractive personality." Cornelia Jenner, Bellingham's appointment secretary, also stressed hidden assets, "I feel that anyone interviewing Miss Nelson might not realize at first what unusual ability she has. . . . [she] is very original and has a keen interest in a large number of worth while activities."[5]

In the spring of 1926, Miss Jenner wrote a letter recommending "our six best" for the cadet program. She had "found some unusually good teaching material" among graduating students, and choosing only six had been hard. In their teaching careers Margaret Westin and Marguerite Siggelko, two of those chosen, proved worthy of her trust.[6] Her letter underlined the qualities that Seattle did seek in all applicants for teaching jobs. She noted that Marguerite Siggelko had been an assistant in first grade, "a full time teaching position [that] calls for initiative and resourcefulness above the average." In addition to her "being a good teacher, Miss Siggelko is very attractive in manner and appearance." Both Miss Jenner and Miss Mildred V. Moffet, esteemed supervisor of student teaching in Bellingham's training school, rated Miss Westin "exceptional in her teaching ability and in the steady, intelligent manner in which she meets all situations."[7]

Margaret Westin spent her cadet year at Interlake School and remained there until 1932; she transferred to B. F. Day, where she taught until well after World War II. Evaluations of Marguerite Siggelko, written by Emerson School's cadet supervisor, credited her with building "a splendid spirit of helpfulness and cooperation. . . . [and] getting excellent reading results" and showing the potential to "become one of our superior primary teachers." The principal of T. T. Minor School, where Miss Siggelko next taught, declared himself "very much pleased" with her work and "attitude toward the children," their parents, and her colleagues. Perhaps most telling at a time when many Seattle teachers were older veterans of the classroom, he wrote, "She has brought to this building the enthusiasm of youth."[8]

Others shared his assessment of cadets' youth as an asset. Elizabeth Tharp, who had long presided at Coe School, wrote of a cadet in 1922, "Her spontaneous enthusiasm lends itself to those older in the work. I think every building needs an enthusiastic cadet to add new life to the building." That cadet, a graduate of Lincoln High School, was herself a product of the Seattle Way.[9]

The cadet program did bring much younger teachers into the system, and lower cadet salaries produced financial savings. Records for the twenties indicate a growing reliance on cadet teachers; 11 percent of those hired between 1920 and 1930 had no teaching experience, and more than half came from Washington's normal schools; 58 percent were between twenty and twenty-five years of age, whereas 23 percent were in that age bracket a decade earlier.[10]

The case of Marguerite Siggelko also calls into question the wisdom of the district's ban against married women teachers. When she resigned to be married in February 1936,[11] Seattle lost a superior, successful teacher and all that it had invested in her career. As the age of teachers went down, the number lost to the district's marriage policy went up. Of those hired in the 1920s, 43 percent would resign to be married; only 16 percent hired a decade earlier had. In the cadet program's first ten years, losses to marriage affected the scope of its overall success. Of 199 cadets who had come to Seattle since 1917, 48 percent remained in the district in 1927, compared to 58 percent of those hired through regular channels. In reporting these findings, the superintendent underlined the former cadets' ability, saying that among those still in the system three were then teaching at the demonstration school, where superior teachers were assigned, and two others had turned down the opportunity to do so.[12]

In the spring of 1927, Amelia Telban, graduating from Ellensburg Normal School, feared that her age would count against her in her initial cadet interview. Eighteen years old at the time, she long remembered the assistant superintendent Frank Willard's exact words, "Well, youth is not a fatal flaw."[13] Her age was not fatal, but her first year was a trying one. She was assigned with five other cadets to Bailey Gatzert School, where Principal Ada J. Mahon did not welcome them, fearing that the school might "suffer by having so many inexperienced teachers." Bailey Gatzert was then a rapidly growing six-year grade school with a predominantly Nikkei student body of a thousand. These first cadets there had "one supervisor—Helen Laurie—and she was with us all year long. . . . So we really had the benefit of a lot of supervision and a lot of help." Amelia Telban recalled the cadet program decades later:

It was hard to get into Seattle in the 1920s. . . . I think they wanted to train their teachers in the way they should go. We had all the responsibilities. We were teachers. And we had the same kind of contract that any other teacher would have had. Same number of days. Our pay was a little less. I started in at $1260 for the year, but a regular teacher would have been hired at $1440, which I received my second year.[14]

The program's salary discrepancy would have appealed to the district from the start. The school board considered the cadet year "an additional year of training," hence, "a smaller salary is paid."[15]

Teachers who had been cadets felt solidarity with cadet newcomers. One of two cadets at Bryant School in the late thirties said that, when Edith Tucker, their supervisor, came to observe, teachers who had been cadets asked their new colleagues for some signal "so they would know she was in the building; they were afraid that she would stop in their rooms."[16]

Not all supervisors were dreaded. By the midthirties a number from the district's Central Office worked in different areas of the city, and Elizabeth Neterer was one both admired and loved. Gladys Charles Perry, who had come from Cheney Normal School as a cadet in 1935, considered her "a super woman—just, you know, so kind, but so helpful to a beginning teacher."[17] That relationship formed at Concord School; Gladys Perry recalled being assigned there at ninety dollars a month—"I thought I was rich!":

> Seattle was going to the teachers' colleges and selecting people . . . to bring into the school system. And I happened to be one of that group. . . . I never applied for a school. . . . I was hired. They did that then. . . . [in] really tough times. We didn't get full salary. They hired us at lesser salary—that's why we were recruited.[18]

Thirty years later as president of the Washington Education Association, that appreciative one-time cadet mused to an audience:

> Somehow we must find ways to enhance human dignity as we experience the dehumanizing [technological changes]. . . . I am well aware that only the ignorant have simple solutions to complex problems; however, I am going to offer what may seem to be a rather simple suggestion, . . . I submit to you that Kindness, which is not an instinct, but one of the civilized virtues that must be learned, encompasses many, if not all, of the characteristics necessary for human understanding and well-being.[19]

The career of another midtwenties cadet from Bellingham perpetuated the Seattle Way with its rooting in solid teaching methods and a democratic, child-oriented philosophy. A graduate of Ballard High School, twenty-year-old Doris Patrick started the 1924 school year teaching a first-grade class at Fairview School under the watchful eye of the principal, Eunice Copeland. Having long experience working with cadets herself, and steeped in the Seattle Way, Miss Copeland needed no supervisor in her school. At one point, concerned that Doris Patrick's work had become "too formal," she recommended that the young teacher apply to the director of primary method, "for help in technique in reading." With her principal's blessing, Miss Patrick subsequently took a year's leave to study at Washington State College; on her return Miss Copeland noted "growth in technique and pupil control." When the former cadet resigned in 1944 to be married, the veteran principal rated her "superior" and "second to none" in "up to date methods of teaching democratic relationship with pupils," with a sense of humor and a "personality that invites confidence."[20] Fortunately for a later generation of Seattle children, Doris Patrick returned to teach another eight years, retiring in 1964. During her second stint, her abilities had not diminished: the record commends a "strong teacher . . . [who] uses a variety of teaching techniques and methods" even with "some very difficult children in her class."[21]

Fairview School under Eunice Copeland epitomized the Seattle Way in its emphasis on sound teaching technique, character development, and democratic relations. In 1922, Miss Copeland had rated a cadet "a desirable member of a corps in which character is considered the best fruit of all teaching." She explained in a later interview that "the school of today is a social institution . . . the first lesson civilized society must learn is the ability to live together in amity." She wanted teachers "to stimulate the child's mind . . . [and to] search for the child's most absorbing interest." Because those interests usually lay "in some field of creative activity," she urged teachers to encourage hobbies and to "subtly expose" pupils to "the best in literature" in the school library. The school should provide access to a "rich and varied world," and discipline, she noted, was part of that world. Her interviewer expressed some amazement: "And yet underneath this rich texture of modern school life thorough education goes on."[22]

Seattle's schools had come to be seen as laboratories for democracy. In the fall of 1926, the Seattle Grade Club Magazine urged returning teachers to join their professional organizations with the following admonition:

As we enter our school rooms this autumn, do we realize that well-equipped laboratories are being furnished us, in which to try-out [sic] the most wonderful of all experiments? Are we almost surprised at receiving pay—instead of having to pay—for this opportunity of experimenting in these interesting laboratories? Are we so absorbed in our work that no other vocation could tempt us to forsake it? Are we planning to hold faithfully to the tried and true . . . while trying-out conscientiously the promising new; noting carefully the effect on the physical, mental and moral well-being of our pupils? Are we remembering, always that, "Character is higher than intellect" and that "Education without good manners is but half education"?

Do we apprehend clearly that the honesty and trustworthiness of our future citizens will be of even greater importance than their [academic] skill. . . .

Are we welcoming the privilege of enlisting in our . . . greatest army—fighting to make the world safe for democracy—by paying . . . [to be] on the membership rolls . . . of the local, state, and national education associations.[23]

Principals other than Eunice Copeland may have overseen their own cadets, but in most schools, including a majority with male principals, a growing number of cadet supervisors oversaw cadet performance. By 1925 Helen Laurie, Jo Hodges, and Ida Hermann were supervisors charged with the "Training of Cadets." All three continued in the cadet program into the thirties; Margaret Breen, Edith Tucker, Hazel Myers, Elizabeth Neterer, and Dorothea Jackson joined them over time. The position often led to administrative promotion. Helen Laurie became district supervisor of elementary education in 1931 and held that position until she resigned in 1949.[24]

Seattle had hired Helen Laurie to teach first grade in the spring of 1918; she came from Walla Walla by way of teaching jobs in North Dakota and Baker, Oregon. Committed to professional advancement, the Minnesotan from Brainerd had pursued the "advanced course" at Mankato State Normal School, took a leave of absence in 1920 to study at the University of Chicago, and received a sabbatical to study in 1926. She began working with cadets in 1923.[25]

During Miss Laurie's sabbatical, Ida Hermann moved into the cadet supervisor job after eleven years in Seattle, teaching most recently at University Heights. A graduate of Michigan's Ypsilanti State Normal School, after teaching fifth through eighth grades in Sault Ste. Marie in her home state, she had moved west to Boise and then on to Puget Sound in 1915. Like Helen Laurie, she received a sabbatical leave to study; after five years as supervisor she became a principal. She supervised cadets in her buildings herself, while acquiring a reputation as a formidable and demanding principal, and retired from McDonald in 1958 at the age of seventy.[26]

Recollections of the cadet program and its supervisors vary. Wilbert Nuetzmann came as a cadet from Cheney in the late thirties, by which time Helen Laurie was no longer supervisor of cadets but of elementary education for the school district. Nonetheless Miss Laurie "was in my classroom. Everybody when you were a cadet teacher, . . . everybody had a chance to come into your classroom . . . [we] were fair game." As for Edith Tucker, his actual supervisor, he remembered her as "always this kind of mousy person" who coauthored "an excellent book for fourth grade on the history of Seattle."[27]

Margaret Houston spent her cadet year, 1931–32, at Fauntleroy School, where Miss Laurie

> was my supervisor . . . she kept a pretty good finger on us. . . . She told me how she wanted me to teach—and I *taught* that way. Some of it I thought was superfluous, but it was a good idea in some ways. . . . She was very pleasant—she didn't demand, but she expected. . . . would explain very clearly.

In addition to the cadets, Miss Laurie "would gather her primary teachers together and talk educational philosophy—to try and get at any particular problems that had cropped up." She held one or two meetings a year, and although Miss Houston "felt I could get along without them pretty well—I assumed it was part of teacher training, you see, trying to bring the great number of teachers up to a certain philosophy of education."[28]

Cadet supervisors surely took satisfaction in the success of their charges. Dorothy Percival, a Broadway High School graduate, began as a cadet at Interlake School in 1924. Miss Laurie had found her somewhat weak in "recognizing and holding up her children to the best that they can do" yet predicted that, if she "continues to be interested in her work, . . . and maintains an open mind for suggestions, there is no reason why she should not become a superior teacher." Miss Laurie was pleased to note at the end of the year that "my prediction that [Miss Percival] would become a superior teacher has come true." Dorothy Percival retired in 1969, after twenty-seven years at Franklin High School; in forty-four years of teaching she had not missed a day of work.[29]

Not all cadet experiences ended in success. In 1922, Helen Reynolds, head of the Department of Primary Method, had reported that one cadet sent from Bellingham with the usual favorable recommendations

seemed unable to control her class and to secure the cooperation of the children in their study and work. The help of the principal over a period of several weeks did not bring about a condition satisfactory enough to warrant Miss B——'s continuance in the teaching position or the continuance of her training.[30]

As a new supervisor in 1926, Ida Hermann had found that a cadet from Ellensburg had done "very unsatisfactory work the first month[,] lacked a sense of classroom management [and] did not sense the bigness of her position." Nonetheless, Miss Hermann thought that she had made progress and had "confidence in her growth and success." The cadet went on to a full-time position, but more than a decade later, her principal "talked at length about what a very poor teacher she was. . . . [and] said over and over that she wondered why she had to have" her on her faculty.[31] These two failed examples are exceptions to the general rule that the program served district and cadets well.

The case of Helen Roberts, on the other hand, proves the rule. A product of the normal school in Moorhead, Minnesota, she spent her cadet year under the supervisor Jo Hodges and the principal Ida Vetting, who found her "promising" and believed that "with the help of Miss Hodges['s] supervision we can feel assured of her success." According to her evaluations, "she is strongest in teaching content subjects" although she "seems to realize that growing in appreciation has its importance." Miss Hodges cautioned that the young teacher not be "over serious about her work and should allow herself sufficient time for needed recreation." Miss Roberts fulfilled their prophecy that she would be a strong, successful teacher. When she resigned to be married in the spring of 1941, Helen

Roberts echoed many others: "Although I am turning to a happy future, it is not without regret that I leave the system in which I have served with pride since I was a cadet in 1926."[32]

Being selected for Seattle's cadet program was more than a privilege by the thirties: it was a godsend for young graduates of normal schools and colleges. Margaret Houston, who came in 1931, recalled her route from California. "Seattle had an agreement with San Diego State College that they would take one of their graduates as a cadet."

> I was walking down the hall one day and the secretary of the college . . . hailed me and said, "Margaret, would you go as far away as Seattle?"—I said I'd go to the moon—there were no jobs. . . . I had no idea I was even being considered—so I was very fortunate.[33]

By the time Margaret Houston arrived with her new bachelor's degree, Washington's teacher certification requirements and normal schools had changed. The state's three normal schools—at Bellingham, Ellensburg, and Cheney—now furnished a majority of Seattle's new teachers. They had standardized their courses of study, and the original mandate to provide high school instruction as well as the normal course had long since been phased out. Model training schools had operated at each since 1900. By 1920, grade teachers earned either certificates for the one-year program or diplomas for the two-year. Holders of either received a Normal School Life Diploma "upon evidence of 24 months of successful teaching experience."[34]

Early in the century prospective grade teachers took such courses as rhetoric and literature, algebra, United States and ancient history, drawing, "familiar science," vocal music, bookkeeping, oral expression, civil government, school law, and philosophy of education and did practice teaching in the model training school as well. Both Cheney and Ellensburg offered special preparation for teaching in rural schools. By 1925 the curriculum leaned toward educational methods, psychology, and social science. By then, courses of study included a third-year option to specialize in home economics, physical and health education, music, and fine or industrial arts, all of which had long been taught in Seattle.[35]

With few exceptions, the Seattle School District had hired only grade teachers with the two-year diploma and high school teachers with a bachelor's degree. By the midtwenties, state certification requirements for elementary teaching had risen to a minimum of two years' education, and throughout that decade, the normal schools sought to become four-year degree-granting institutions. They told their students that there was "growing sentiment in favor of paying the elementary school teacher [with] training equivalent to the four-year college course the same as the high school teacher of like training and experience."[36] That growing sentiment had motivated any number of Seattle elementary teachers to pursue degrees at the University of Washington.

A normal school degree bill passed both houses of the legislature during the 1925 session, only to be vetoed by the antieducation governor, Roland Hartley. A second bill passed both houses in 1929, and Hartley surprised a school community that had grown overoptimistic when he vetoed it as well. The matter came to a vote again in 1933 when Senate Bill 112 passed that chamber by a 41-to-2 margin and the House by 93 to 5. A Cheney Normal School alumnus, Clarence Martin, now occupied the governor's chair, and he promptly signed the measure into law. In September 1934, "the elementary diploma based on two years of training became a thing of the past." He signed another measure important to teachers in March 1937, designating the three normal schools as colleges of education.[37]

In 1938 the Eastern Washington College of Education in Cheney sent twelve more cadets to Seattle, among them Mary Heaton from Spokane. She recalled that "this was supposed to be a real big deal, you know—you get to go to Seattle. . . . They got us at a bargain. We got $1,000 a year." All twelve served as cadets for three years, and all twelve had Edith Tucker as cadet supervisor.

> We got into her clutches, and she would come around unbeknownst to us—
> we'd never know when, . . . and she'd sit back there writing on a pad. And
> you know, that's disconcerting to somebody, when you know that they're
> checking on what you're doing, and you feel . . . at a disadvantage, along
> with being a neophyte.

Edith Tucker notwithstanding, Mary Heaton thought cadet supervision was good for new teachers, since every school district "has its own little peculiarities" that new teachers should learn "without having to find out the hard way."[38]

By the time Mary Heaton and her eleven colleagues from Cheney arrived, Edith Tucker and Dorothea Jackson were the only two remaining cadet supervisors. The others had been reassigned—Helen Laurie to central administration; Jo Hodges to the child guidance center; Elizabeth Neterer and Hazel Myers to the demonstration school now located in the Seward building on north Capitol Hill. All had helped inexperienced cadets learn the district's "little peculiarities," and the two reassigned to the demonstration school continued there to groom newcomers and indoctrinate them in the Seattle Way. Beth Neterer, the daughter of a longtime superior court judge, Jeremiah Neterer, worked in the primary grades at the demonstration school, having taught citywide since 1918. Hazel Myers had been in the district since 1917, supervising cadets in the upper grades and serving on curriculum committees.[39] At the demonstration school, they joined forces with the original cadet supervisor, Principal Ida Vetting.

In the spring of 1926, the district stressed "greater individualization of teaching" as its emphasis on democracy increased. Superintendent Thomas Cole outlined curriculum and methods changes and how he would "give teachers direct assistance" with them. The school board voted unanimously to establish "demonstration classes" and to convert one of the grade buildings into "a demonstration school open to visitation by teachers throughout the year." It also approved "selection of the best teachers in the corps" to staff the new school and authorized additional salary "for the extra service." Prior to that time Helen Reynolds had conducted demonstrations of teaching methods in a series of Saturday morning meetings that had drawn overflow crowds.[40]

The demonstration school, first located in the Summit building, was a feature of the Progressive school system. Intended neither as a model school nor an experimental school, it was a place for "demonstration of established teaching techniques." Summit School, a typically equipped grade building on First Hill near downtown, was easily accessible from all parts of the city and presented "all the major problems which confront the great majority of the teachers."[41] Although the demonstration school did not open during Frank Cooper's tenure, Thomas Cole, Helen Reynolds, the principal W. Virgil Smith, and ten of its original teachers were Cooper disciples. Six of those ten still taught in the demonstration school in 1941; Ida Vetting, hired by Cooper before World War I, replaced Smith as principal in 1929 and served through the 1940s.[42]

The demonstration school moved into the Seward building in 1931, "because of changes in the distribution of population." The school was organized on the platoon system, in which each teacher taught one subject and students moved from room to room. Cadets and newcomers attending demonstration classes observed master teachers in their subject areas. Its purpose remained: "to carry out the principles basic to . . . the Seattle Public schools . . . to endeavor to exemplify these principles and . . . to [make] modification as our schools strive to keep abreast of this changing civilization." The Seward location not only provided more room, it allowed a view of Lake Union and the Olympic Mountains— "glimpses of typical Northwest scenery and Northwest industry." Progressive educational professionals believed that "there is much of educational value in the surroundings of the school." Indeed, as Ida Vetting observed:

> On the lake boats ply, while along the shore rise the smokestacks of industrial plants. These glimpses of activity are objects of curiosity and question, which lead to investigation. The settling and lifting of the fog over the lake, the picturesque craft seen through the trees, . . . and the changing mountains inspire poetic and artistic expression.[43]

Demonstrations were intended primarily for the indoctrination and professional benefit of teachers new to the district, but experienced Seattle teachers attended also. Amelia Telban recalled, "As a rule, we got to go to demonstration school once a year and observe a teacher. I think it was a good thing [and] very helpful." Occasionally, teachers "in need of assistance" were required to attend the sessions. During the school's first month of operation, six demonstration sessions had drawn observers from school districts as distant as Los Angeles and Paterson, New Jersey. In the 1928–29 school year, demonstrations attracted 171 out-of-town observers.[44]

Demonstrations, scheduled well in advance, lasted through a morning, and the number of observers was limited so that "classroom conditions may be as near normal as possible." A conference before school prepared observers for the day's activities, which hewed to a tight time schedule. The observers were "asked to aid in . . . maintaining a natural situation for demonstration teacher and pupils, but [were] directed to move about freely and to ask questions of individual children" about their activities. The demonstration teacher led an evaluation session afterward; the school's principal and a supervisor from the central administration always attended.[45]

The district chose teachers for the school "on the basis of professional training and teaching effectiveness." Close liaison remained between the school and the district curriculum department, and what "the demonstration teacher taught was more or less exactly what Seattle wanted [taught by] the kind of teacher Seattle wanted."[46] Although being selected to serve in the demonstration school was an honor, and some teachers had long tenures there, not everyone enjoyed the experience. Margaret Houston taught three years at Seward during World War II. Asked to transfer to the demonstration school, she recalled,

I didn't want to, but I was flattered of course. . . . I didn't like it. It was such an artificial set-up. We had to say a month or two ahead of time what lesson [we] were going to teach on a particular day and make up a lesson plan and get it out. How would I *know* what I was going to do two months from then. [Observers] were all around there watching—I was on stage, and I didn't like it.[47]

Gladys Charles Perry taught at Seward for one year during the 1940s, chosen by Dorothea Jackson, one of the two cadet supervisors "instrumental in selecting people to teach at the demonstration school."

I didn't want to stay there—you could stay there several years if you wanted to—it was incredibly time consuming—the teaching part was not hard— it was just that . . . it was like being on stage—pressure was hard. It was grueling. . . . They expected you to be perfect because they were bringing people to watch what *they* wanted done in Seattle.[48]

Others obviously enjoyed being on stage and thrived on the challenges presented by the demonstration school. Frances Montague, a native of Minnesota and graduate of its normal school in Moorhead, had six years of experience when she moved to Seattle in 1912. She taught first grade at B. F. Day School until selected for the demonstration school in 1929, where she remained through 1941, the year she went into central administration as a primary assistant, having failed two years earlier in a bid for a principalship (by then the district was filling those posts primarily with men). She died in 1946 at the age of sixty, clearly a loss to the school system at a time when postwar societal changes called for stability and experienced leadership.[49]

Helen Tompkins also began at the demonstration school in 1929, teaching kindergarten. She moved into the Central Office in 1943 but returned to Seward in 1946 for another eight years. A 1913 graduate of Broadway High School, Miss Tompkins had absorbed the Seattle Way at an early age. After graduating from normal school in Bellingham, she taught in Vancouver, British Columbia, and Portland, Oregon, then spent six years in Bellingham as a critic teacher at the normal school before moving to Seattle in 1927. From the very beginning she received superior evaluations. By the end of her second tour at Seward, the district had disbanded the demonstration school. She taught four more years, retiring in 1958 at the age of sixty-six after thirty years in Seattle classrooms.[50]

The school and the demonstration process influenced countless teachers and students and helped perpetuate the Progressive Seattle Way. Over time a mystique grew around the demonstration school. As one cadet from the late thirties put it, "I was young enough at that time to really believe that that was God's world and I really felt privileged to have this opportunity."[51] Many who were students in the twenties and thirties echoed the belief that the Seattle schools were nearly perfect. Teachers seasoned by the cadet program and the demonstration school had stabilized childhood and adolescence for their students, opening doors of imagination and opportunity even as they instilled a strong sense of responsibility and service.

5 / Principals

Saints, Ogres, and Legends

Grade schools defined most Seattle neighborhoods in the interwar years, and their principals came to personify the schools.
The stability that characterized the city fairly oozed from the
offices of grade school principals in those decades when strong and capable women occupied many of them for long tenures. Beginning with the
appointment of Adelaide Pollock in 1902, the number of women grade
principals in Seattle grew steadily until the mid-1930s. Always in the minority, in 1919 they headed 29 percent of the grade schools; in 1930 the percentage stood at 44; and by 1940, in line with a national trend that saw
men moving into elementary education in greater numbers, the percentage
had dropped to 30.[1]

Women principals were neighborhood icons. Parents admired them,
respected them, and backed them to the hilt in dealings with their
offspring. Children feared them, respected them, obeyed them, and loved
them. They were admired, esteemed, respected, and occasionally feared
and loathed by the teachers in their buildings. Leadership styles varied,
but most "ran a tight ship," and their buildings reflected that. A cadet
from the late thirties considered the interwar era "a time when Seattle
principals had a lot of power."[2]

Although women had headed small grade schools in the city in the
nineteenth century, soon after Frank Cooper arrived in Seattle he chose
Adelaide Pollock to be the first to head a larger school with age-graded
classrooms; the graded grammar school was then "still something of an

innovation in American schools." Miss Pollock had recently graduated, with a Phi Beta Kappa key, from Stanford University. Her family had brought her as a four-year-old by wagon train to Oregon from Cedar Falls, Iowa, in 1864. She completed the course at San Jose Normal School in 1888, taught briefly in Seattle, and in 1895 broke new ground in Stockton, California, as its first woman principal. She retired from the Seattle district on her return from war service in France with the Red Cross but continued to influence her former colleagues and their younger successors. Adelaide Pollock, who traced ancestors to the American Revolution, embodied the white Anglo-Saxon Protestant values that stamped the Seattle school system and its corps of principals before World War II.[3]

Within two years of Adelaide Pollock's hiring, L. Maxine Kelly had arrived from Iowa to head Interbay School, and Annie L. Gifford had embarked on her thirty-three-year reign at Longfellow. Emma C. Hart, along with five others, rounded out the ranks of Seattle's women principals in 1904. When Miss Pollock died in 1938, at the age of seventy-eight, eighteen of Seattle's twenty-three women principals at that time had been with the district since 1919. Seven who had been Miss Pollock's fellow principals before the war still served, including Maxine Kelly.[4]

The principals were consummate professionals. The earliest came to join Cooper in building his school system and to carve careers in a new and growing profession. Cooper's somewhat intuitive hiring practices elevated women with only one or two years of normal school preparation and some, as in the case of Eunice Copeland, with none at all. Many, if not most, returned to school for further study. The state's normal schools hosted many during summer sessions, and some of these women pursued degrees at the university and elsewhere. Virtually none of the interwar women principals resigned to be married. Perhaps the only exception was Carolyn Stevens, who had come to Seattle before World War I; she was principal of Washington Irving School when she resigned in August 1940, giving marriage as her reason. Irving School closed at that same time; hence Stevens, unlike most of the veteran women, did not see a man replace her in the principal's office.[5]

The professional bent of the principals surfaced early. Adelaide Pollock invited some of her colleagues to dinner in 1910 to discuss educational philosophy and the problems they encountered in their schools.

Her primary motive had been to address the isolation that women principals experienced in their separate buildings, and by the end of the evening they had agreed to meet regularly as an informal study group. Adopting a name, constitution, bylaws, and officers, they elected Anna B. Kane their first president. Other principals in the original group of diners whose Seattle careers extended into the interwar years were L. Maxine Kelly, Elizabeth Tharp, Lydia Lovering, Annie Gifford, Jessie Lockwood, Henrietta Mills, and Emma Hart. In the autumn of 1915, Miss Pollock helped organize a similar group on the state level and served as its first president. A year later, a national organization of like intent gained affiliation with the National Education Association[6]; this National Council of Administrative Women in Education reflected the aims and aspirations of Adelaide Pollock and her Seattle associates.

The Seattle Principals' Association, primarily a men's group organized in 1912, held monthly business and professional meetings that covered a wide range of topics. It elected its first woman president, Jessie Lockwood, in 1924; three other women served as president during the interwar years—Anna May Matheson, Dora Herren, and Lulie Nettleton.[7]

Women principals had two study groups. The Fortnightly Club met on alternate Monday evenings; it evolved from a group that gathered occasionally to study problems encountered in "the supervision of instruction and building administration." Membership was limited to eight, insuring that discussions remained informal and that everyone could join in. Programs included reports on school visits and discussion of current educational literature: at one point the members undertook a "study of the revisions of the curriculum."[8]

A second group arose in the midtwenties—the Monday Evening Club, also known as the Monday Night Study Club. Limited to twelve members, it existed "for the purpose of promoting good fellowship, of knowing better the school system, and of stimulating each individual to higher professionalism and growth." Its dinner meetings featured roundtable discussions and committee reports. One year's agenda centered on "The Technique of Leadership," a topic that would "take [members] far enough away from immediate problems to give a broader perspective to their entire work."[9]

District records do not exist for all the early principals who joined Adelaide Pollock for dinner in 1910, but the records of Annie Gifford, L. Maxine Kelly, and Anna B. Kane are illustrative. Miss Kane began her Seattle career in 1901 and Miss Kelly in 1902; both retired June 14, 1940.

Annie Gifford, born in 1861, not long after the firing on Fort Sumter, came to Seattle in 1898 with her certificate from Iowa's Buchanan County Normal School. She had taught five years in Independence, Iowa, before moving west for a seven-year stint in Grand Forks, North Dakota. Her first Seattle teaching assignment was at B. F. Day School. By 1902, her leadership qualities propelled her into the principalship of Lake School, newly opened near the end of the streetcar line that served a growing population in Madison Park. In January 1903, Frank Cooper named Miss Gifford principal of the new twelve-room Longfellow School on the east side of Capitol Hill, where she endeared herself to parents.[10]

In the spring of 1921 the Longfellow PTA requested that the school board "grant a leave of absence of one-half year, on half salary, for study and travel, to our beloved principal, Miss Annie L. Gifford." Even the attraction of paying only half salary could not move the parsimonious board, which did not grant the leave.[11]

Although the board did not see fit to recognize her worth with a leave of absence, the administration had long rewarded her with admiration and no small degree of autonomy. Jessie K. How, a longtime teacher at Longfellow, recalled being hired in 1926: "They wanted Miss Gifford . . . to interview me . . . and she gave me a vivid picture of what life was like at Longfellow school. And you could tell from the beginning that she was enthusiastic about Longfellow." Supervisors working out of the district's Central Office had such faith in Miss Gifford that they rarely visited Longfellow. Her teachers had high regard for her; even though Annie Gifford did "run a tight ship . . . , nobody resented the tight ship. They knew that she knew what she was doing." Her teacher evaluations reflect great thought; she stereotyped no one and did not hesitate to raise her assessments when she saw progress.[12]

Longfellow served a wide social spectrum. Jessie How recalled, "We really had about three levels of children." One group came from families west of the school that "had money, either from the past, or they had businesses, . . . they were fairly well to do." A second category was the offspring of what she described as "a sort of middle group of people who worked in regular [jobs] . . . hardworking people of many kinds." The third group of students came from "rather poor people" who lived east of Longfellow, "down below the hill, where rents were much cheaper and the houses were much smaller, in the vicinity of Madison Street." During the Depression, many Longfellow families had "a very difficult time, and . . . the PTA, or others, would supply clothing or whatever was needed."[13]

The school also had racial diversity. African-American families "had lived in that area for many years," and some of the parents had attended Longfellow themselves. The family of Edward Pitter was among those longtime residents. Mrs. Marjorie Allen Pitter, a Seattle native and a graduate of Broadway High School, championed children in any eventuality when it came to the schools. As her daughter Constance said, she frequently called on Annie Gifford, who from her office window could "see my mother marching to school, and she knew that some child there of color had been called a name or been slapped, or had been insulted, and my mother was on her way there to defend this child." Constance, a Longfellow pupil in the twenties, remembered Miss Gifford as

> a tough principal, but she was also a principal who listened to parents, and if a parent was right, and felt they were right, she would certainly . . . [deal with] teachers who were not good. I know when I was slapped [by a teacher] because I couldn't spell a word, . . . she really followed through on discipline.[14]

Miss Gifford "often referred to the Longfellow School—teachers, and children, and parents—as her family." The family analogy arose frequently, as in 1933 when a school board member, John Shorett, praised her as "'one of the finest women in the world,' illustrating her devotion to her pupils by the care she had taken of the little children of his own brother when they were left motherless, saying that she had 'been a mother to them.'"[15]

Her long tenure ended on August 28, 1936, when she retired at the age of seventy-five, "on advice of her physician." A year earlier, former students, "many of them now active in Seattle's civic life," had attested to her influence in honoring her at a testimonial banquet. Then Superintendent Worth McClure lauded her for her "remarkable influence in the building of character," saying that her "interest in each child was deep and genuine" and that she had "faith in them . . . [and] joy in their success." He offered as proof of her lasting influence his own experience as "a new principal in Seattle, over twenty years ago, [when he] visited her school more than once to observe her ideals in action."[16]

Like Miss Gifford, Anna B. Kane had taught in Grand Forks, North Dakota, before coming to Seattle. She had received her certificate from the normal school in River Falls, Wisconsin, in 1900; a year later the thirty-two-year-old was teaching seventh grade at Cascade School, just north of downtown. After assignments at Green Lake and T. T. Minor, she moved into the principal's office at Brighton School in 1910—in time to receive Adelaide Pollock's dinner invitation. Two years later she began twenty-eight years as principal of Colman School.[17] Until 1910, Miss Kane lived at the Otis, a First Hill residential hotel popular among teachers. When her sister Margaret joined her in Seattle, they moved into a house on Capitol Hill, just a few blocks north of Longfellow School, where they remained for the rest of their lives.[18]

Anna Kane stood a commanding five feet seven inches tall. Her photographs show an austere face tempered by kindness, but *motherly* is not a word anyone associated with her. Respect mingled with fear and some warmth colors the memories of her students. One former pupil who spent the years 1911 through 1919 at Colman said:

> Miss Kane was wonderful. . . . She was nice to us—but she played the role. She was the principal—we all respected her—when you would see Miss Kane coming, . . . you didn't run in the halls . . . and believe me, before we even walked by her [office] we walked so nice. We were kind of afraid of her, so we wouldn't do anything wrong.

A watchword at Colman was "You be careful—Miss Kane might see you."[19]

Stability marked the Colman neighborhood; children who started out together in kindergarten stayed together through all eight grades. It was primarily an Italian community in which "the families knew each other . . . they helped one another—they got along fine." Parents sent their children to Colman with an admonition to "be good" and to respect all their teachers. Since Anna Kane "was a little older," remembered one of those children, "we kind of respected her more—we were taught that older people" were entitled to more respect.[20]

In an era when few ever questioned corporal punishment in the schools, rumor had most principals keeping a paddle or a yardstick for disciplinary purposes. Anna Kane reportedly had a stick, but few tested her willingness to use it. As one early Colman pupil said, "I think if we did that when we got home we'd have got another beating."[21]

An episode in the late twenties validates that supposition and suggests that Miss Kane might have been somewhat ambivalent toward corporal punishment. She spotted the son of Colman's custodian among a group of boys throwing gravel on the playground and from her window summoned him to her office. His father followed him and reached the office just as the principal, armed with her "fancy hair-brush type paddle," told the boy to bend over. When he asked what she was doing, she replied, "I'm going to give your boy a spanking." At that, he pulled his son away, told her, "No, no, no, I'll do it!" and proceeded to knock him about. Horrified, Miss Kane said, "Mr. Patricelli—control yourself!" As they left the office he told her not to concern herself further and assured her that "he would take care of it." His son vividly remembered that he did just that.[22]

Although Colman's teachers are remembered as never differentiating among children along ethnic lines, one account of corporal punishment at the school around 1915 did involve ethnic differences. When the African-American newspaper, the Seattle *Republican,* fell on hard times, its editor and publisher moved his family from affluent Capitol Hill to blue-collar Rainier Valley. He enrolled his children at Colman, where his son Horace recounted that his "report card was filled with A's, [but he] consistently received D's and F's in deportment." The move had been traumatic for the sixth-grader, who recalled, "The children in my room at Coleman School looked different, talked differently, and behaved differently from any children I had known. Up to this time I had never fought. Now I was constantly being chased home by the rougher Italian boys." One day at school his younger brother reported that the principal was going to whip him after recess. Horace told him to run home and tell their mother and recalled that,

When Miss Kane, the lady principal, found out about this, she sent for me and told me that I would get the whipping instead. When I refused to bend over the chair, she sent for the janitor.

He threw me to the floor, face down, and sat on me, but before the principal could apply the paddle I bit his hand. When he jumped up from the pain, I got out and ran home.

He recalled, too, that "the affair was somehow smoothed over by my mother, who did not approve of school whippings, and my brother and I returned to school as heroes." This story indicates both that Anna Kane took parental intervention and involvement seriously and that her commitment to physical punishment may not have been wholehearted.[23]

Teacher evaluations written by Anna Kane show a principal steeped in Progressive values and a careful administrator who did not make effusive remarks or rash judgments. In 1920, a teacher forced by family illness to return home to Illinois, wrote, "I have enjoyed my two years work in Seattle very much and regret that I cannot continue"; Anna Kane surely regretted it more, having earlier said simply, "Miss Ott has the master touch in everything." In the case of one of Eva Ott's successors in the first-grade room, ultimately dropped for less than satisfactory service, Miss Kane did not rush to judgment, preferring "to rate Miss W—— after she has had time to adjust herself to the abilities and needs of these children." In finally rendering an evaluation, she remained evenhanded, saying the teacher was "very well trained, show[ed] a fine cooperative spirit," yet seemed "quite lacking in the power of organization." The principal asked for help from the Central Office "deciding what to do in this case."[24]

Even toward the end of her long career, her teacher evaluations were considered and concise. One, written six months before she retired and bearing a rather feeble signature, was characteristic: in the subject's classroom, "Children are taught to be courteous and orderly. Explanations are clear and to the point. Each child progresses at his own rate. Worthwhile character traits are developed, such as kindness, courtesy, etc. The teacher is encouraging and friendly in her manner." Never one to lavish praise, Miss Kane ranked the teacher only "very satisfactory."[25]

After twenty-eight years, Miss Kane relinquished the Colman principal's office in 1940 to James F. Shannon, principal at neighboring Rainier School, which closed that year. At the age of seventy-two, she wrote to the school board that "it is always difficult to give up a work you love and feel that you still do with ease and snap. . . . I shall always hope to be a part of the school system which I helped to build and part of the life of the city that I love." She expressed the interwar teachers' continuing optimism and belief in the idea of progress in the face of a worsening international picture:

> When one has lived to see empires rise and fall and to see the darkening clouds of war hover over our own land on at least three different occasions, it is with a conviction born of experience and faith that I step out into the now troubled world feeling very much assured that "God is in His heaven and all will be right with the world."[26]

Principal L. Maxine Kelly came to Seattle in 1902 after teaching ten years in Marshalltown, Iowa. Frank E. Willard, the superintendent there, supplied a reference. Willard himself came to Seattle as assistant superintendent for elementary schools in 1907; he proved a staunch administrative ally of Frank Cooper. Serving in that position until 1940, Willard provided a stable link with the early years; he wholeheartedly championed women teachers and won their admiration and support.[27]

Born September 20, 1867, Maxine Kelly graduated from high school in St. Joseph, Missouri. In Marshalltown she taught grades one through seven, and although she held no normal school credential, by 1902 she was also the principal in her building. Adelaide Pollock maintained that Cooper brought Maxine to Seattle specifically to serve as the first principal of newly opened Interbay School.[28]

Long after she retired, Miss Kelly recalled that when she first came to Interbay, "cattle roamed all over the place. The little tykes often got 'buffaloed' by the cows on their way to school. . . . Some of the teachers weren't so fond of those cows, either." Five teachers had greeted her in the new building on that "rather foggy, dreary day" in 1903 when she assumed command. She described that first trip by streetcar from her residence at the foot of Queen Anne Hill: "Much of the way the street car passed over trestles along the water front and up Smith's Cove . . . to a low gulch . . . where the tide flats and marshes of Smith's Cove and Salmon Bay almost met."[29]

Located between those two bodies of water, Interbay School stood where a sandspit had once hosted Native American summer encampments. After dredging and filling, the land between Queen Anne Hill and the Magnolia neighborhood accommodated switchyard, roundhouse, and shops for the Great Northern Railroad, which employed many residents of the area. Although the railroad came to dominate Interbay, streetcars made downtown accessible, and "clerks, laborers and other workers found Interbay a convenient" place to live. Essentially an immigrant community during Miss Kelly's tenure, Interbay hosted many from what became Yugoslavia and from Finland. At one time the school population also included Austrians, Canadians, Danes, Germans, Icelanders, Italians, Japanese, Latvians, Lithuanians, Norwegians, Poles, Russians, Scots, and Swedes.[30]

The polyglot community appreciated and supported its school, its teachers, and its principal. Miss Kelly remembered, "The residents out Interbay way were so happy to get a school that they treated the teachers like queens—brought us food and all sorts of treats." The largess continued through the years; one parent in the late twenties raised rabbits, and whenever the family enjoyed one for dinner, he always sent a portion to Clide O. Fisher, even after his son had left her second-grade classroom.[31]

The principal also recalled that everyone "took part in school life in those days. . . . We knew every parent and were frequent guests in every home . . . [and] every instance of discipline in school was noted and applauded at home." There is little to suggest that Miss Kelly leaned toward corporal punishment, although one former pupil did recall that she once "took him to the basement to whip him," saying, "she'd swing and I'd jump—she never did hit me." Others noted the use of a dunce cap and banishment to the hallway from class as two accepted practices in her building.[32]

Influenced by the principal and the fourth-grade teacher, Nina Moore, Florence Soderback Byers began her own teaching career in the Seattle schools in 1927. Saying that Miss Kelly "knew our family," she recalled her years as an Interbay pupil before World War I and attested to the trust and mutual respect between teachers and the community. The Misses Kelly and Moore lived together

on about Queen Anne Avenue and First [Avenue] West, just south of Mercer Street. I only know that because Miss Kelly . . . would not bother to
send a note home to my family [asking] would I please be allowed to do
something—she was in charge—she would say, "Florence, I'll give you
my key now, and you go to my apartment and you'll see some papers on
my desk there, and I need those." I took the streetcar. You see, . . . I was
a little girl from a family that they knew.[33]

Miss Kelly lived at 326 Queen Anne Avenue until her retirement.
Others agreed that "she was in charge," but one early thirties first-grader
also considered her "the grandmother type." Most agreed that "Interbay
was a happy school" in a neighborhood where you could "play in the streets
after dinner" and where "we were all poor but happy." A teacher in a neighboring school corroborated on the poverty:

> These kids were poor . . . but [Miss Kelly] had all kinds of clothing for kids—
> any size, any shape, and she would get just everything she could. She *really*
> felt that she had a responsibility for those poor kids—she was almost like
> a saint in [that community] . . . a Mother Theresa figure.[34]

Interbay School remained fairly stable under L. Maxine Kelly; a core
of strong, long-tenured teachers buttressed her against inevitable staff
turnover. She had as much empathy for her teachers as she did for the
pupils. A poem that she probably wrote indicates that she appreciated the
gulf that separated teachers at Interbay from those in more affluent schools
atop Queen Anne Hill.

> One sister works on the terraced hills
> And one in the gulch below,
> And it rests with the gods who grind their mills
> That the gulch work will ever show.

> The sister who works on the terraced hills
> An earthly crown will wear,
> But the crown of the one who toils in the gulch
> Will be but her own gray hair.

For the soil of the gulch is strong and coarse
And results are hard to see;
But the goal of the gulch is the human soul,
So hurrah for the gulch, say we.[35]

She wrote terse evaluations, but teacher morale would have soared with such praise as she gave Rubie Carlson in 1929: "General Estimate— excellent. A person of much enthusiasm. Responds quickly and resource- fully to any calls made. A splendid teacher." Rubie Carlson compiled a forty-two-year record in Seattle, carrying the influence of L. Maxine Kelly well into the postwar years.[36]

When the principal of Cascade School died in 1932, the school district transferred Miss Kelly to replace him. Its working-class population akin to Interbay's, Cascade seemed a logical assignment. She stayed at Cascade with such longtime teachers as Grace McCauley and Myrtle Kiger until she retired in 1940 at the age of seventy-three. She had been a force in the drive to establish a home for Seattle's retired teachers; one such opened on Queen Anne Avenue in the midthirties, named for a recently deceased fellow teacher, Ida Culver. It seems fitting that in 1951 when she moved from lower Queen Anne where she had lived since 1903, L. Maxine Kelly was one of the first to move into a larger Ida Culver House, newly located in the Ravenna district. She died three years later at the age of eighty-seven.[37]

Although principals received respect, admiration, and affection, there was some public antipathy toward a woman in the principal's office. In 1915, the school board heard "from 'A Father' urging the Board to con- sider . . . [appointing] men principals." Twenty-three years later, on the retirement of the Alki School principal, the PTA asked "that he be replaced by a young, alert man." Even L. Maxine Kelly received less than total support when she transferred to Cascade; one school board mem- ber voted against her assignment because he believed that the school should have a male principal.[38]

The typical road to a principalship for a woman in Seattle was through the classroom, and that helped to perpetuate the Seattle Way. If Frank Cooper did bring an experienced principal to Seattle specifically to open Interbay School, it was a rare departure from his usual practice of pro- moting grade teachers like Annie Gifford and Anna B. Kane.

Any number of women principals of long tenure had their first administrative experience as an acting principal or head teacher.[39] The size of a building determined not only whether a principal or a head teacher directed it, but also her salary. Since a head teacher taught in the classroom and administered the building as well, that designation for smaller buildings also allowed the district to pay less in salary. In 1923, Superintendent Thomas Cole told a school board demanding draconian budget cuts that "head teachers in the smaller elementary schools have been substituted for the more expensive principals." That year a head teacher did "the regular teaching work and receive[d] $120 a year extra for the additional service rendered." In May five women who later became principals were named head teachers for the coming school year: Charlotte Graham, Lulie Nettleton, Eugenie Pariseau, Myra Snow, and Blanche Tanner.[40]

Principals were vulnerable to salary reduction. In 1918 the school board adopted the policy of basing a principal's salary on the building's average attendance rather than on the size of its teaching staff. Should a school lose population, the principal's salary would not drop, but she might be "assigned to another building and . . . paid a [lower] salary in accordance with the attendance at such building." A year later a delegation of grade principals protested that policy only to be told that it was "impracticable to re-open the question of salaries for the current school year."[41]

L. Maxine Kelly recalled $700 as her annual starting salary in 1903. A salary schedule adopted seven years later would have paid her $1,500. According to the 1919 salary scale based on school population, principals of schools with more than 700 pupils received between $2,760 and $3,360; those with 490 to 700 pupils received $2,400 to $2,880; those with 280 to 490 received a minimum of $2,040 and maximum of $2,400; and for those with fewer than 280 pupils, a minimum of $1,920 and maximum of $2,160. Interbay in 1919 would have fallen in the third category, so Miss Kelly likely earned $2,400 maximum after sixteen years with the district.[42]

By 1925, the salary scale for grade principals ranged from a low of $2,400 in smaller buildings to $3,660 in the largest. The Seattle Principals' Association broached the question of increases with the board in late 1927, as the movement to organize a union gained momentum and the entire teaching corps grew more aggressive in the matter of salary. In March 1928, the superintendent recommended that minimums and maximums for grade principals be set at $2,960 and $3,960; for head teachers, at $2,300 and $2,700.[43] On this scale, Miss Kelly would have received approximately $3,160 that year; her transfer to the larger Cascade School in 1932 would have moved her into a higher category just as Depression-mandated salary cuts began.

Each school came to reflect the style, talent, and inclinations of its principal. Personalities and leadership styles did vary among them, but all principals maintained strict control in their buildings. The day began with saluting the flag in each classroom. Virtually every principal utilized student hall monitors to keep order, and her own presence in the hallway indelibly imprinted the memories of interwar pupils. Helen Shelton, a native Seattleite who went on to a long career as a high school Spanish teacher, attended Coe School in the early twenties. She remembered the principal Elizabeth Tharp:

> I can still see her office between the first and second [floors]. . . . [She was] "old school"—well, she'd have to be in those days. . . . She was imposing— you could say that. . . . I don't remember any stories about people being sent to the Principal's office. But I'll tell you what I did do, . . . they had a piano on the second floor . . . and at noon or at the end of school . . . I played the piano, and the [whole student body] marched out.[44]

In that era of great structure, pupils moved as a group in orderly fashion, and they exited more than one building to music that reflected the principal's taste.

At Montlake School in the thirties, Principal Dora Herren, always properly dressed and wearing "sensible shoes," utilized music to maintain order; pupils "never ran out the door."

> At the end of the day, the bell would ring and we would go to the cloak room and get our coats and line up outside the door. Then Mrs. Herren would put some music on the phonograph in the hall—"Washington Post" march by Sousa . . . that's what we walked out to.[45]

One teacher at Bailey Gatzert in the 1940s said that Ada J. Mahon always "had the kids marching out of the school to the beat of a drum." The regimentation would continue beyond the building to a "particular telephone pole . . . [but] at the telephone pole, all hell broke loose."[46]

Corporal punishment came with the principals' portfolio, but some, if not most, eschewed it. By maintaining control and discipline in their buildings they avoided many instances of extremely bad behavior that might have brought the proverbial paddle into play. Interwar discipline included sending miscreants out into the hall, to the principal's office, or as one said, "into the cloakroom. [And] I think there may have been some [teachers] who used a ruler."[47]

Most principals cared about their teachers and found ways of cementing good relations with them. Operating within the framework of the Progressive Seattle Way, most—even in dealing with teachers—kept their emphasis on the children in their buildings. In 1941, Etta Minnig, who had been at Van Asselt since 1925, conceded that a difficult teacher whom she had long wanted removed from her staff "was getting along better and . . . loving the children a little more."[48] Her statement reflects not only concern for children but a willingness to try to achieve harmony in the school. Miss Minnig, who never shed the head teacher role, gave her teachers strong support even as she continued to teach sixth grade until she resigned in 1942. One of them, whose Seattle career started at Van Asselt in 1928, recalled that support, both real and moral: the school

> was clear out on the end of Beacon Hill [and] busses only went as far as Jefferson Park. [So] we rode with our Principal, Miss Minnig. . . . She had a car, and she picked all of us up. . . . We roomed [on First Hill] . . . and she picked us up there and brought us back. The Superintendent at the time [once] told her, "I was out to your school about 4:00, and nobody was there." And she [replied], "That's right. If you'd been there at 8:00 in the morning, you'd have found everybody there."[49]

Amelia Telban always felt that Ada Mahon had not welcomed her group of cadets to Bailey Gatzert in 1927 but also recalled that the principal had her staff's best interest in mind. She made a practice of socializing with her teachers and introducing them throughout the district:

I think that was the day of the woman Principal. And Miss Mahon had many friends among the women principals, and we got to know them. Got to know them socially. For example we were staying at [her] cottage at the beach at West Port, and there were times when the entire body of teachers at the school, plus principals from the other schools—women principals—would go down there for a weekend. And so we got to know each other.

Miss Telban had spent more than five years at Gatzert when Miss Mahon told her that, for her "own good as a teacher, [she] should try another school." Principal and teacher—"both wept at our parting [when] I moved to Columbia School."[50]

A principal would all too often see a promising teacher forced to leave the profession when she married. It is difficult to determine how they reacted, but the *Grade Club Magazine* reported many engagement celebrations and wedding showers with principals as active participants. Mary Heaton never forgot the reaction of Fairview's Eunice Copeland when she married a junior high teacher, Fred Ingalls, in 1944. "Miss Copeland ate that stuff up . . . she was so excited when I got engaged." She also took a hand in the "activities at the church" the day of the wedding, which most of the Fairview teachers attended.[51]

A dedicated professional with time invested in a young woman's success, and perhaps a desire to see a replication of her own career, surely would have had mixed emotions when the district ban on married teachers forced a protégée to resign. One can imagine what went through the mind of Bella Perry, principal at Youngstown School, in the spring of 1935, when two teachers she regarded highly left to be married. Neither effusive nor sentimental, Miss Perry wrote of one: "Miss Beairsto came to Seattle as a cadet eight years ago. She expects to be married in June. Seattle will lose an excellent teacher." Mary Beairsto and Jean Nicol had both been at Youngstown since 1927. Successive evaluations written for Miss Nicol show that her principal considered her "a desirable member of any corps of teachers," a leader among her colleagues, and, finally: "An excellent teacher; popular with other teachers, loved and admired by pupils and parents. Leaving in June to be married."[52]

The following year, Bella Perry transferred from West Seattle's blue-collar Youngstown to William Cullen Bryant School in a rapidly growing middle-class professional neighborhood near the university. An incident early in her Bryant tenure hints at her curiosity, if not a latent romantic bent. Mary Gasperich and Wilbert Nuetzmann, two young cadet teachers, taught in adjoining rooms. "All of the students were trying to match them up, [and] any time they had a conference in the hall, why—eyebrows were raised and smiles emerged." Both planned to marry at the end of the school year. Not immune to building gossip and unwilling to be excluded, Miss Perry confronted them: "Mary and I happened to be in the office at the same time," recalled Nuetzmann. Miss Perry said,

> "I want to talk to you two" . . . and so we sat down and she was kind of quiet about it, and then she said, "I understand you two are getting married"— and . . . she didn't want to be the last one to find out about anything. I was *embarrassed*—Mary was embarrassed. I was getting married, but I wasn't getting married to her. So [Miss Perry] never ever said anything [else] about that.

He mused decades later that the principal "wanted to let the community know" about anything involving her teachers. He also thought "she would have been excited about it had it been true."[53]

Some teachers took exception to the bond between teacher and principal if they perceived it as tyrannical, obtrusive, and restrictive. Individual principals ranked from beloved through accepted to tolerated by their teaching staff, and a few were considered beyond tolerating. School district lore is rife with tales of "The Seven Devils," a group that remains elusive because more than seven women were identified as members of that group. Apparently, the devil was in the eye of the beholder, or perhaps one person's devil was another's strong leader. The Seven Devils stories also reflect changing generational reactions to unyielding leadership.

Evidence about the Seven Devils is anecdotal and comes from teachers who began their careers in the late thirties when longtime principals neared retirement. One who started teaching in Seattle in 1927 speculated that the devils "were probably *very* professional women, maybe they were demanding."[54] Personnel records tend to validate her theory.

The school district records contain a small number of requests for transfers to a building with a male principal; such requests were usually granted.

Late in her career, Anna May Matheson, who began teaching in Seattle before World War I, provoked such a request from at least one who taught at Muir School while she was principal there in 1941. Happy to transfer, that teacher gave her new principal at Summit School the impression that "she always appreciated me for no particular good reason other than I was a man" and not Anna May Matheson. He recalled that she never mentioned Miss Matheson by name, "but she said 'I will not teach for another woman principal after I taught for *that woman*.' And it was always '*that woman*.'"[55]

Recollections and the record of Eugenie Pariseau, whom many nominated as one of the Seven Devils, fail to clarify the puzzle. At the age of thirty-one, she had come to Seattle from Michigan in 1914, as executive clerk in the superintendent's office. In 1923 she was named head teacher at Harrison School; following a brief time as principal at Ross, she moved in 1926 to Bagley School where she stayed for the rest of her career. Florence Byers arrived at Ross in 1927, just missing her; she later said, "I heard all kinds of stories about her. . . . I think she was on the 'bad list' of some teachers."[56]

Miss Pariseau's teacher evaluations were the work of a dedicated professional who made candid observations, and they provide a clue to her priorities. One was "nice character building work"; she also praised a teacher for setting "high [student] standards of workmanship and arous[ing] unusual interest in what is going on in the world about them." Even when being critical, she tried to remain objective, saying of one teacher in 1940, "Personally I like her very well," but "much of the satisfaction which would usually come from physical education is lost because of her lack of discipline . . . [which] is the source of the trouble."[57]

In 1936, she wrote of a teacher who had begun teaching in 1900, "Miss Hootman is an older teacher who endeavors to keep up with present day practices." Miss Pariseau's commitment to professionalism showed in her praise of Genevieve Rogers, who "reads professional literature, [and] attended Dr. Kilpatrick's conferences." Both Miss Hootman and Miss Rogers appreciated her leadership. On resigning to be married in 1940, the latter wrote, "It has been a great satisfaction for me to have taught in Seattle, and particularly a privilege to serve at the Daniel Bagley School where you have an exceptionally fine corps." Mary Hootman retired in 1947, saying "The fine spirit of cooperation and helpfulness I have enjoyed in working with Miss Pariseau and the splendid corps of teachers of the Bagley School is something I shall always remember."[58]

Eugenie Pariseau retired in 1954. Former Bagley students remembered her as a force—a presence in the hallways. Jim Shelton, later a long-tenured principal himself, agreed: "I went to Bagley and I remember this woman very, very well . . . but I remember her also as a kind, benevolent woman." Parents, too, had high regard for her; one from the last years of Miss Pariseau's career remembered Bagley as well-organized and tightly run, saying of its then white-haired principal: "She was very much into everything with everybody. I was active in PTA—she knew everything that was going on. My kids liked her. She was a little busy-body—always around doing everything."[59] The Eugenie Pariseau story does not shed light on what qualified a principal to be one of the Seven Devils.

Bella Perry made the list of Seven Devils largely "because of the fear that she generated . . . and the demands that she put on people."[60] Even so, in retrospect, she also received grudging credit for positive influence on the careers of her teachers. Arabella Perry arrived in Seattle early in the twentieth century. In 1911, after two years under Annie Gifford at Longfellow, she moved to Hawthorne as vice-principal. In 1927 she transferred to Youngstown School in West Seattle, then in 1936 to Bryant, where she literally died on the job—in the Bryant building during the 1945–46 school year.[61]

Bryant parents had high expectations for their children and, though never showering her with affection as parents did Annie Gifford, they respected and responded to Bella Perry. According to one of her teachers, they felt free to come to the school: "Oh the parents came! . . . Even if you might [just] *think* about talking to [them] they would be there. . . . The kids in that school came to school to learn and for the most part they did a good job of it."[62] When a behavior problem or academic concern brought parents to Bryant, they met with a no-nonsense principal who included all of a student's teachers in such conferences. Bryant had subject matter teachers in the upper grades, and Miss Perry elicited the perspective of each, intimidating though the practice could be:

Here were all of the student's teachers sitting in [Miss Perry's] office—the whole bunch of us. And so she would sit at her desk and . . . [ask each teacher] "what do you have to say," right down the line. And so we would all say our piece and then she would say to the parent, "And now what do you have to say?"[63]

Bryant was as tightly run a ship as any in the school district. Pupils from the interwar years remembered Bella Perry less vividly than teachers did; their descriptions range from "stately" to "short and kind of roundish." Stature aside, they agreed that she was a commanding presence and that order reigned. She wore a whistle around her neck, which "gained instant attention" in the halls.[64]

Rumors of corporal punishment circulated. Miss Perry did believe in corporal punishment, but questions remain about how firmly she applied it. Wilbert Nuetzmann recalled the time she asked him to witness a paddling:

> She talked to the kid for a long, long time and just about harangued him to death. [Then] she deliberately took [two yardsticks] and put them together with rubber bands. She had the kid bend over, took this ruler and just whaled it and banged it on the table. There was a great big noise and the kid couldn't realize what was happening . . . she didn't hit him at all, but that kid was scared to death.[65]

Her relationship with the faculty remained strictly professional: teachers "called her Bella behind her back—never to her face, it was Miss Perry, always." She did not encourage faculty socializing, and her teachers seldom saw a less formidable side of their intimidating principal, though one would later say that she was very kind. She held few official meetings. Instead, at lunchtime, "she would come into the teachers' room, . . . [and] tell us some things we had to do . . . it seems as though we had a building meeting every noon." Few teachers ever clashed with her; Hilder Erickson, Bryant's upper-grades librarian and reading teacher, was remembered as a rare exception. The outspoken Erickson, long active in the Washington State Federation of Teachers, had "whatever it took to be able to stand up to" her and did not knuckle under; "at some of these lunch meetings she would actually question" things that Miss Perry mandated.[66]

A teacher evaluation she wrote in 1919 clearly shows Bella Perry's philosophy, her style, and what she considered her mission. It also reveals what the district considered acceptable class size:

> In this room are forty-six little citizens who are tending strictly to business every minute of the day and enjoying it, too. This teacher is very resourceful, and works with definite plan and purpose. All work is closely supervised and as a result quality is showing. The type of citizen that is being developed under the guidance of Miss Felzer is very desirable.

Genevieve Felzer resigned three years later, perhaps to return to her native Minnesota; she probably never knew how highly Miss Perry regarded her work. Wilbert Nuetzmann did not expect "much of a recommendation from Bella" when he applied for a principalship not long after leaving Bryant. Not until he saw his personnel file in the district archives after he retired did he realize that her evaluations of him "were just about as good as you could get—even in the first year she said 'you should look at this young man for a principal'—yet she would never let me know." Miss Perry demanded a lot, but Bryant's structured environment and high standards offered a good early experience for young teachers. More than a few who taught for her went on to principalships and administrative posts. For the most part they respected her, but she "would never let her guard down . . . [or let them] know that she was a pretty soft person underneath.[67]

Another of the reputed Seven Devils was Charlotte Graham, who succeeded Anna May Matheson as principal at Emerson in 1930. Like her predecessor, Miss Graham provoked transfers among her teachers. After ten years teaching reading in Emerson's upper grades, Emma Groves decided during World War II that she "couldn't take the war and the Principal together" and moved to University Heights in 1943. Her greatest grievance was the principal's treatment of teachers in front of their pupils: Graham would "storm at" an offending teacher right in the classroom. Miss Groves put on plays and dramatized stories. Once, she said,

> something happened on the stage and the children laughed. [Miss Graham] went into a Screaming Mimi—"I'm tired of being the Principal of a school

where the teachers don't make the children mind.". . . of course, they all stopped laughing and . . . we went back into the library, and we just sat. We didn't even talk, the kids or I.[68]

Emma Groves herself had a reputation as a strong teacher, "devoted to reading . . . [but] a tartar—she was demanding." One former Emerson student remembered "no funny business" in that school; "class discipline was maintained from the first grade right through the eighth grade. There was no unruliness in class—ever." He vividly recalled that "Miss Graham was legend. She was a redhead . . . a no nonsense Principal, and to go down to Miss Graham's office—boy, I'll tell you, that was the end of the world. And she ran that blue collar school with an iron hand."[69]

At least one Emerson teacher had a positive view of Charlotte Graham. When she resigned to be married in 1938, after twelve years of teaching, Agatha Shook wrote that "it has been a privilege to work with Miss Charlotte Graham, my principal, and I wish to express my appreciation for the help and cooperation I have received from her."[70] Little else suggests that Graham may not have been one of the Seven Devils. Other principals so designated, however, had even less clear cut reviews from teachers who taught under them.

Blanche Tanner, principal at Concord in the early thirties, made the list for Mary Luch, who said Miss Tanner "was a demon, but I learned a lot." Yet Margaret Houston welcomed a transfer to Highland Park, where Miss Tanner had moved in 1936. Having come from Fauntleroy and an intrusive principal, she said of Miss Tanner,

I liked her—some teachers didn't, but I liked her very much. . . . When I went to Highland Park I was given a reading-library assignment. . . . I had only taught up to third grade, and here I had fourth, fifth, and sixth graders. When I visited the school . . . [I told her] "I never taught 5th and 6th graders, I don't know how I'm going to go about it." And she laughed at me and she said, "You teach them just like you taught the 3rd graders." And you know, that dear soul—she went away and she never stuck her nose in my room for six months—but she probably knew what was going on just the same. . . . It was such a joy to be able to do things—to start in and *do* it, without worrying about somebody coming in and criticizing.

She had just spent three years under Ida Hermann, another contender for Seven Devils status; said Houston, "We couldn't do anything without telling her. . . . [she] had to know every little thing I was doing."[71]

Ida Hermann had been a cadet supervisor in the 1920s. Although teachers found her hard to deal with, when she went to Hawthorne as head teacher in 1937, parents there highly approved. They wrote the school board a letter of "thanks for sending them such a 'lovely principal, Miss Ida Hermann,' who 'has accomplished so much in addition to teaching all day.'" They added, "We mothers and fathers do so appreciate Miss Hermann's cooperation, and we want you to know that all the children just love her."[72]

She finished her career as principal of McDonald School, retiring in 1958 at the age of seventy. Military veterans who in postwar years taught at McDonald were less appreciative, forgiving, or indulgent of the older woman than those Hawthorne parents. One, whose first teaching assignment was there in the early fifties, remembered that "At noontime all the teachers would sit around the lunchroom table, and Ida Hermann would come in with her tray, and everybody would stand up. And then she would go over to the end and sit down. . . . just like Queen Victoria." Another teacher, a former marine, left the school district rather than deal with Ida Hermann; he "went down and taught at the jail for years."[73]

Reflecting decades later, Margaret Houston said of the Seven Devils phenomenon, "I think that was a way of phrasing your own frustrations."[74] Having served under Ida Hermann, Blanche Tanner, and Ida Vetting, all of whom earned mention as one of the Seven Devils, she may have learned from them "what not to do." Reluctant to accept a principalship, she finally yielded and took over at Northgate School in 1958. She brought an ordered yet benign management to the building. A former teacher there remembered Miss Houston as a teachers' principal: "A gem! A really strong woman who backed her teachers 150 percent and helped you in every imaginable way."[75]

Rather than recruit principals from elsewhere, Frank Cooper and his immediate successors had promoted from within; they relied on current principals to recommend prospects who reflected their own philosophy and priorities. The case of Thelma Thompson Randall illustrates this practice. In 1946, teaching at Madrona School, she impressed her principal,

Dora Herren, who sent the superintendent an unsolicited, enthusiastic endorsement, saying that Thelma Randall:

is in a class by herself, so far as superiority is concerned. . . . she is extremely versatile in her abilities.

She has personal appearance, health, tact, sound judgment, the ability to meet both parents and pupils; all coupled with an outstanding personality.

She is certainly material from which an excellent school principal evolves. I commend her to your notice.

Since entering the Seattle system in 1929, Thelma Randall had taught under both Charlotte Graham at Emerson and Eugenie Pariseau at Bagley. During her stint as acting principal at Ravenna in 1952, she captivated the teachers, all of whom signed a testimonial letter saying she had "won the love and respect of teachers, children and parents." There was surely rejoicing in 1955 when she returned as principal. Mrs. Randall stayed at Ravenna through years of social and educational change; she retired in 1968.[76]

Another teacher whose administrative potential was recognized early by more than one strong principal was Janet Dewhurst, whose career also spanned the interwar years and decades beyond them. She had graduated from Broadway High School in 1918 and spent the next year at the Seattle Kindergarten Training School, a first step for any number of teachers. Its director soon judged that "Miss Dewhurst will make steady growth in her profession." After completing the normal course at Bellingham, she worked informally at Longfellow while attending the University of Washington. Annie Gifford said, "She has been in our building so much . . . that I have had opportunity to judge of her ability. . . . She is a student and capable of a good deal of growth. She has manifested great interest in the profession." After receiving her bachelor's degree in 1921, Miss Dewhurst taught as a cadet at Harrison under Eunice Copeland, then spent two years at Ravenna before resigning in May 1924 to study at Teachers College, Columbia University.[77]

A year later, master's degree in hand, Miss Dewhurst returned to Ravenna; two years later the district tapped her for the demonstration school. She stayed in demonstration teaching under Ida Vetting until 1942, then moved to Bryant. Bella Perry evaluated her in 1943, saying that she was vitally interested in her profession and that her

> work is of the highest character. . . . Her patience and her sense of humor are appreciated by the pupils and the parents. . . . [Fellow teachers] admire her frankness, honesty, and democratic viewpoint. . . . She is good material for promotion.[78]

When she made that assessment, Miss Perry surely knew that, as president of the Seattle Association of Classroom Teachers, Janet Dewhurst found herself deep in political and legislative affairs. The Washington State Federation of Teachers commended her, a nonmember, that year for her cooperation during a disappointing legislative session: "Miss Dewhurst and her associates worked with the W.S.F.T. in its major efforts to the extent that no small measure of the credit for such gains as were made are due them." She had been active in the Better Schools Council, composed mainly of union leaders, which had worked to reelect the labor leader James Duncan in the most recent school board election. One study of teachers unions said that such participation "showed that teachers, though unwilling to affiliate with organized labor, nevertheless desire[d] its support."[79]

Miss Dewhurst had also led the fight for equal status for married teachers. In January 1943, she appealed to the school board to make no distinction in salary for married teachers hired for emergency service during the war:

> These teachers are loyal to the system and will remain so despite opportunities for more lucrative employment. They desire to continue . . . to expend their best efforts to help preserve the educational standards of the Seattle Public Schools. We need teachers of maturity and experience to preserve these high standards.

By the end of the year, although still considered emergency hires, married teachers were "paid in accordance with the [regular] Seattle salary schedule."[80]

In 1951, going against the mostly-male trend, Janet Dewhurst finally applied for a principalship. Old-line Cooper disciples, now retired, closed ranks behind her with superlative recommendations. Helen Laurie, noting that she had "known Janet since she was a cadet with Eunice Copeland," wrote from Florida to say, "In comparison to some [principals] we have appointed in the past—she soars." Helen Reynolds and Ida Vetting had known and worked with her for thirty years and both rated her "outstanding." Walter Marshall, Bella Perry's successor at Bryant, had come to Seattle in the midtwenties. His slightly less glowing recommendation alluded to Miss Dewhurst's political activism:

> I have often thought that it was unfortunate that Miss Dewhurst wasn't given administrative responsibility earlier in her Seattle career. She would have been a valuable ally on the administrative side of the various questions which have arisen. To be quite frank, it would have been much better to have had her "for us rather than agin' us."[81]

When the civil rights movement reached Seattle, Janet Dewhurst, the political activist now principal of Leschi, became a neighborhood leader. One of the first to propose community organizing, she took her strong, child-oriented voice into planning the Leschi Improvement Council, which held its first meeting in January 1959 at her school. Her concern remained with children who "come to school ill clad, poorly fed and needing sleep." She retired in 1964 after forty-three years with the district. By then demographic change had created a 90 percent African American student body at Leschi; a year later the school district included Leschi in its first program of mandatory student reassignment to relieve overcrowding and racial imbalance. In her letter of resignation, she mentioned "dealing with the rapidly emerging problems of the civil rights revolution and its tremendous effects upon elementary school boys and girls," and added, "Unless one is actively engaged in a central area school it is difficult to imagine or to realize these problems. However life has been interesting and challenging with very few dull moments!"[82]

Janet Dewhurst served on the board of trustees of the Seattle Education Auxiliary, which, in 1929, had begun a drive to establish "a home for retired and convalescent teachers," leading to the creation of Ida Culver

House. When she died, Miss Dewhurst left a substantial bequest to the auxiliary; as the Janet Dewhurst Fund, it became an endowed source of aid for residents of Ida Culver House "whose current resources can no longer provide a reasonable quality of life."[83]

Another principal who rose from the teaching ranks and had a lasting effect on the city was Jessie Lockwood, who arrived in Seattle in 1908 at the age of thirty-two. A graduate of Maine State Normal School, she taught six years in Orono and Augusta and then seven years in Somerville, Massachusetts. In Seattle she taught eighth grade, and in 1910 she was named principal of York School located in the Mount Baker area where English immigrants had settled. A dedicated conservationist and a disciple of the naturalist John Muir, in 1921 she succeeded in having York renamed John Muir School.[84]

Muir students from the 1930s remember an imposing figure who "put the fear of God [in us] . . . she *was* God to us." A trip to her office "was about the worst thing that could happen." A proper New Englander to the core, at a time when women had long since adopted short skirts and informal clothing, "Miss Lockwood wore skirts down to the floor. She wore . . . a navy blue serge skirt and high-necked blouse."[85] Although not on the cutting edge of fashion, she won acclaim from Superintendent Worth McClure as one of "the pioneers in the use of student government in schools." Her students took this exercise in civics very seriously. They ran campaigns complete with campaign managers and electioneering signs. Chief justice was the highest in a wide spectrum of offices. Miss Lockwood's system had teeth in it; the chief justice would adjudicate cases when a commissioner reported rules infractions. Fittingly, the officers included a conservation commissioner who "could give a ticket to anybody . . . found picking a trillium . . . [because] if they're picked, they don't bloom for another seven years." Emphasizing that students took their student government experience to heart, a former Muir officeholder said, "Not one person you'll ever find who went to John Muir . . . has ever even *dreamed* of not voting! My goodness, that would be right up there with having to go to [Miss Lockwood's] office!"[86]

The tone at John Muir was reinforced by chivalric pictures that hung in the hallways. A former student spoke of the atmosphere Jessie Lockwood created and "the great Sir Galahad paintings [that] were all over John Muir":

> They were a major part of our schooling, because they were there, and we had lots of stories about them . . . it was the whole ambiance of Sir Galahad, and the courtesies to each other, and the reverence, really . . . the chivalry of it all. Quite grand. And we thought we were quite grand.

Although "all the other schools in the area thought we were just terrible snobs," Muir pupils took enormous pride in their student government and all that they absorbed in Jessie Lockwood's school.[87]

The Muir mystique included the school's nature pageant, "Forest Trails." A regular event in the twenties when pageants were popular, it headlined the program at the National Education Association convention in Seattle in 1927. Originally written by pupils as a means of making John Muir's life "a vital force in [their] lives," the pageant was adapted by present and former faculty for the NEA presentation. Jessie Merrick, a longtime friend of Miss Lockwood's and head of physical education in the district, created the "interpretation of the episodes in rhythmic expression." Florence Keller Brooke, who had recently resigned as Muir's English teacher when she married, wrote the speaking parts, using Muir's own words.[88]

Given the opportunity to guide the school in a direction she wanted, Jessie Lockwood appreciated the considerable autonomy she enjoyed. In 1935 she told the school board, "It is a rare privilege to teach in a system in which development of one's ideals is encouraged and recognized."[89] Her ideals remained deeply embedded in former Muir students. Among them, Katie Houlihan Dolan and James Ellis represent a long list who helped shape the Seattle community for decades. Dolan took those ideals into a career as an advocate for the rights of the developmentally disabled. Ellis, "the father of the Mountains-to-Sound Greenway" and prime mover in combating environmental pollution, returned to the school in June of 2000 to "talk about how Muir turned students into environmentalists." Ellis had spent eight years absorbing Miss Lockwood's ideals during the 1930s.[90]

Jessie Lockwood died November 26, 1936. In eulogizing her, Superintendent McClure said,

[She] lived in deeds, not words. . . . She identified her life with the school, and her school with the system. . . . Jessie Lockwood had faith in her ideals. She saw their power so clearly that the short-comings of human nature never daunted her. She believed passionately in America and in the ultimate triumph of great principles to make its dreams come true. . . . [She] never once forgot her great purpose to fashion a school where the great loyalties could be planted in growing lives.[91]

The following year, John Muir School parents commissioned a stained-glass window for the school in her memory. Dedicated in 1938, the huge window bears the likeness of Sir Galahad and incorporates school mottoes that mirror her philosophy. It depicts the Quest for Purity, Justice, and Loyalty, leading to Achievement and Wisdom.[92]

Most of the interwar principals identified their lives with their schools and their schools with the system. They never abandoned the idea of progress and continued to plant "the great loyalties . . . in growing lives." From the beloved Annie Gifford and L. Maxine Kelly, through the feared yet respected Bella Perry, to the widely disliked Charlotte Graham and Ida Hermann, women who occupied the principals' offices in Seattle grade schools during the interwar years left their mark. Neither those who attended their schools nor teachers and principals whose careers they had helped to mold forgot them. Their hopes and beliefs continued to influence the schools, and, indeed, the city through the social upheaval and demographic change of two more decades.

6 / Dealing with Diversity

An important element of the Seattle Way was assimilating into the mainstream the children of immigrants new to America—in Seattle, a relatively small group during the Cooper years. Frank Cooper wanted no separate school for those who arrived with little or no ability in English. Pacific School, a standard grade school on First Hill, accommodated newcomers in four special classes where they gained sufficient English fluency to enter regular classes in their neighborhood schools.[1]

Seattle's ethnic communities gradually moved from their original areas of settlement near Pioneer Square, and by 1920 their children predominated in some schools. The residences of Japanese Americans—Nikkei—had "spread eastward up First Hill and mingled with those of Jews, Italians, and groups who had settled earlier."[2] "Wealthier Temple de Hirsch Jews lived in fine homes on Capitol Hill . . . around Volunteer Park," and their children attended Lowell and Stevens schools; children of Orthodox and "later-arriving East European Jews and Sephardic immigrants" attended in growing numbers at Rainier and Horace Mann.[3] Seattle's small African-American community had become concentrated along Madison Street east of First Hill, an area served by T. T. Minor and Longfellow. Students at Colman in Rainier Valley came primarily from the Italian community. Nikkei were the majority among Asians at Bailey Gatzert and Washington Schools. Grade schools that fed into Ballard High School—Ross, Adams, and Salmon Bay, among others—served Scandinavian groups. School patrons from Ballard once petitioned the school board to include Scandinavian languages in the high school curriculum.[4]

Rebecca Waxman, by all accounts Seattle's first Jewish teacher, began at Seward School in 1911 after six years at P.S. 55 in Brooklyn. A graduate of the Normal College of New York, she took a leave of absence in 1917 to complete her bachelor's degree at Hunter College. When she returned to Seattle, the district assigned her to Horace Mann School, where she taught until retiring in 1955 at the age of sixty-nine.[5]

June Droker, a pupil there in the early 1930s, remembered her as "a little woman with glasses, and also very strict." She said many in Horace Mann's large Jewish student body felt that Miss Waxman was harder on them than she was on the other children: "because we were Jewish she was trying not to be so nice to us. We all had that feeling, I think." She also recalled moving from Miss Waxman's third-grade class to that of the fourth-grade teacher, Alice Robertson, whom they all liked:

> Miss Waxman was rigid and strict, and Miss Robertson was just the opposite . . . tall and thin, and very soft-spoken. . . . She lived with her elderly mother, just the two of them. . . . right around the corner from us. . . . My father had a meat market, and she was one of his customers, and he . . . [delivered] to her house, so I'd go with him to her home, and we were good friends. She was one of my favorites. . . . Everybody liked her.[6]

Rebecca Waxman's membership in the Temple de Hirsch may have contributed to her unpopularity, because "Orthodox Jews of Yesler Way/Cherry Street regarded the [Reform] Temple Jews with a wariness that bordered on suspicion."[7] Or perhaps, as June Droker suggests, she overcompensated to guard against any hint of ethnic favoritism.

The interwar teacher cohort mirrored Seattle's middle-class population; the women who taught in schools with children of various ethnic makeup were virtually all white, Anglo-Saxon, and Protestant.[8] Some schools, such as Interbay, were widely diverse, but scattered throughout the city were many non-English-speaking children who never attended the classes at Pacific School. They faced hurdles both academic and social when families did not speak English at home, but their teachers coped with language as best they could in classes that ranged in size from thirty to forty-two pupils.

At Rainier School in the midtwenties, the language barrier cost one young pupil an extra semester in Amelia Reible's first-grade classroom. His family spoke Yiddish at home, and his sister recalled that when he entered school he "really didn't know much English," but Miss Reible helped him overcome that hurdle, and he ultimately had a successful career as a nuclear scientist. Rainier School is remembered also as having a sizable number of Japanese pupils and a few African Americans among its Jewish majority in the late twenties and early thirties.[9]

Among those few African-American children at Rainier was Vivian Austen, who had happy memories of pre–World War I Rainier teachers, most of whom continued their service into the interwar years and were "very, very nice." She said, "They were always talking courtesy. In that day and time people talked an awful lot about courtesy and manners—good behavior—and [other] children treated us fine." She, her brother and sister, and three other youngsters made up Rainier's African-American contingent at the time. Their fellow students brought parents' racial attitudes to school, but the teachers, especially Lillie P. White, were "very, very liberal" and conscientious: "All we had to do was just tell them [of racial harassment] and they must have gotten after them because the thing smoothed right over and we learned and got along fine."[10] Lillie White taught eighth grade at Rainier from the turn of the century until she retired in 1922. Elsie Judd, who taught sixth grade when Vivian Austen was there in 1910, transferred later to T. T. Minor where she taught third grade past 1941.[11]

Not all schools were so enlightened. By the time Maxine Pitter reached fifth grade in the late twenties, her family had moved, so she transferred from Longfellow to T. T. Minor. As there were only two African-American families with children at Minor, the Pitters were definitely in the minority, and Maxine Pitter Haynes, who remembered Longfellow with pleasure, said, "I was tormented daily at T. T. Minor—daily, by the students." She considered Minor teachers "derelict in their responsibility" on the playground. Other students "would call me names—terrible names," and even when "they would trip me up," no teacher would intervene.[12]

Decades later a former pupil said that polyglot Interbay School in the midthirties "must have been a big challenge to the teachers." Regardless of the language problem, Elsie Hill Fell remembered the school fondly: "I had cousins and an older brother who went there before me and we all spoke Finnish. I finally learned to read in third grade. I was mixing English and Finnish." Interbay's Finnish community flourished throughout the decade; at the big Finnish Brotherhood Hall on the west slope of Queen Anne Hill, regular Saturday night socials drew many Finns to musical programs and dancing, followed by dinner.[13]

Gladys Wheeler had taught first grade at North Queen Anne School since shortly after it opened in 1914; in 1920, she introduced an unhappy child to English and to America. After their mother died, Alli Benson and her sister joined their father in Seattle. She had not wanted to leave Finland and recalled:

> I had to start school right after New Year's and I did not like that. I was twelve years old and started in the first grade [at North Queen Anne]. . . .
> It took me about four years to go through grammar school. I [was] fifteen or sixteen when I graduated from eighth grade.

Miss Wheeler finished her long career in various schools in predominantly Scandinavian Ballard.[14]

Policy on non-English-speaking students lacked uniformity. Lowell School on Capitol Hill would not accept a newcomer from Copenhagen in 1921. Laura Foss and a cousin came to Seattle to live with their aunt and uncle; she recalled that when it was time to go to school they had to go to Pacific School:

> We were enrolled in this class with Chinamen and Russian girls and Greek and you name it. . . . we had to start all over again, writing A's and B's. . . .
> We caught on very fast and the teacher was so proud of us when we had done something, she would send us in to the principal with our papers and he would pat us on the back.[15]

The cousins very likely attended Margaret J. Thomas's class for "newcomers with no English vocabulary, and whose residence in Seattle has been of short duration." Margaret Thomas had begun her Seattle teaching career during World War I at Interbay, with its rich ethnic mix. By fall 1921, she had transferred to Pacific to teach one of four "foreign" classes. In teaching the newcomers, she observed, "work must be accomplished through the use of objects, pictures and actions. . . . [but] Phonics and word drill are stressed . . . with special care as to lingual difficulties." Reflecting both the patriotism of earlier Progressives and the school district's emphasis on democracy and Americanization in the twenties, Miss Thomas noted that "American and Christian ideals are taught to make these future citizens appreciate the advantages given here, as well as to inspire in them true Americanism and the highest ideals of living."[16]

Teaching immigrant children required a sensitivity that teachers may not always have possessed or communicated. The Grade Club reminded its members of special burdens and obligations: "To receive pupils of so varied inheritance and customs, and melt them into true Americans[,] proves the teacher a genuine refiner. The interest, tact, courage, and confidence that she must constantly evidence add heavily to the ordinary classroom service."[17]

Laverne Nelson Anderson, who might well have profited from some time at Pacific, learned English at Green Lake School. Her immigrant parents spoke Swedish at home until, as she recalled, her teacher told them, "You can't do that any more; we can't understand the children . . . they disturb the whole class—they answer in Swedish." Her mother "started to read the newspapers aloud so she could get the knack of the English language," but the daughter keenly felt her disadvantage. By the time she reached eighth grade in the midtwenties, Green Lake had implemented an ability-tracking system of sorts, and "I cried so hard because I was just on the border line—and wanted to go with the top." Only the art teacher, Louise Judges, ignored the language problem and provided a bright spot. Years later, Mrs. Anderson said, "She thought I was great—she used to send my drawings downtown to the central office; she thought I had lots of talent in art—well I *did*, and I've been kind of an artist all my life."[18]

Art classes cut across language barriers and ethnic divides. Bryant School's Florence Porter was "a fantastic art teacher [who] . . . produced several commercial artists." One of the most successful was George Tanagi, whose Nikkei family cultivated large vegetable gardens on the present site of University Village. After Miss Porter's tutelage, the boy went on to Roosevelt High School, where his schooling ended abruptly with the internment of Japanese Americans in 1942. Tanagi's postwar career produced such landmark Seattle images as logos for Starbuck's Frappucino, K2 Skis, and the Seattle Sonics. The inspiring Florence Porter saw beyond ethnic difference and gradations of ability. "Everyone got to work on her projects, . . not just the artists," and a lone Nikkei boy's talent gave him memorable status.[19]

Patriotism permeated life in Seattle schools during the first four decades of the twentieth century, and nowhere more than in schools with large immigrant populations. Children in Louise Rathbun's Americanization class at Pacific sang their own anthem, written by her and set to the tune of "America":

> Our chosen country, thee,
> Thou hast a welcome free
> For all who come;
> Guide us forever on,
> Thou canst depend upon
> Our steadfast loyalty
> To thee, our Own.

Louise Rathbun had come from Iowa early in the century. She began her Seattle career at the new B. F. Day School, then moved to Pacific and on to Youngstown; with the advent of junior high schools, she transferred to Hamilton Junior High in Wallingford where she taught social studies until retiring in 1940.[20]

An article in the *Seattle Grade Club Magazine* in 1920 spelled out the Seattle Way of educating children of immigrants:

If we will plant the children of our immigrants in American soil, give them American companions, teach them in the American language, let them breathe American literature, discipline them in the American art of self-government, . . . and always respect the nature which God has given them, however it may differ from ours; they will grow up loyal, patriotic, devoted Americans.[21]

The article stated that Seattle grade teachers had "been sharing in Americanization work [since] long before World War days made the subject a popular term," especially those in Colman, Washington, Main Street (Bailey Gatzert), and Pacific. Colman's predominantly Italian kindergarten and first grade were 40 percent non-English-speaking, and 50 percent of all its students came from homes that did not speak English. At Washington, 55 percent of the children were from "Turkish and Russian-Jew families, 15 per cent . . . Italian, and 3 per cent Japanese." At Pacific School, children brought "the immediate influence of twenty European, three Asiatic, two North American and two South American nations. . . . [and] 75 per cent of tots entering kindergarten spoke no English." The article concluded "that Seattle has her Americanization problem, and that the grade-school classroom is a veritable crucible."[22] Of the schools cited, all but Colman were in the International District and, apart from Pacific's foreign classes with their ethnic variety, had largely Asian student bodies. Japanese Americans constituted Seattle's largest minority group until 1942, and Bailey Gatzert and Washington schools accommodated a majority of the Nikkei children.

The journalist Bill Hosokawa recalled a varied population at Washington School and memorialized one of its interwar teachers in his 1969 book, *Nisei: The Quiet Americans:*

Her name was Miss Bohan, and a barely perceptible brogue in her speech hinted of not distant Irish forebears. If she had a first name, none of her charges were aware of it. She was a lean, lank, red-haired maiden lady who had grown old in the thankless profession of civilizing children—other people's children—who . . . were both required and privileged to enroll in first grade.

Miss Bohan enforced a strict discipline and whetted the children's native curiosity into a keen desire for learning. . . . She was a dedicated teacher of a type that has all but disappeared.

More than half of her pupils had pale white skins, brown curly hair, and on Saturdays they dressed in their best clothes and went to the synagogues with their parents. There were other children with German, Scandinavian, Polish, Italian and Russian names. And although some of them did weird things to the English language . . . Miss Bohan, somehow, understood them all.

Julia K. Bohan left Hosokawa with "a faint memory of patience, kindness and warm understanding, the first person among many outside his family to help shape the course of his life."[23]

Julia Bohan had earned a two-year certificate at Oshkosh State Normal School in 1903. She taught eight years in Wisconsin before moving to Pocatello, Idaho, Port Angeles, Washington, and Portland, Oregon. She visited Seattle in the summer of 1913 and applied to the school district, so impressing Frank Cooper that he hired her as a substitute immediately; in January 1914 she began a six-year stint at South Park School. In 1920 she requested a transfer to a school closer to her hotel residence on First Hill. Miss Bohan anchored the first grade at Washington School for seventeen years before moving to Harrison for the rest of her career. That move spared her the wrenching experience of seeing Nikkei children removed from her classroom in April 1942, to be sent to relocation camps. Miss Bohan died on April 9, 1945, one day before her fifty-ninth birthday.[24]

Washington School was the quintessential Progressive laboratory of democracy during the twenties. It "became a site for the negotiation of public culture across social differences of race and culture" in the interwar years. Principal Arthur G. Sears emphasized "living a dignified life . . . through an understanding and an appreciation of one's ethnic identity." Under his leadership, teachers at Washington sought to cultivate in their students a sensitivity to ethnic heritage and toleration of diversity. Sears had spent twenty-one years as principal of Ross and Adams schools in Ballard before transferring to Washington in 1928.[25]

Recalling his own years there, Bill Hosokawa said that he was by "sixth grade, enough of a student and class leader to be assigned the role of George Washington in a patriotic play about the travail at Valley Forge." He learned later that some in the larger community who "were not ready to have a 'Jap' boy take the role of Washington" had confronted Sears with strong opposition to his selection. To Sears's credit, "he stood by the teacher's choice, and together they shielded the boy from this exhibition of petty bigotry."[26]

This episode occurred in 1928, Sears's first year at Washington. The teacher would have been either Maud Thompson or Mary Calder. Miss

Thompson had taught in Seattle since 1910, transferring to Washington from Summit School in 1926. Miss Calder had been at Washington since coming to Seattle in 1915, and she continued to teach there beyond the interwar years.[27]

Maud Thompson, who retired in June 1938, had spent her 1929 summer vacation touring China, Japan, and Korea and visiting schools at every stop. In reporting on her trip, she noted that "only eight per cent of Chinese Children" had schooling opportunities but that in Japan "less than eight per cent of the children of the land are without school advantages. This is according to . . . the Minister of Education," who entertained her touring group "right royally at his palatial residence." After observing one Japanese kindergarten, Miss Thompson had found it hard "to believe that a wide ocean separated these children from their little brother and sister Kindergartners in America." She also proudly reported that two "Japanese men of note in Tokyo, who had gone through Broadway High and the University of Washington, spoke in highest terms of the educators of the Evergreen State."[28]

Frank Cooper's successors built on his model of inclusiveness and worked to foster the role of the school as melting pot. Although making good, loyal citizens of *all* children remained a primary goal in the interwar decades, the district's teachers were motivated to appreciate "the gifts which our immigrant friends bring" and to conserve them. In 1932, Superintendent Worth McClure reminded the grade school corps especially to inspire the children of immigrants "to respect and admire also the art, the music, the religion, the folklore of their parents, whose hardihood has brought them to the new land of opportunity."[29]

Seattle teachers responded with considerable pride to this multicultural approach. A thirty-year district veteran, Huldah Olein, who taught at Central School, shared this pride at the 1932 convention of the World Federation of Education Associations. Appearing on a panel about "Conflict Produced in Pupils by Divergent Aims of Home and School," she countered the "very gloomy view . . . that in this melting pot too much was lost and not enough gained" with evidence from her own school, where 59 percent of the students were Japanese. The vice-president of the PTA, she said, was a Japanese gentleman who at the monthly meeting . . . translates . . . for the benefit of those who do not understand English well. . . . [We have] afternoon classes for foreigners where the mothers may learn to read and write English, and . . . programs for the P.T.A. which the Japanese furnish a certain number of times during the year. I mentioned [our] exhibits of Japanese toys and dolls . . . and the Japanese dances forming part of our program on many occasions. I tried to indicate to them how we avoid conflict by showing a sympathetic appreciation of the culture and art of Japanese people. We hope in this way to convert the love and loyalty [that pupils] have for the country of their parents into loyalty for their adopted country.

Except for two years at Lowell School before she retired in 1937, Hulda Olein had spent her entire career in ethnically diverse schools, including five years at Colman with its large Italian student body, and twenty-one years at Central.[30]

The Seattle School District had long acknowledged Asia's importance in the Pacific Northwest. A 1926 revision of the high school curriculum added an elective course in Pacific Rim history that continued on through the thirties. Mary E. Knight, Garfield High School's history department chair, described it as "a survey course designed to acquaint pupils with historical and geographical . . . social, industrial, and international problems." She went on to say:

It recognizes the Pacific as the future trade mart of the world; that contact with people on its shores will be more and more frequent; that these commercial, political, and social contacts can be constantly marred by prejudices and misunderstandings. The schools must prepare the nation's citizens for the task of expansion on the Pacific, for they will be responsible for the blunders an uninformed citizen body is sure to make. The problem has a particularly local appeal.[31]

Asian children went from the relative shelter of neighborhood grade schools to high schools that drew students from a wide geographic area. There they "began to mesh with the majority community . . . [and] encountered a largely positive experience all around, although there was little interracial mixing after school hours as students returned to their respective neighborhood enclaves." Broadway and to a lesser extent both Garfield and Franklin had sizable Asian populations.[32]

No Seattle grade school serving Nikkei children in the interwar years had greater, longer-lasting influence than Bailey Gatzert. A kindergarten-through-sixth-grade school, it sent children on to Washington, Pacific, and Central schools for grades seven and eight, thence to high school. And no principal stood higher in Nikkei community esteem than Bailey Gatzert's Ada J. Mahon. As the sociologist Frank Miyamoto observed: "The public schools . . . in and around the Japanese community were the one aspect of the community's institutional life beyond the direct control of the residents. Nevertheless, the community exerted influence even here." In Ada Mahon, the community and its children had a champion; her "teaching philosophy won community approval," and mutual admiration between principal and community grew over the years.[33]

When Frank Cooper arrived in Seattle in 1901, Emma C. Hart presided over the small Main Street Annex; two years later Main achieved full status as an elementary school. Located on Main Street not far from Pioneer Place, it had always served Seattle's immigrant children. In 1910, Ada J. Mahon began her thirty-five years there as principal. Eleven years later, a regrading project forced the school from the original building.[34]

More than one former Gatzert student remembered the day of the move to Twelfth Avenue South and Weller Street. Shigeko Uno, a first-grader at the time, remembered everyone lining up and walking to the new building some eight blocks away, "on a rainy, rainy day." Ada Mahon led the entire student body into what Henry Itoi described as a "spread out, airy, well-lit Bailey Gatzert School, built attractively in the modern style . . . a really neat school."[35] Itoi's sister, Monica Sone, remembered morning treks to the new building:

> We meandered through the international section of town, past the small Japanese shops and stores, already bustling in the early morning hour, past the cafés and barber shops filled with Filipino men, and through China-town. Then finally we went up a gentle sloping hill to the handsome low-slung, red-brick building with its velvet green lawn and huge play yard. I felt like a princess walking through its bright, sunny corridors on smooth, shiny floors.[36]

All agree that Ada J. Mahon kept that handsome, sunny building under tight control. Parents appreciated "the authority and devotion with which she ran her school. . . . To the Issei, education required disciplined attention to teachers . . . [who] were regarded as founts of knowledge and authority." Gatzert's playground rang with boisterous physical activity, but there was seriousness in the classrooms. Miss Mahon "symbolized educational leadership in the community. . . . [and] commanded respect not only for her intellectual efforts but . . . for her moral influence on the students."[37] Bill Hosokawa, who had attended Washington School, noted, "Under [Miss Mahon's] direction Caucasian teachers took Nisei youngsters, many of whom spoke no English, and prepared them for life in America."[38]

One of those youngsters later thought that "our teachers must have been very patient and kind. We really marvel, those of us who were students in those days, at how they taught us. We didn't know even one word." Shigeko Uno allowed, however, that Miss Mahon "was kind of harsh on some of the Nisei boys, though, who were mischievous. Many of my friends, the boys, tell me they didn't like Miss Mahon. Strange, but we girls didn't see that side at all." Henry Itoi said that they "weren't fearful of her."[39] Although she did not forgo corporal punishment, even the critics among former Gatzert students agree that she tempered her authoritarian style with kindness and caring.

Aki Kurose, a Gatzert student from the early thirties who went on to a successful teaching career in Seattle herself, remembered Miss Mahon as a short, "kind of stately woman—[who] walked with great authority" and made pupils "toe the mark." "Some of the fellows would say she was a mean one. But the parents loved her." According to Kurose, Asian parents felt "beholden" to Ada Mahon and gave her gifts—"even the poorer parents." She recalled that children whose parents "felt they had to monetarily reward her all the time" were treated deferentially. "And yet we all loved her! . . . the thing I remember most about her is her caring."[40] However individual parents may have rewarded the principal, the Japanese community "honored her on many occasions . . . [and] expressed its gratitude by giving her an elaborate tour of Japan."[41]

She returned from that tour to start fall semester 1931 even more appreciative of Japanese culture than before. Her account of her travels reveals a gentler side of the autocratic principal that few ever saw. She told her

Seattle colleagues, "I loved it all and I'll revel forever in the recollection of it and my wonderful experiences in that interesting playland of the far east." She had visited schools in all the major cities but enjoyed most a kindergarten in Osaka: "I was greatly touched by the innocent yet intelligent manners of the winsome children[,] and my party could hardly tear me away." One of her hosts thanked her for what he called "the inestimable service rendered the educational cause of Japanese children on the other side of the Pacific." She summed up:

> I shall always remember the day I spent at Nara. The beauty of the scenery, the exquisite beauty of the carvings, the trees, the deer, the mystery of the shrines and temples, the presence of old and cherished friends—all appealed to my Irish nature and I responded with a love for it all and a delight that was pure joy.[42]

She carried her enthusiasm back to Bailey Gatzert. A former pupil said that she returned "so impressed with Japanese custom that she had all the kids . . . bowing to teachers" to show courtesy and respect. Chinese parents did not appreciate this and objected—"it was a Japanese custom and their children were *not* Japanese."[43]

Ada Mahon was born in New Brunswick, April 11, 1875; her family moved to Seattle in 1888, a year before Washington statehood, and she graduated from Seattle High School in 1894. For five years she taught in the King County schools; the superintendent there had commended her to the Seattle district, writing: "I can say without reservation that she is one of the most successful young teachers in this county. I know of no better disciplinarian than Miss Mahon, and her work as an instructor is of a high order. . . . If you decide to employ her, I can assure you that you will never have reason to regret your action."[44] Throughout her career she lived in the family home, two blocks east of Horace Mann School, to which she transferred in 1907 from Denny.[45]

One of few extant teacher evaluations she wrote sheds light on Miss Mahon's priorities. She wrote of Clara Hermanson, on March 24, 1924, that the second-year teacher out of Minnesota's St. Olaf College "Trains pupils to discipline themselves by appealing to the best that is in them. These pupils are invariably an example to the rest of the building." A "near superior" teacher, Miss Hermanson was "a great help to me and to the rest of the corps."[46] Miss Mahon no doubt considered it a great loss when the young teacher resigned two years later to be married.

Miss Mahon's authority met a challenge in the midtwenties when the first cadets assigned to Gatzert arrived fresh from normal school, bringing a cadet supervisor into her building. The principal and the supervisor, Helen Laurie, "didn't mesh too well, because Miss Mahon was of the old school, and was exceedingly strict, and wanted a schoolroom that was traditional. . . . Whereas Helen Laurie had . . . [attended] Columbia, and she was influenced by the John Dewey School." The two compromised on a cadet's role in the classroom: "in the end . . . Miss Mahon took care of the discipline and the math, and Miss Laurie handled everything else."[47]

Ada Mahon believed in strong discipline, but, in at least one instance, she showed disapproval of a teacher's intemperate actions. Rae Lewis, who ranks by consensus among former Gatzert students as the meanest teacher, predated the principal by at least a year in the school. But that seniority did not prevent Miss Mahon from siding with a parent from the Chinese community whose daughter Miss Lewis shook so violently that she tore buttons from her coat: William Mar recalled the day his mother "marched my sister Ruby back to school" and in the principal's office declared "that if her children needed spanking *she* would do it." Miss Mahon agreed, and Miss Lewis never touched those pupils again.[48]

A study of multiracial Bailey Gatzert in the late twenties reported that its faculty was "selected with care," which might explain Miss Mahon's reluctance to have cadets in her building. A new teacher was "told explicitly just what the situation is, and is questioned as to attitude toward race or color." During Ada Mahon's administration, there was little turnover, "and the principal cause for leaving is marriage."[49] Teachers' greatest problem was "to overcome the language difficulty, if there is one." In 1926, Gatzert's student body included 741 Nikkei children, 63 Chinese, 2 Philippino, 5 African American, and 19 Caucasian. The district gave Caucasian parents, mostly recent immigrants from southeastern Europe, "the privilege of transferring their children to some other school," but, apparently, there was only one transfer, in 1927.[50]

Most of the women who taught at Bailey Gatzert shared Miss Mahon's devotion to the community and her desire to respect the cultures of the students' families. Parents taught their children to respect and honor the teachers; by and large, the children did so and delighted in meeting their teachers outside of school. Monica Sone attended the Japanese language school, *Nihon Gakko,* every afternoon following her day at Gatzert. She wrote of its picnic held every June in Jefferson Park, which the entire Japanese community eagerly anticipated: "Sprinkled here and there in the crowd were strange Occidental faces. . . . Now and then some public school teachers appeared. Whenever their Japanese-American students spotted them they were instantly surrounded with cries of welcome."[51]

Not all teachers were beloved, however, and not all exhibited patience, tact, and sensitivity. Sally Kazama, cochair of the Asian Pacific Women's Caucus, told the 1981 congressional redress hearing in Seattle of being told "as a six-year old taking my mother to my first Open House that I should be ashamed that she could only speak 'Chinese.'" Kazama said that she had interpreted for her mother on that occasion and did not correct the teacher, but "I did not ask my mother to another Open House, and I did not speak Japanese for many years."[52] She soon transferred to Beacon Hill School where she was one of only four or five other Nikkei children in her class.

Its annual Japanese May festivals ranked as the most popular and enduring tradition at Ada Mahon's Bailey Gatzert School. Those events, described by one former student as "a combination of a bazaar and open-house," constituted something of a showcase for Japanese culture. They drew huge crowds. Amelia Telban's sister, then a teenager, went to the festivals while the elder sister taught at Gatzert. She remembered that each room was "beautifully decorated [and] lots of parents came—very devoted parents." Ethel Telban's strongest impression of Ada J. Mahon was that, "she *loved* those children—she wanted them to become good citizens."[53]

Former students corroborate both of Ethel Telban's observations. Sharon Aburano remembered Miss Mahon from the early thirties: "She had the Good American Citizenship club . . . [that met] before school started. She's the one who really Americanized us all, I think. She taught us what democracy really meant." Miss Mahon also instituted an early meal program for the neediest children, and during the Depression, she managed to clothe them, too.

She would have the messenger go to the room and tell the children to go to the office. [They] tell me today that they went, but were very embarrassed, because every time they went they would get these clothes, and would . . . be sent back to the room with them on. They knew everyone knew they were poverty stricken. That was Miss Mahon's doing. For some then, it was a negative thing. But . . . it showed me a compassionate person.

Gatzert teachers also held periodic inspections and reported "who needed what." For example, the science teacher, Ava Chambers, "had kids line up and show the bottoms of their shoes" and reported any to the principal whose shoes needed new soles.[54]

The Good American Citizenship Club met Wednesday mornings with the object of making "its members better citizens by . . . obeying the rules and laws and by being attentive and prompt." Students served on such committees as the basement committee, the clean grounds committee, and the safety patrol. Individually, they helped "teach younger children to share building responsibilities." An equal opportunity principal, Miss Mahon had "boys and girls alternate" in presiding at meetings, which began with the Flag Salute and singing of "America," followed by a short program usually geared to a current event.[55]

Caring, compassionate, and a strict disciplinarian, Ada Mahon returned from Japan in 1931 to say, "I love and . . . believe in boys and girls, the men and women of the great tomorrow. . . . [N]either Japan nor America need fear to leave the nation of tomorrow to the youth of today." The bombing of Pearl Harbor left her shaken, but it also may have strengthened further her devotion to Bailey Gatzert's children. One former student recalled the December 8 school assembly: "The usually composed Miss Mahon shook with emotion. [She told them] 'You are all my children' . . . and warned that friendships would be tested and that difficult times loomed ahead."[56]

It can only be imagined what anguish the patriotic principal must have felt the following spring when the federal government herded all Nikkei, citizens and noncitizens alike, into relocation centers inland from Puget Sound. As each group of internees that included Bailey Gatzert pupils was scheduled to move out, the school held "special assemblies, timed with their departures, calling them to the stage, so everyone could say goodbye." On one of the days of departure for the internment camps, the Nikkei assembled "with suitcases and duffel bags tagged with preassigned numbers. Among the friends who came to say goodbye was Ada Mahon, [who]. . . . wept openly at the sight of her departing students."[57]

Japanese Americans returned to Seattle after the war to an unwelcoming if not hostile environment in the city. Ada Mahon remained uncompromising in her love for "her children" and their families. Henry Itoi recalled having come back

> to help my father restart his life and a small hotel business in Seattle. So it was on a late afternoon in February of 1945, my father and I were walking [on Jackson Street]. . . . Suddenly I heard a car screech to a stop on our side of the street. The driver . . . came out of the car. It was Ms. Mahon who had suddenly spotted us. She welcomed us back warmly and then asked, "How can I help you?" We ended up borrowing two blankets from her.

Itoi himself had a long teaching career in Seattle; in fact, while he was a student at the university preparing for practice teaching,

> I got lucky, for I was assigned to my former school. . . . Bailey Gatzert hadn't changed much inside or out.
> All the time I was there cadetting I had a weird feeling that I'd run into Ms. Mahon in a hall somewhere, so strong was my recollection of her."[58]

Ada Mahon retired in 1945 at the age of seventy. She died June 11, 1951, at the place in Westport where she had hosted countless groups of Seattle teachers over the years.[59]

The school district and individual principals counseled calm and tolerance after the attack on Pearl Harbor, but classrooms reflected attitudes students brought from home as well as any prejudices teachers themselves harbored. Theresa Machmeier had taught in Queen Anne area schools since 1929, moving to Coe in 1935, which had few Nikkei children. "The day after Pearl Harbor was a somber Monday," she recalled. "The Japanese students were badly treated. It was terrible to see the other children put [them] down . . . merely because of their race." In February 1942, four mothers at Gatewood Elementary in West Seattle began a successful campaign to rid the schools of Nikkei clerical employees, saying that their presence put their children's safety at risk: there was "the possibility of sabotage if Japanese-American clerks were free to work in or near school cafeterias . . . [and they] should not be trusted to answer the telephones." A long-held motive surfaced when they told the press, "We always had a white girl until last fall and we resent the change particularly because we have no Japanese students in our school. This is a white district."[60]

Ella Evanson assigned Washington School seventh-graders an essay about their principal's remarks the day after Pearl Harbor. She asked them to write again at the time of the evacuation, which later caused tears among classmates saying goodbye. The students' writings offer a glimpse of those grievous days and reflect the school's atmosphere, spirit, and feeling in March 1942:

> I am very sorry that I will soon be leaving Washington School and the teachers I have. As you know we have been asked to evacuate. . . . Wherever I am going I hope there will be a school like Washington School. I don't want to leave . . . I have been in Seattle from the time I was a little baby. . . . I know I am going to miss everybody. I am hoping the trouble will be over soon.

A classmate wrote in a similar vein:

> Because of this situation, we are asked to leave this dear city of Seattle. . . . There was never a school like Washington School and I sure will miss it. As for me, the one I will miss most will be you. You have been very patient and kind throughout my work. . . . [M]y memories will flow back to the time I was attending this school and the assemblies which were held in the hall.
> Wherever I go I will be a loyal American.[61]

Even at Washington School, with its record of harmony and fairness, pupils' attitudes echoed those in the community. Miss Evanson discerned "a general acceptance of the evacuation as justified." One Caucasian girl expressed a position widely held:

We are all sorry to see the Japanese leave for we know if they do not leave that the white people who don't like the behavior of Japan will start beating up on the American Japanese so that is why they are leaving. . . . One of my best girl friends . . . said that she was leaving to a more safer place. . . . [we had] a farewell party for the Japanese who were leaving. I think that it is best for them to leave and go to a much safer place inland.[62]

Ella Clarissa Evanson began teaching in Seattle in 1926 at Fauntleroy in West Seattle; she transferred to Washington School in 1938. A North Dakota native, she had received a normal school certificate in 1910 and taught in her home state. During the First World War, she spent three and a half years as a "clerk in [the] office of Adjutant General of the Army" in Washington, D.C.[63] With this background, she lent support to a parent incarcerated in the first arrests of Seattle's Nikkei leaders in December 1941. Two months later, an envelope postmarked Fort Missoula, Montana, and stamped "Detained Alien, Enemy Alien, EXAMINED, U.S.I. & N. S." brought his handwritten thanks:

I wish to thank you very much for your kindness for sending me a statement concerning my past endeavor in cooperating with the school education of my children.

I have just mailed the statement to the F.B.I. Office on my behalf. The Board hearing was over in so far as I am concerned and I'm confident . . . as I have done no wrong to any lessons or instructions but only tried my best to bring up my children to the best tradition of the American ideal and principles.[64]

When Miss Evanson retired from teaching in March 1956, she left immediately "on a freighter trip across the Pacific," a reprise of voyages to Asia taken by countless of her colleagues and predecessors during the twenties and thirties.[65]

Seattle's ethnic picture changed completely during World War II. Those interwar teachers who taught beyond 1941 confronted a different set of challenges in dealing with diversity. Nikkei children returned to a school system bursting with newcomers and short of teachers. Demographic change created predominantly African-American student bodies in some elementary schools. By 1957, 81 percent of all elementary age African-American pupils were enrolled in nine schools, eight in the Central Area. By the end of that decade, the city had taken on classic characteristics of a de facto segregated school system.[66]

As the school district slowly moved to address that racial imbalance, women of the interwar cohort dealt with changed relationships among children and with organized pressures from the adult community. For principals such as Janet Dewhurst at Leschi and Margaret Houston at Northgate, the 1963 implementation of a student transfer program created both problems and opportunities in their "sending" and "receiving" schools. Teachers who had earlier worked toward the goal of developing good, loyal, English-speaking citizens of immigrant children had taken seriously the charge to respect and admire "the art, the music, the religion, the folklore of their parents." They now had a similar charge in accommodating African-American history and culture in the schools.

7 / Genteel Militants

Early in the twentieth century, women teachers bent on careers began their long tenures in the Seattle public schools, drawn by Frank Cooper's progressive new system. Seattle salaries equated with the best in the East and Midwest, but even before the World War I economy created a salary crisis, most grade school teachers acknowledged, albeit reluctantly, the need for a unified voice in dealing with the school board. The Seattle Grade Teachers' Club served as their advocacy group throughout the interwar years. They did not consider their club a labor union: although salary and working conditions remained top priorities, they held it to professional goals. The club president Freda Libbee in 1930 reminded members "to bear in mind that the purpose" of the organization was not only to secure "financial advancement, but [also to promote] intellectual and social welfare and [to maintain] highest professional standards."[1]

Lack of an adequate sick leave policy had proved a catalyst for districtwide organization of all teachers in 1911. Superintendent Cooper requested that teachers "give financial help to those colleagues experiencing extended illness"; an estimated three-fourths of the corps responded by forming the Seattle Teachers' Association. A teacher absent because of long-term illness could then receive ten dollars a week from association dues. The STA came into being that spring basically as a self-insurance organization, but it soon became an advocacy group.[2]

The grade teachers had launched the short-lived Primary Teachers'

Association in 1897. Some of those same women attended a mass meeting of grade teachers in the basement of the First Presbyterian Church on November 15, 1912, prompted by a problem relating to salaries. May Hurd, who would teach English and social studies for another thirty years, recalled that evening:

> I remember how the crowd stood around the stove. This is the way the conversation ran: "Who told you about the meeting?" "Where's the chairman?" "What will the School Board say?" "I don't think the administrative office will approve of this." "We'll be called on the carpet." "Sh—who's that on the platform?" "That's the chairman?" "Who is she?" "What's her name?" "Why doesn't she take off that linen duster?"

The meeting came to order "after a fashion [and with] some confusion temporary officers were chosen," including the chairman in her linen duster—Annie C. Brayton, then teaching seventh grade at Denny School. Applause greeted one teacher's suggestion that they needed an organization "through which to express themselves," but a motion to organize was followed by one "not to organize [which] received a second and doubtless could have been carried, if it had been put to a vote."[3] It had taken two previous meetings to reach this point.

Earlier, a large group had appointed a committee to proceed toward a permanent organization. But "since the majority of the committee [members] were not in sympathy with the movement they had done nothing, and recommended the matter be dropped." A second committee was named, and it reported to that November 15 meeting. Its proposed constitution was "adopted and personally signed by those present," who, before adjourning, set November 22 as the date to elect officers.[4] A special meeting of the school board on November 20 would have stiffened their resolve: "the Board at this time did not see its way to make the [salary] advance requested by the grade teachers."[5]

From such a weak and confused beginning, the grade teachers built an impressive and successful organization. They were fortunate in selecting strong and capable leaders throughout the interwar years. Their modus operandi—patient, nonthreatening communication well within what the school system allowed—proved move effective over time than a more militant and demanding approach might have. Nellie Sterret, the first president, said, "The biggest work and the greatest care of the first administration was to keep in the middle of the road—so to speak—to build a good foundation leaving the super-structure [for] those who would follow."[6]

The newly formed Seattle Grade Teachers' Club did conduct other business after electing officers on November 22. It accepted with thanks a report from the STA salary committee, then chose three representatives to call on the Reverend Mark Matthews to offer thanks "for the use of his church." It also chose a committee of three to visit Superintendent Cooper "to acquaint him with the names of the officers of the Club, and to assure him of our support and assistance."[7]

The club need not have worried about his approval. Cooper often asked Miss Sterret about the membership numbers, and told her that when he could "say to the board, . . . 'It is a club of [so many] members, 90 per cent of whom attend the meetings,' then your club will have power." Cooper possibly smoothed the grade teachers' path with the school board by characterizing the club as an organization to "promote sociability among its members; to raise the intellectual and professional standard; to guard personal interests; to improve working conditions; to procure desirable legislation on all school questions; to be an instrument for good in the community." The superintendent accepted an invitation to address the club when it met at Broadway High School on December 17, 1912, and, at the business meeting that followed, salary headed the agenda.[8]

Salary remained a prime concern, and Bertha Coleson, eighth-grade teacher at Warren Avenue School and chair of the STA's salary committee, kept the club apprised of her group's activities. The matter of working conditions appeared on the agenda in February 1913. Members resolved "that a committee be appointed to investigate heating conditions in all Grade Buildings, and to act according to their findings." The club did not neglect public relations. President Sterret spoke with an editor of the *Seattle Post-Intelligencer,* and accordingly "it was resolved that a press committee limited to five members should be appointed" with the president as chairman.[9] By the end of March, the club considered forming its own salary committee. Bertha Coleson reported again, and within two months the Grade Teachers' Club took a salary petition directly to the school board.[10] Once again the board invoked poor economic conditions to deny the request, and in October that year, the club voted to appoint a five-member salary committee of its own.

Club membership continued to grow. Members considered political action beyond the school district, but whether to "bring a bill before the next Legislature limiting the number of pupils that might be assigned to a teacher" was temporarily deferred.[11] Class size had joined salary and physical plant conditions as a priority.

The club unanimously reelected incumbent officers, including Nellie Sterret, in December 1913. The matter of class size arose again, and members voted "to investigate the number of pupils per teacher in the Seattle schools at present." Of more immediate concern, they voted to "request Mr. Cooper to change the date of the Christmas holiday vacation" so that it would run from December 23 through January 4.[12]

The committee on class size reported its findings in April 1914. Three hundred sixty-four teachers in grades one through four dealt with an average of just over thirty-eight pupils. Sixty-five of them had up to forty-eight in class, and eleven handled more than forty-eight children; only ninety-four taught in classes of fewer than thirty-six. Classes of the 293 teachers in grades five through eight averaged thirty-seven children each; 10 coped with more than forty-eight; and a fortunate 105 had less than thirty-six.[13] Class size would remain high among grade teachers' concerns.

That autumn, the club turned its attention to provisions for retirement. Members met in October to select grade representatives for a committee appointed by Cooper "to work in the interests of the Teachers' Retirement Fund Bill" then before the legislature. In what may have been a first, two businessmen "addressed the meeting and pledged their support to the bill."[14]

The year 1914 also marked the beginning of a long working relationship between the Grade Teachers' Club and the Seattle Federation of Women's Clubs, a component of which became the Parent Teacher Association. The grade teachers had joined the federation the previous year, and their association with those "women of vision . . . doing big things in the civic life of the city" and their "feeling of admiration and respect" would grow. This connection became so important that in November 1917 Superintendent Cooper granted rare permission for three grade club delegates to be "excused from school to attend the meetings of the Federation."[15]

Never abandoning the social side of things, the club voted that April to "arrange for a dinner." Whether the event occurred is unknown, but the combination of meeting and meal became part of the club's style. In 1915, the well-attended April meeting "took the form of a luncheon at the Rathskeller." In addition to representatives of the Seattle Teachers' Association, the Federation of Women's Clubs, and an organization of women principals, guests included the assistant superintendent of schools, Almina George, and the state superintendent, Josephine Corliss Preston.[16] The club had weathered its first two years in good fashion under Nellie Sterret and continued to grow in strength and influence under her successor, Nina O. Buchanan.

During Miss Buchanan's tenure, grade teachers appear to have become more political. Nina Buchanan herself epitomized political activism, not only chairing the committee to draft Seattle's first teacher retirement law, but also working statewide for legislation that enabled large districts to establish similar plans. She played a leading role in founding a statewide organization of classroom teachers, served two years as its president, then moved onto the national stage when its national counterpart later elected her president. A first-grade teacher her entire career, she taught at Coe Elementary while serving as president of the Grade Teachers' Club, and then taught for twelve years at T. T. Minor. She was elected superintendent of King County schools in 1935.[17]

In 1902, at the age of twenty-seven, Miss Buchanan had arrived in Seattle, having asked on her application only "One week's notice, and a compensation of at least $70 per month." The Illinois State Normal School graduate had taught seven years in rural and small-town schools of Illinois and Indiana. A former Coe pupil remembered her as a tepid believer in corporal punishment, saying, "She kept in the bottom drawer of her desk a slipper. I can remember a little boy getting a little spanking." A far more zealous advocate in the cause of teacher rights, she took a month's unpaid leave in 1917 to lobby for the teacher retirement bill. At one time or another she served on virtually every committee of the Grade Teachers' Club.[18]

The club had been targeted early on by candidates and others with agendas. At first it promised to "listen to those who cared to appear before it" and to make no endorsements. But three years later members voted to join the King County Women's Legislative Council.[19] The intervening years saw the teachers' increased political awareness and active involvement in school district affairs. In 1916, they discussed the Keating-Owen Child Labor Law, which the United States Senate then had under consideration, and voted to send a resolution in favor to Washington's senators. Later that year they agreed to send representatives to public meetings of the school board, though many felt trepidation lest their action be misconstrued. One of their number, Grace McKechnie of Greenwood School, had earlier "laid before the board the request that teachers out for illness receive the half pay due them at the end of the school month instead of in June." The first club delegation to attend a meeting "was made welcome," and the administration eventually sent copies of board minutes to each school.[20]

By the spring of 1917, the Grade Teachers' Club had gained confidence and broadened its scope. Membership stood at 737, forty-three schools reporting 100 percent membership. The number of committees multiplied. One committee had oversight of a fund from which it made interest-free loans to individual teachers, and that April, from donations of $345, it issued a check for $200 to a member in need of financial help. The fund originally relied on contributions, but by 1921 it received a $500 allocation from the treasury. Ever prudent, the club required that any loan "which exceeds $200 must be properly secured."[21]

Also in the realm of teacher welfare was the April 1917 discussion of "the advisability of establishing a Rest Cottage for temporarily disabled teachers." In May, the legislative committee reported passage of the law allowing school districts throughout the state to establish retirement funds for teachers, essentially the same measure that Seattle teachers had supported since 1914.[22] Club members would later be glad for having determined that their "time-worn and toil-worn sister teachers must not be left to the mercy of a rude stream that was drifting them . . . to a helpless and penniless old age" and having worked "for a Retirement Law which has since proved a blessing."[23]

The nation's entry into the First World War brought new concerns but did not alter priorities. Even though the grade club budgeted financial support for a French war orphan and supported such war-related concerns as Red Cross drives, it placed greatest stress on salaries affected by the inflation that accompanied war industries to Seattle. Other salary-related issues that had smoldered for years flared to life when the school board debated ways to retain and recruit qualified teachers being lured by the private sector. Different pay scales for men and women teachers and for grade and high school teachers were two of the inequities that the club targeted.

In October 1903, the school district had engaged Maud Thompson, an experienced teacher, at $700 per year paid on a ten-month schedule. Other grade teachers hired that month were offered between $650 and $800; for high school teaching, the district signed two men at $1,000 and $900, respectively, and two women at $800 and $900. When it was revised in April 1906, the salary schedule called for grade teachers to receive up to $864 with a $540 minimum, and high school teachers up to $1,080 with an $840 minimum. Perhaps that high school minimum gave experienced grade aspirants the $840 target that appeared in so many of their applications. By 1910 annual schedules ranged from $810 to $1,050 for grade teachers and $1,020 to $1,380 for those in the high schools.[24]

A young Seattle teacher earning the minimum $810 in 1910 had to stretch her monthly $67.50 for food, clothing, and shelter. A five-room flat on Capitol Hill rented for $20; sharing with at least one colleague would have helped. She could eat lunch at the Newport Café and Grill on the corner of Second and Madison for 25 cents. If she cooked for herself, she could find bacon at 25 cents a pound and white bread for 15 cents a loaf. Newspapers carried numerous ads for clothing suitable for a teacher. The Frederick and Nelson department store offered tailored suits for $25; the Bon Marché sold serge walking dresses for $12.95 and coats for $14.50. Hosiery cost 25 cents a pair. A long white underskirt sold for between $3.50 and $6.00, but a young woman on a budget could find "under muslins" at $1.45. She need not have spurned the latter, for the "corset covers" came with "deep yokes of Valencienne lace" and the drawers were "wide with dainty hemstitched ruffles."[25]

When wartime inflation hit, grade teachers who earned the minimum salary suffered most. At the school board meeting on April 30, 1917, Robert

Winsor moved to raise the minimum to $900 and to improve salaries at the upper levels. His efforts failed. But two weeks later, the board voted for an annual increase of $60 for grade teachers in the lower and middle brackets and $100 for those at the top of the schedule, and on May 23, it adopted the long-sought $840 minimum.[26]

Steps on salary schedules were based on experience and years of service in the district. War industries offered excellent wages that drew men teachers from the high schools. In an attempt to stem the loss, on December 7, 1917, the board added an eighth step to the high school pay scale, effectively granting an increase in salary. The board made no distinction between men's and women's salaries in the high schools, but this accommodation widened the gulf between the grade and high school teachers. For the past year, the grade teachers had sought additional steps for their own salary schedule. Some minimally paid grade teachers attended that December meeting, and the board told them to submit their requests in writing.[27]

Before returning with a written request, they documented the hardships of those on the lowest rung of the salary ladder. Within a week, the committee presented Superintendent Cooper with results of a questionnaire returned by a majority of those queried. Their responses confirmed the dire straits those women found themselves in month after month. They reported an average bill of $37.50 for room and board, with an increase of up to $10 looming. Insurance, which only a minority still carried, cost them an average $5.60, and they asserted that their economic state made "them poor risks for insurance companies." They reported little money left each month for either recreation or for charitable and church-related giving; the average for the former was $1.85 and the latter, $3.80. Many had bought no new clothes for that 1917–18 school year, and the monthly cost of laundry and dry cleaning ran an average of $3.86. Other costs directly related to their jobs included $3.06 for carfare and $3.40 for "professional expenditures." The committee lamented "how few are able to avail themselves of courses offered in our University" and concluded that "they lose joy in life and their work assuredly suffers."[28]

When the board met in January 1918, it voted an additional step for grade teachers, to $1,200, but minimum salary remained at $840. Other pay issues arose at that meeting; Broadway High School's Adella Parker raised the question of discrepancies in salary between men and women.[29] Two major grievances of grade teachers now came together, and they would begin to openly campaign for a single salary schedule for all teachers—men and women, grade and high school.

At a special meeting of the grade club on February 1, the gulf between high school and grade salaries moved the members to take a stand: focusing on grade teachers paid at the fifth level, $1,080, they noted that their high school counterparts earned $1,380; the $300 difference became the maximum that they would deem acceptable. Why the club chose to contest the fifth level is not clear, for the differential varied at lower levels,[30] but the rationale for a differential rested on the requirement of a bachelor's degree for high school teachers, which involved greater cost than a normal school certificate.

In April, the grade teachers' resolve hardened. At least 300 club members unanimously "promise[d] to give their individual support to whatever action the members of the Grade Club decided upon." To bolster their case for pay equal to high school teachers', they launched a survey to determine the number of grade teachers "qualified for high school work . . . [and] the number who held more than the grade school requirements." The salary committee received instructions to "get as little difference as possible between" grade and high school salaries at all levels, the "difference not to exceed $300."[31]

The problem of retaining male teachers grew worse, and the board entertained the notion of giving them a wartime bonus; grade teachers began their fight to keep the differential from surpassing $300. They gained support from both the Women's Legislative Council and the Seattle Federation of Women's Clubs. Throughout the spring of 1918 community leaders ranging from Temple de Hirsch's Rabbi Samuel Koch to Mayor Ole Hanson supported the teachers' cause at school board meetings.[32]

The board did not budge on basic salary for grade teachers, but on May 20 it approved a bonus schedule that increased lower salary levels. With a bonus of $216, a minimum-salary teacher would receive $1,056; a $72 bonus meant that the highest-paid teacher would receive $1,272. To avoid setting any precedent or raising expectations, the board stressed that the bonuses would be granted only for the 1918–19 school year. Its spokesman, the miserly Ebenezer Shorrock, called the new salaries "substantially equal" to those paid anywhere in the country "and far above the average."[33]

Maintaining "the proper differential" between grade and high school salaries, the school board took up the matter of high school bonuses. Because "virtually all our high school men instructors are married, with families, and the increased burden of the high cost of living has affected them to a much greater degree than the women," Shorrock proposed a bonus of $300 per year to men teachers and none for high school women. His board colleagues agreed, except for Evangeline Harper, recently appointed to replace Anna Louise Strong.[34] A few days later, the board met again and extended the $300 bonus to newly hired male teachers, with Mrs. Harper again dissenting; and it set the salary for cadet teachers, all women, at $900 with no bonus.[35]

By October, when the men teachers received bonus-enhanced salary checks, the outraged high school women had sent the school board a letter of protest signed by every one of them. Tame by late-twentieth-century standards but unprecedented at the time, it said, "For the first time in the history of our schools a group of teachers face a discrimination on the ground of sex." All high school teachers had to meet the same requirements and taught the same subjects for the same hours and to the same number of students; therefore, the signers made "vigorous protest against this unfair discrimination." Saying they did not ask for themselves alone, "but for the future of education in this city. . . . [and] because a sex discrimination is an injury to our profession," they asked for the same bonus as the men.[36]

The women had one champion on the board—Evangeline Harper. A month after receiving their protest letter, she offered a resolution that would grant them an equal bonus, to take effect retroactively. The board men deferred action, and when it came up again three weeks later, it lost by three to two, Judge Winsor having joined her cause. In a rare move, the majority offered explanation: Nathan Eckstein considered it "illegal" to appropriate money for the women's bonus; Shorrock concurred and said that any further increase "should be distributed among all the teachers, both high school and grade"; and George Spencer went along "mainly because he considered the grade school teachers more entitled to consideration than the high school teachers."[37] In effect, the three school board men had pitted the grade teachers against the high school women, who remained the only group to receive no bonus, and grade teachers still endured the differential that paid them less.

But the grade teachers also saw equal pay for men and women as an irritant. Other than the few men who taught manual training in schools with large vocational programs, the grade women had no direct male competition in the salary wars. Yet, at a grade club meeting in May 1918, members had instructed the salary committee to draft a resolution "concerning equal pay for men and women," and they soon adopted it and took it to the board.[38]

The school board election that fall had a critical impact on teacher salaries. Held in November when the flu epidemic had closed facilities, it produced a school board more in tune with Ebenezer Shorrock than with Evangeline Harper. Beginning in January 1919, a more resolute and persistent Grade Teachers' Club pressed its case. The differential then stood at $510, and the club wanted it reduced to $300, if indeed there had to be one. In March, Superintendent Cooper took the question of grade salary to the board, saying that the $840 minimum was "quite insufficient to be attractive to the kind of teachers we have been accustomed to employ." He proposed a revised schedule placing the differential between $240 and $300, depending on experience.[39]

By April 30, 1919, the board had been persuaded to fix grade salaries at $1,200 minimum and $1,800 maximum; to add salary steps; and to set the differential at $300. A delighted Agnes Parker, eighth-grade teacher at T. T. Minor and chair of the grade club's salary committee, reported that the goal of limiting the grade–high school salary differential to $300 had at last been obtained, and when Walter Santmyer of the school board joined her at that May 11 meeting, "all rose and gave him a most hearty welcome." All no doubt cheered when "he gave one extremely good suggestion: Why any differential?"[40] This oblique sanctioning of the grade teachers' ultimate goal could have stiffened their resolve to place a single salary scale at the top of their agenda.

Even as they celebrated an improved salary schedule, another income-related issue returned. Since at least 1915, school board policy had forbidden teachers to engage in any other employment, even during vacations. Frank Cooper could not sway the board with his belief that "some work or some study or both during the twelve weeks' vacation period is far preferable for teachers in general than for them to spend the vacation in aimless abstinence from employment." The board routinely denied teacher requests for exceptions to the rule. It even used the 1918 flu epidemic to rationalize, saying that the ban on summer jobs was intended to "protect teachers from contagion."[41]

The next year there were further skirmishes over the vacation employment issue. With Cooper's help, the teachers won a one-time waiver from the board for holiday work.[42] The matter took a slightly different turn in 1920. The otherwise intransigent board allowed the assistant superintendent, Thomas Cole, to accept a teaching appointment at the University of Washington, but it denied the request of Ethel Henson, supervisor of music, to teach that summer in Centralia. In fact, it rejected all summer work requests from women teachers, including those of

1.—Rebecca S. Knight—. . . no reason for granting her request. Nearly everybody, in the vicissitudes of life, has some relative to assist.

2.—In the application of Lulu A. Brown, there is nothing but the assertion that an additional increase in earnings is needed. I presume this is true to a certain extent of every teacher.

Even the laudable goal of paying off debt did not move the board to make an exception for "Mabel M. Carson [who] claims to have borrowed money and wants to earn more money to repay it. This may be literally true of a number of our teachers, although we are paying fair, if not liberal, salaries."[43]

Mabel Carson presumably took the board's rebuff in stride; she had started at West Seattle High School before the war and continued at Broadway into World War II. When family obligations led her to seek permission to work during the summer of 1920, Rebecca Knight was teaching at Brighton School; she retired from West Woodland in 1940. Lulu Brown had taught in Seattle only a short time before she needed the "additional increase in earnings" she sought in 1920; apparently less sanguine than the others, she did not return to the district that fall.[44]

The crux of the outside employment matter lay in board members' belief that "to compete with workers in other fields of labor is generally unwise,

unfair, and unprofessional." Nevertheless, in the spring of 1921, they modi-
fied their ruling after Superintendent Cooper pointed out that the rule
could not really be enforced and that it undermined morale. The board
now decreed that no employee of the district "shall engage in any occupation that will interfere with his or her professional obligations or
efficiency" and required that anyone who took other work must "report
the fact" so that the board could ascertain whether it "interfere[d] with the
efficiency of the one so engaged."[45]

Five years later the board reaffirmed that "as a general policy it is not
for the best interest of the schools" for teachers to hold outside jobs "during the time of the regular school year." Further, teachers now "are expressly
forbidden to tutor or give private lessons during . . . the regular school
year to pupils who are enrolled in the Seattle Schools."[46] Whatever the
underlying motive, the board found it hard to relinquish complete control over the time and incomes of teachers. The corps was more or less
at the board's mercy and became even more vulnerable with Cooper's resignation in 1922.

In 1920, before the advent of such groups as the Voters Information
League and the Tax Reduction Council, Cooper had persuaded the
tightfisted board to adopt another improved salary schedule. A year earlier, $1,080 had replaced the long-sought $840 as the grade teachers' minimum to help offset 74 percent wartime inflation in Seattle. The new 1920
minimum stood at $1,500 and the maximum at $2,100. The differential
between grade and high school salaries remained at $300.[47]

Frank Cooper resigned March 17, 1922, and teachers lost their best friend
and advocate. The Grade Teachers' Club president, Myra Snow, urged her
colleagues:

> To hold our morale in the face of depression, to "come back" when it would
> be easy to "slump," to be loyal to the children and to each other, whatever
> comes, all this requires courage and conscious determination. We need
> organization and association. The Grade Club next year should be more
> alive than ever before in its history.[48]

Her call to action did not come too soon.

In June the school board voted to cut teacher salaries by $150. The decision won applause from the likes of the Building Owners' Association, the Tax Reduction Council, and the Voters Information League, although the PTA and mothers clubs had urged the opposite. Protests came from every teacher organization, the Central Labor Council, civil service workers, and individual property owners.[49] But the antitax groups prevailed.

The Tax Reduction Council claimed that "surely there is nowhere else in the world so privileged a working class of folk" as the teachers. Not content with the school board's cuts, the TRC urged "still other reductions of salary," and the board gave assurance that it expected "to continue its policy of retrenchment."[50] Within two years that policy meant lengthening the grade school day by twenty classroom minutes without any additional compensation for teachers. District hiring practices also came under fire. The school system's strength had long rested on hiring the best candidates from throughout the country. In August 1922, the TRC questioned "employment of teachers from the outside," preferring to see local graduates hired. Cooper's successor, Thomas Cole, provided statistics for the coming school year: twenty-one grade candidates employed from Seattle, fifteen from elsewhere in the state, and thirty-two from outside. Defending quality as a hiring criterion, he pointed out that the number of grade positions to be filled exceeded the number of Seattle applicants, regardless of their merit.[51] And salary remained the way to secure superior teachers.

All teacher groups continued to petition for restoration of the 1922 salary schedule. Finally, in 1925 they formed a joint salary committee—George Porter from Garfield High School, president of the Principals' Association; A. L. Kaye, history teacher at West Seattle High School and president of the Seattle High School Teachers' League; and Mabel V. Wilson, eighth-grade teacher at John Hay and president of the Grade Teachers' Club. That spring the board adopted a salary schedule giving grade teachers a minimum of $1,440 and a maximum of $2,100. High school salaries paralleled that range, and the $300 differential remained. Mabel Wilson modestly reported that the committee "claims only a small part of the credit of securing the last step in the full restoration of the salary schedule. . . . The Superintendent and a majority of the Board recognized the justice of the request . . . and readily gave the issue their support" once they determined how to fund the raises without a special levy.[52] Adding salary levels to the schedule appears to have been a part of the solution.

The superintendent offered praise for the "splendid spirit of the Seattle corps during the three years following the reduction in teachers' salaries"; he found it "most commendable." But those three years had taken a toll in goodwill and morale. Women teachers, though hardly radical, had become increasingly political. They joined in the move to unionize the high school ranks, took a greater interest in taxation, and added tenure to their goals.[53]

During the early twenties, restoration of the differential to $300 had been considered a major victory for the grade teachers. The *Seattle Grade Club Magazine* contained articles decrying the public perception that grade teachers had a less important role than their high school counterparts. Indeed, attempting to win popular support, the grade club called attention to "the value of the teachers of the first four grades." At a joint meeting with representatives from the Seattle Principals' Association, the grade teachers agreed to "unite for a just [salary] schedule and . . . participate in a publicity campaign to get the facts before the public."[54]

In 1926, saying that "elementary teachers provide the foundation for all higher education," the grade club defined the goal as "equal salaries to all classroom teachers having equal training and experience, regardless of" the level they teach. Significant numbers of its members began to pursue secondary credentials, and high school colleagues wanted the club to join in "investigat[ing] further the Single Salary schedule."[55]

By then, high school teachers were ready to move further. Seattle's teacher union movement came from within the high school teaching corps. In the spring of 1927, the High School Teachers' League reported that members with dependents could not live on the maximum salary of $2,400, adding, "The typical high school teacher is not a young woman, living at home and partly supported by her parents as seems to be the popular notion. . . . Citizens, when acquainted with the facts, will rally to our support." Local 200 of the American Federation of Teachers came into being the following November. Spearheaded by men faculty at Queen Anne and Roosevelt high schools, the union gained the support of many women teachers, including the Ballard botany teacher Leah Griffin, who signed the Local 200 charter. Franklin's Lilah Hunter served as the union's vice-president, and West Seattle's Belle McKenzie, its corresponding secretary; both taught English. One founder recalled that Local 200 "was formed mostly out of frustration and the realization that we needed the support of the laboring people."[56] Not since the 1918 protest over the bonus for male teaches had an internal school district issue become so public.

The day before creation of Local 200, all teacher groups had petitioned the school board for salary increases. They returned on November 27, with President Mamie B. Stoecker and the redoubtable Nina O. Buchanan representing the Grade Club, but the board stalled, declining to "deal with any class or petition separately."[57] In the coming months, the campaign for better salaries continued; the Central Labor Council president, David Levine, welcomed the teachers union; the school board president, E. B. Holmes, allowed that forming a union was "merely a matter of personal liberties—just as long as service to the schools and the contract are not tampered with"; and the attorney John Shorett filed for a school board seat with the backing of labor and teachers.[58]

On February 17, 1928, in something of a surprise, the school board adopted a single salary schedule. The maximum for all teachers would be $2,700; the differential between grade and high school would exist only at the minimum level—$1,600 as opposed to $1,300.[59] The surprise lay in the board's timing, since salary announcements had historically come with budget hearings in April. One scholar calls the early concession part of the board's "campaign to reelect the incumbent board member" at the March election; Shorett failed to defeat the incumbent Caspar Sharples by fewer than 2,000 votes.[60]

Arguably, the grade teachers' constant and comparatively nonthreatening petitions for a single salary scale gave the board a way to blunt the union's efforts. In fact, by late spring, again invoking efficiency in the schools, the board adopted the resolution of its president: "That no person be employed hereafter or continued in the employ of the district as a teacher, while a member of the American Federation of Teachers, or any local thereof, and that before any [hiring] shall be considered binding, such teacher shall sign a declaration" to that effect. Contracts would now include the statement, "I hereby declare that I am not a member of the American Federation of Teachers or any local thereof and will not become a member during the term of this contract." The school board thus effectively destroyed Local 200; the yellow-dog contract was in force until January 1931.[61]

In its first dozen years, the Grade Teachers' Club had gained enormous credibility and strength as an advocacy group. In 1920, membership stood at 927, and the membership committee boasted of 100 percent membership in fifty-six of the city's sixty-eight grade buildings.[62] It had enjoyed outstanding leadership from the capable, talented, professional women who served it as president. Committee chairs had steered the club's agenda skillfully and persistently toward its goals. The club became a tangible part of grade teachers' lives when it acquired physical headquarters, and the *Seattle Grade Club Magazine*'s appearance on the scene in 1920 insured reliable communication among all the members.

Agnes Winn, fifth-grade teacher at Coe School since before the war, assumed the presidency in 1919. Both the magazine and club headquarters materialized during her tenure, and she led the fight to keep the salary differential at $300. She recalled that advertising made the magazine "a financial success from the beginning," but it took a sharp increase of dues—from one to four dollars a year—to establish the club's office, pay a part-time executive secretary, and support "other constructive projects." Agnes Winn's leadership ability and accomplishments caught the attention of the National Education Association, and she moved from Seattle to Washington, D.C., in 1921 to join the headquarters staff of the NEA.[63]

From the outset, Miss Winn thought the magazine held promise as a means not only to communicate with members but also to "get and keep in touch with our patrons and citizens." Its second editor, Amy Estep, agreed. Looking back in 1928 she spoke of the grade teachers' contacts with the "outside world through the magazine":

As an organization our interests became linked with other civic and social organizations of the city such as the Chamber of Commerce, the Business Women's Club, and the other women's clubs of the city. . . . [Thus the magazine] served to link our professional life with other civic interests.

The *Grade Club Magazine* became one of the two more prestigious publications of grade teachers nationally.[64]

The Grade Teachers' Club had convened its early meetings in school auditoriums and the YWCA and later in the chamber of commerce auditorium. Executive business had operated from the president's home; committees had no central meeting place. In April 1920, Agnes Winn announced temporary headquarters in the Colman Building downtown, made possible by the generosity of the businessman D. B. Trefethen. The following fall the club moved to the Central Building for a short stay, and then to larger quarters in the Wintonia Hotel on First Hill that allowed for expanded program opportunities, including classes for members. Classes in parliamentary procedure and community problems proved most popular in the first year, but by December 1921 some teachers were asking "would not a dancing class [add] to our pleasure!" The club rooms did bring members together socially, "partly through the Thursday evening informals, in which every building in the city [took] part and a turn in entertaining." The new location expedited publication of the magazine and made committee meetings easier; as one committee chair put it, members "no longer [had] to chase each other up and down the corridors of the Central Building looking for a place to hold a meeting."[65]

While Agnes Winn went on to national prominence with the NEA and Nina O. Buchanan later won elective office, Nellie B. Sterret, the grade club's first president, gained citywide renown as a parliamentarian. She acted as parliamentarian for schools and teacher associations; other organizations in Seattle frequently sought her advice on parliamentary questions as well.[66] Described as "a precise little person," Miss Sterret had left Iowa for Seattle in 1906 at the age of thirty. She joined her childhood friend, Louise Rathbun, who had begun teaching at B. F. Day School a year or so earlier. Miss Sterret had taught eight years in her native state after graduating from the normal school in Cedar Falls. She taught eighth-grade mathematics first at Mercer School and then at Lowell; she completed her bachelor's degree at the University of Washington in 1925. When John Marshall Junior High opened two years later, she was named to its first faculty. She continued to teach math and algebra to Marshall teenagers until she retired in 1946 at the age of seventy.[67]

Nellie Sterret and Louise Rathbun, who shared an apartment on First Hill throughout their careers, numbered among those few teachers who owned an automobile in the 1920s. A friend recalled that their two-door sedan, "was her pride and joy." The two teachers, along with scores of their colleagues, attended Plymouth Congregational Church. During summer vacations they participated in professional meetings and spent time at their "nice little summer cottage . . . down the beach a few miles" from Rosario Resort on Orcas Island.[68]

Another Grade Teachers' Club president was Myra Snow (1921–22), who, after the resignation of Frank Cooper, presided over "a year of intense application to the cause of the . . . profession from the standpoint of the teachers' interests." Those interests included aggressive pursuit of the single salary schedule and increasing the club's loan fund.[69]

Myra Snow began teaching sixth grade at McDonald School during the First World War. She had graduated magna cum laude from the University of Washington and counted Phi Beta Kappa among her honors. Long an active, "faithful worker in the University Methodist Church," in 1928 she accepted a position in a girls mission school in Tianjin, China. Her harrowing account of traveling "Third Class through Bandit Land" appeared in the *Seattle Grade Club Magazine* in 1931. She wrote that a bandit waylaid her party's car and at gunpoint demanded,

"Give us your money." . . . I handed over my coin purse full of silver dollars. . . . he kept the gun cocked . . . and a nervous watch on the road in both directions. He got our watches and some more money, then began taking off my rings, my big moss agate and the ring mother always wore. . . . Then the thing happened that saved us from losing all. A bus returning to Tainan came in sight around a bend in the road.

The group finished the journey by train, thankful to be alive, but she stoutly declared, "I do not regret having had the experience." Miss Snow returned to Seattle in 1932 to teach another two years at McDonald before leaving again for the Tianjin school. Sources do not show her activities or whereabouts after the Japanese military incursion into China and World War II.[70]

The first club president to serve a full term without Frank Cooper in the superintendent's office was Dora Smith Herren, whom he had hired in 1907. She had applied in Seattle while teaching first through fifth grades and serving as principal in Kent, Washington; her marital status was "Widow (reside with parents)." Having taught four years in Oregon's Marion County schools, she confidently wrote, "Am competent and willing to take any grade, to show my ability."[71]

Dora Smith was born in Cloud County, Kansas, in 1882. Her pioneering parents moved to Salem, Oregon, where she graduated from high school. She completed the freshman year at Willamette University and earned a certificate at Capital Normal College. While teaching, and during her two years of marriage, she studied another two years at Willamette; she completed her bachelor's degree at the University of Washington in 1928, acquiring a Phi Beta Kappa key along the way.[72]

Mrs. Herren spent sixteen years teaching the upper grades at Green Lake School, and in 1922, the grade club elected her its eighth president. Salary increases that signified progress "toward restoration of the former salary schedule" were among her accomplishments in office. She also oversaw club contributions to "a home for girls . . . released through the juvenile court" and the establishment of both a grade teachers choral group and a dramatic club.[73] When Laurelhurst School opened in portable buildings in 1924, Dora Herren moved in as head teacher; two years later she transferred to the Montlake principal's office where she remained until 1942. She finished her career as principal of Madrona School. After she retired in 1951 at the age of seventy-one, she was chosen to head the Seattle Retired Teachers Association in 1953 and 1954.[74]

Mabel V. Wilson was the grade club's ninth president in 1925, after teachers' salary levels had been restored from the 1922 cuts. During her term (1924–25) the club turned to such matters as instituting tenure, granting sabbatical leaves for grade teachers, and empowering state normal schools to grant the bachelor of arts degree.[75] The club's Cooperative Council Committee, a noteworthy addition during her tenure, helped heal the breach between classroom teachers and administrators that followed the departure of Frank Cooper. The seventeen-member committee—the club president and two representatives from each grade level—met regularly with Superintendent Cole to discuss "problems of [mutual] interest."[76]

Born in Iowa in 1886, Mabel Wilson had earned a normal diploma at that state's Simpson College. After four years teaching sixth grade in Creston, Iowa, she taught three years in Salem, Oregon. She began in Seattle in 1913 at Brighton School, and then moved to the top of Queen Anne Hill to teach ten years in John Hay's eighth-grade classroom. Following her term as grade club president, she spent one year at the new Summit demonstration school before succeeding Dora Herren as head teacher at Laurelhurst, where she became principal on completion of the two-story brick building in 1927.[77]

Laurelhurst's parents and pupils alike held Miss Wilson in high regard. She wrote teacher evaluations that reflected her concern for the community, frequently noting favorable parental reactions. She remarked upon one third-grade teacher's "keen sense of justice in dealing with individual pupils" and praised her for being "fearless but tactful in handling 'problem parents.'" Although former students recalled that she was a strong presence in the school, an episode from her year as head teacher suggests authority tempered by human kindness: called to a meeting at district headquarters downtown, she boarded a bus and left her class on its own. On the return trip she stopped at a chocolate shop and brought "a treat back to the kids 'because she knew how nice they had been.'"[78]

Her colleagues, too, esteemed Mabel Wilson. Teachers applauded her leadership; she welcomed discussion and did not "in the least object to having teachers disagree" with her. Election to the grade club presidency confirmed confidence in her judgment and ability. Further confirmation came in October 1929, when the 12,000–member Washington Education Association elected her president at a two-day Seattle meeting that occasioned a school closure, a rarity. Perhaps even rarer, the school board granted Miss Wilson a paid leave of absence to preside that day and on days of regional meetings that followed. She left Laurelhurst in 1936, finished her career as principal at E. C. Hughes, and retired in 1947 at the comparatively young age of sixty-one.[79]

Her successor as club president, Mamie B. Stoecker, saw efforts to achieve a single salary schedule come to fruition in 1928. Under her leadership, the club helped to secure and make local arrangements for the 1927 NEA convention; she credited "the splendid work of the individual members . . . [and] the committees" for such accomplishments.[80]

Twenty-six-year-old Mamie Stoecker came to Seattle from Terre Haute, Indiana, in 1908. With a three-year normal certificate from Indiana State

Normal School, she had taught second through eighth grades in Terre Haute. Her Seattle career began at Columbia School in newly annexed Columbia City in southeast Seattle. She held seven other assignments throughout the city. While club president, she taught eighth grade at Central School, and after her term she transferred to Fauntleroy in West Seattle as head teacher. In 1932 she was named principal of McGilvra School in Madison Park, where she served until 1941, and she retired in 1947 as principal of Green Lake.[81]

When Mamie Stoecker passed the gavel to Margaret J. Thomas in the spring of 1928, she did so with the hope that the club would "continue to progress honorably, sanely, altruistically, harmoniously, professionally . . . [toward] a better school for a better teacher." For her part, Miss Thomas promised a year of "professional growth, mutual understanding, and pleasure derived from association with coworkers engaged in child welfare."[82] Having won their long fight for a single salary scale, the grade teachers, under Margaret Thomas, worked toward gaining an accident, health, and casualty group insurance plan, which finally went into effect in May 1930. Miss Thomas still taught one of the four classes at Pacific School for newcomers who spoke no English. She moved to Bailey Gatzert in 1940, where she would experience the wrenching evacuation of Japanese pupils to internment camps.[83]

Freda Libbee followed as president and continued to emphasize the welfare of children, high professional standards, and club members' "intellectual and social welfare." She did not hesitate to chide teachers who did not join the club yet "willingly accept[ed] any benefit . . . such as salary increase, sabbatical and sick leave . . . [and] enjoy[ed] the protection and prestige of their group." Accordingly, she worked to build membership in the depths of the Depression, writing in 1931, "If teacher organizations have been important in the past, they are increasingly essential under present conditions."[84] She left office in 1933, just as the first Depression-mandated salary cuts hit Seattle teachers:

I have given my best in attempting to hold as much as possible of the advantages gained so far and to advance, perhaps ever so little, in the face of many problems which at times have seemed overwhelming. How I wish I could report no mistakes, no retrogression, but steady progress.

Freda Libbee had taught at Horace Mann since before World War I. She transferred to Washington School in 1938, on the eve of the second war, where, like Margaret Thomas, she found herself painfully affected by the 1942 internment of many of her pupils.[85]

Throughout the difficult years of the Depression, teacher organizations merged and changed as the economic situation deteriorated, but the Grade Teachers' Club, holding to its basic mission, remained apart. In the spring of 1934, the High School Teachers' League became simply the Seattle Teachers' League, opening its membership to all teachers, but few grade teachers joined. Two years later, the Seattle Association of Classroom Teachers emerged as an amalgamation of earlier groups. Some friction stemming from the 1928 single salary arrangement lingered, and not until 1958 did the grade club merge with that group to form today's Seattle Education Association.[86]

President Mabel Wilson had restated the mission of the Grade Teachers' Club in 1924. Beginning with the assertion that "the American child is the most priceless possession of the American people," she said that the club was established "for the unselfish purpose of promoting the professional, the social and the material welfare of the American teacher, in order that she might be more efficient and happy in the service of the American child."[87] Under the leadership of women who devoted untold hours of unpaid service, the club's genteel militants promoted, with grace and tenacity, all three phases of teacher welfare throughout the interwar years.

8 / Beyond the Classroom

She will, of course, follow the dictates of good taste.

—J. FRANK MARSH, *The Teacher Outside the School* (1928)

As they molded its children in the interwar years, women teachers left their mark on Seattle. They filled church congregations, worked in volunteer groups devoted to the arts and social welfare, and fostered the growth of recreational and social organizations that endured beyond the end of the century. One of the few fringe benefits they enjoyed was the opportunity for travel afforded by long summer vacations. Many of them traveled extensively and, never forgetting students, returned to enrich their classrooms with artifacts, souvenirs, and intangibles from their adventures.

Teachers performed the mundane chores of housekeeping, their weekends absorbed by laundry, cleaning, and sundry other chores for which the school week left no time. For many, the accustomed role of single woman included ongoing responsibility for parents and siblings. Family obligations often dictated a return to homes in the Midwest for every holiday and summer vacation. They spent leisure time much as the rest of the population—enjoying movies, plays, concerts, indoor and outdoor sports, dancing and card playing. Although it mandated decorum and good judgment, the role of teacher did not totally impede social life. As evidenced by the number who resigned to be married, they enjoyed freedom of action and association. Just as in other spheres, socializing tended to occur primarily among colleagues and coworkers, but they formed lasting friendships beyond the school district as they participated in the city's rich variety of clubs and organizations.

The annual Inter-Club dinner brought women together from those groups, "united for an evening of exchanging good will across the banquet tables." Teachers had helped found many of those groups. Freda Libbee, the Grade Teachers' Club president, presided at the 1934 dinner at the Arctic Club. The program that night had an international flavor; honorees "were outstanding women from foreign countries," and the main speaker addressed "Woman's Place in the Affairs of Nations: Both Yesterday and Today."[1]

By 1913, Seattle had enjoyed rapid growth and a building boom that extended to school construction and annexation. The Alaska Yukon Pacific Exposition had made the city a destination for tourists and businesspeople alike. But, as one writer later observed,

> There were few attractive places in downtown Seattle for women to lunch and dine. . . . When eastern dignitaries came to town there was no appropriate place to entertain them, and the college and university women began to feel that they must have a downtown meeting place all their own.

With the dream of a downtown clubhouse first and foremost, on February 10, 1914, fourteen women applied to incorporate the Women's University Club of Seattle. Among them were three Seattle teachers—Adelaide Pollock, Stanford graduate and principal of West Queen Anne Elementary; Mabel Chilberg, Vassar alumna and mathematics teacher at Broadway High School; and H. Jeannette Perry, a graduate of Smith College, who taught English at Franklin High School. The latter two taught throughout the interwar years.[2]

With 276 charter members, the Women's University Club held its first meeting on May 6, 1914. That September, members enjoyed their first luncheon in a small facility built for them at 1205 Fifth Avenue. The founders had sought to "enlarge cultural and sociable activities for themselves and their contemporaries," and in its first years the club established its practice of drawing on the talents of members as it grew into a literary and artistic center. Lectures, book reviews, and musical programs became standard offerings—in addition to the social events typical of most private clubs. At least thirty-two of Seattle's interwar teachers numbered among the charter members, the majority from the high school ranks because membership required a college degree. Over time, as teaching certification changed, grade teachers met the requirement, and they too joined.[3]

Among charter members were Elizabeth Clarahan, graduate of the University of Missouri and principal of Lowell School since 1907; Lou McKean, with a degree from Columbia, a seventh-grade teacher at Lowell; Lulie Nettleton, graduate of Minnesota's Winona State Normal School, teaching fifth grade at Coe Elementary; Juliet O'Hearn, with degrees from Minnesota and Chicago, teaching English at Queen Anne High School; Elizabeth Rowell, longtime head of the history department at Broadway High School, with a master's degree from Columbia; Helen Vaupell, a University of Washington graduate teaching geometry at Lincoln High School; Rose Glass, another Washington graduate, teaching history at Lincoln; and Blanche Wenner, Wellesley class of 1905, and Broadway's drama coach.[4]

Plans to build what would be the Olympic Hotel on the site of their clubhouse forced members to relocate, and Mabel Chilberg contributed to the project by preparing the construction budget for the new facility. Another member of the planning committee recalled the initial fundraising dinner, which apparently sprang to life with Miss Chilberg's presentation: "When she got through, everyone was waking up. . . . Mrs. De Steiguer wrote on a card, 'I will pledge one thousand dollars.' From that moment I knew we would have a club house." The women bought the northeast corner lot at Sixth Avenue and Spring Street for $30,000; the nearly 600 members opened their multipurpose building, complete with meeting, dining, and living rooms, in November 1922. Over the years, the stately building has hosted innumerable dignitaries, including Lou Henry Hoover and Eleanor Roosevelt.[5]

Mabel Chilberg had left the school district in June 1917 to serve with the Red Cross in France during the war, and after she came back to Seattle she had pursued business interests, during which time she did the budget work for the Women's University Club. In fall semester 1922, she returned to teaching at newly opened Roosevelt High School; two years later she was named girls adviser at West Seattle, a position she held until retiring in 1948.[6]

The daughter of early settlers, Mabel Chilberg was born in Seattle in

1882. She graduated from Seattle High School, spent a short time at the University of Washington, and then taught two years at West Queen Anne Elementary. In 1903, she went east to attend Vassar College, returning in the fall of 1906 with her degree and a Phi Beta Kappa key. Among the first to join the Mountaineers, she was an active member who climbed a number of Washington's peaks. Along with many colleagues, she belonged to Plymouth Congregational Church. In the tradition of teacher travel, she had taken leave from the district between June 1911 and September 1913 to tour Europe. Miss Chilberg, one of the more memorable girls advisers who belonged to the Women's University Club over the years, died in January 1973 at the age of ninety-one.[7]

The school board had created the position of girls adviser in 1913, primarily to oversee the activities of a girls club that existed at Broadway High School; it was soon replicated in other buildings, and by 1915 each high school had a teacher designated girls adviser. Although she taught at least one class, her primary function was to advise and direct the girls club. It is virtually impossible to overstate the advisers' importance during the interwar years. All girls belonged to a school's girls club, but with varying degrees of involvement, and the clubs soon became training grounds for student leaders. Their various committees sponsored teas and other entertainments, student orientation, and service projects such as charity fundraising, food drives, and volunteering at the Seattle Children's Home and Children's Orthopedic Hospital.

The Girls Club Creed, adopted citywide in 1923, clearly states the aims, objectives, and philosophy of the clubs and their advisers:

> I believe, as a High School girl
> of Seattle, I should be
> Joyous, courageous, and courteous.
> Truthful, considerate, and just.
> Loyal and sincere in friendship.
> Too noble to speak ill of others.
> Willing to forgive and forget.
> Prompt and gracious in obedience.
> Ready to do all possible service.
> Quick to appreciate what is done for me.

Respectful of my elders.
True to the best that is within me that
I may become a fine and worthy woman.[8]

Advisers worked with a considerable degree of autonomy and stamped their schools with individual trademarks. No high school reflected the cachet and independent style of its girls adviser more than Roosevelt did during the interwar decades. Rose Glass, another charter member of the Women's University Club, brought her own idiosyncratic approach to the job from the day Roosevelt opened in 1922.

Born October 10, 1880, Rose Glass graduated from Shimer Academy, a secondary school connected with the University of Chicago. She came to Washington and taught a year in Thurston County schools before moving to teach history at yet-to-be-annexed Ballard High School. Along the way she earned a diploma from the normal school in Bellingham and a B.A. from the University of Washington. Her 1905 application to teach in Seattle listed as references three University of Washington immortals— Frederick Padelford, Edmond Meany, and J. Allen Smith. She taught history at Lincoln High School until 1912, taking leave in 1910 for graduate work at Columbia. She returned to teach nine years at Franklin before being named Roosevelt's first girls adviser. She left the adviser role in 1940 and returned to teach history at Franklin until retiring in 1947.[9]

In 1918, she had volunteered for war service in France with the YMCA, saying, "I've got red hair, I know how to rough it, and I hope they send me just as near the front lines as they can!" But the woman who had "ridden horseback for 125 miles at a stretch. . . . gone swimming in icy mountain streams . . . [who could] paddle an Indian canoe as well as she [could] dance, and shoot as well as . . . play tennis" spent her time overseas in Brest, working in the Y's entertainment section.[10]

The somewhat flamboyant redhead turned her hair and her name into trademarks at Roosevelt. Every girls club had a myriad of committees, but only Roosevelt's had the Aurora Guards, composed entirely of red-haired students. Just shy of an elite, this group ushered visitors and guided new students in the ways of school routine and club activities. Another enduring Roosevelt custom bearing Miss Glass's imprint was the annual selection of the Rose Maidens, one young woman from each class named for outstanding scholarship and participation in activities. Every school had a girls club office, but Roosevelt had the Rose Garden. Each spring the Rose Maidens helped install the new club officers and pass the torch in the "mystic rites of the Rose Garden." Any number of Roosevelt graduates would later agree that "*It was a big deal* and [Miss Glass] choreographed the whole thing."[11]

Every high school enjoyed visits of dignitaries, but only Roosevelt hosted royalty. Rose Glass and Queen Marie of Romania had met during the war and become friends; the gregarious American invited the queen to visit her in Seattle. On her grand tour of the United States in 1926, Queen Marie did just that. One student remembered her visit as "Rose Glass's big day," when the entire student body welcomed her friend the queen on the school's front steps.[12]

She and her sister, Florence, had always lived together and after 1947 they moved to Wesley Gardens, a retirement center south of Seattle. There, Miss Glass served as social director, and, not surprisingly, the one-time national president of the Women's Overseas Service League traveled, too. She celebrated her eighty-first birthday during a four-month trip around the world in 1963; former students hosted her on three continents.[13]

Women teachers had affiliated early with the Seattle Federation of Women's Clubs and the Women's Legislative Council. After founding Seattle's Soroptimist Club in 1925, the membership in that service organization strengthened its ties to women in business, the social and artistic realm, and the other professions. Only women with ownership or management status could belong; hence, school women Soroptimists came from the supervisory ranks. Charter members included Ellen Powell Dabney, director of home economics; Nellie Goodhue, longtime director of the Child Study Laboratory; Clara Reynolds, director of art; and Helen Reynolds, head of the Department of Primary Method, who served as president in 1938. Dora Lewis, a later head of home economics, joined the Soroptimists in 1939; she went on to national prominence, elected president of the Soroptimist Federation of the Americas in 1960.[14]

Many applications to the Seattle School District included ministers as references, testifying to the importance of church affiliation to young women teachers. Seattle has borne the label of the nation's least churched city, but women teachers of the interwar cohort could be found on the rolls of most of its mainline Protestant churches. First Presbyterian hosted organizing meetings of the Grade Teachers' Club; early in the century, the fledgling University Congregational attracted teachers; and Plymouth Congregational stands as another prime example.

A pillar of Seattle, Plymouth had rebuilt downtown soon after the Great Fire and in a true sense became the city's social and cultural center. From its inception in 1870, the church had reached out to teachers. In 1882, one influential member of the congregation and his wife established the "custom of inviting all the new teachers of the city schools to spend a September Saturday at their Bainbridge Island summer home . . . [and] many young women of that time found a church home through this gracious act of hospitality."[15]

A succession of eloquent and intellectual senior ministers continued to draw teachers to Plymouth. In 1921, the church enhanced its outreach when it created the Plymouth Girls' Club. It offered social and recreational opportunities for working women, and in an era when the Grade Teachers' Club called its members "girls," teachers joined in great number. The church club provided a social and recreational base for countless teachers for fourteen of the interwar years. By the midthirties, other nonprofit groups offered similar programs that siphoned off attendance and led to its demise, but before it voted itself out of existence in 1935, it had reached a membership in excess of 800.[16]

The Plymouth Girls' Club met every Monday evening for dinner, a vesper service, and a slate of classes. Among its popular year-round activities were dramatic presentations, glee club programs, annual Memorial Day excursions to Victoria, British Columbia, skiing expeditions to Mount Rainier, and a summer camp on the Kitsap Peninsula that members could attend in 1923 for ten dollars a week. Club dues remained minimal, and the cost of dinner never exceeded thirty-five cents. Monday night classes covered a wide range—from swimming and basketball through foreign language and history to millinery and needlework—and both students and volunteer instructors came from the ranks of teachers. Adelaide Pollock had set an example in 1923, offering a class in bird study that she still taught in 1929; Nellie Sterret perennially taught Parliamentary Law; Belle Gleason, Roosevelt's French teacher, introduced that language; and Eva Jurgensohn presented a class in rhythmic movement.[17]

Some teachers, such as Elizabeth Neterer and Helen Vaupell, both Seattle natives, had come into Plymouth Church with their families, but Plymouth Girls' Club drew newcomers and cemented their church allegiance. Many still worshiped at Plymouth more than half a century later. The church in turn benefited enormously from them. Many taught in its Sunday School program, and the church saluted them, as in 1926 when it urged the congregation to "Consider for instance our Kindergarten Department. Miss Elizabeth Neterer, the head of the department is . . . one of the well-known Kindergarten teachers in our city schools. Assisting her are Miss Bessie Dick . . . and Janet Dewhurst." The latter two had just returned from a year of graduate work at Teachers College, Columbia. Bessie Dick taught kindergarten at Lowell School through the interwar years; she had been a Plymouth member since at least 1913. Janet Dewhurst had joined the Plymouth Girls' Club in 1923, early in her teaching career.[18]

Delia Bergstrom, another teacher who maintained decades-long membership at Plymouth Congregational, came to Seattle in 1926 as a primary teacher. Born in Ogden, Utah, in 1895, she moved with her family to Grays Harbor County, Washington, where she graduated from Montesano High School in 1913. She taught two years before earning a certificate from Ellensburg Normal School. After five more years in Grays Harbor and three teaching first grade in Spokane, she joined the Seattle corps, teaching throughout the district, from blue-collar Emerson in the far south end to the affluent Briarcliff and Magnolia schools in the northwest. She retired in 1960. In 1974, the church honored her as an exemplar of stewardship and volunteerism with its Annual Plymouth Award; she had long been a volunteer financial secretary and in her eighty-fifth year still served as the church's wedding hostess. One of the most durable of the interwar cohort, Delia Bergstrom died in the spring of 1999 at the age of 104.[19]

Nonsectarian opportunities for socializing also abounded in the city. In addition to fostering professional growth and opportunity, the Grade Teachers' Club looked to the leisure time of its members. Teachers from various schools rotated in hosting Thursday evening informals at the club headquarters. Open to all, the evenings included musical programs, mixers, and get-acquainted activities, dancing, and card playing.[20] School principals often entertained their teaching staffs. Dora Herren, to note but one, hosted her entire Montlake School faculty at dinner in her home, and her counterpart at Bailey Gatzert, Ada Mahon, frequently invited teachers to spend a weekend at her vacation home on the ocean at Westport.[21]

Beginning in the early thirties, once the single salary goal had been reached, the *Seattle Grade Club Magazine* turned increasingly to reporting social and recreational activities. Throughout that decade, the magazine carried accounts of parties, dinners, luncheons, and brunches; the issue of May 1933 was typical. It reported that Marion Kelly, a teacher at Coe School, invited friends and colleagues to a "May breakfast," after which "the guests enjoyed an afternoon of bridge." Also noted were two "very successful card and dancing parties" held at the Seattle Yacht Club and the Meany Hotel.[22]

Engagement announcements provided incentive for much springtime socializing. Teachers at Coe celebrated the approaching marriage of the office clerk with a luncheon in April 1934. That same month, Agnes Skartvedt invited all her colleagues from Cascade School to her home for a dessert bridge, where, "concealed under the teacups were found tiny silver and blue wedding bells which announced the engagement of Miss [Lydia] Jones." That spring, Marie Nettleton entertained the Concord faculty at her "summer home at Woodinville," hosting a luncheon and kitchen shower for Frances Kernan, who had taught fourth grade since the midtwenties.[23]

As attitudes toward sports for women broadened and opportunities increased, many of the interwar cohort enjoyed active recreation during vacations and on weekends. Teachers themselves formed a recreation committee in 1930, the Magnolia School principal, Zella Allen, serving as its first general chairman. Dedicated to helping teachers "spend the 'after-school hours' and vacations in recreations which entirely make them forget school-room problems," the group sponsored events and competition in badminton, basketball, bowling, cycling, golf, hiking, skating, skiing, and tennis; the less athletic teachers chose organized social dancing, knitting, gardening, or photography.[24]

Throughout the thirties, skating parties met twice-monthly at what became the Seattle Center Arena; skiers trekked to the slopes at Mount Rainier and Snoqualmie Summit. Parties of cyclists rode on park trails throughout the city; on Memorial Day in 1934, the physical education teacher at Broadway High School, Vera Waller, led about twenty pedalers from Alki to the south end of West Seattle's Lincoln Park and back. The municipal course at Jefferson Park welcomed the annual golf tournament and most rounds that teachers played throughout the year. An ongoing ladder-type tournament occupied tennis players until their annual elimination tournament at the end of the school year. Badminton matches and basketball games took place in school gymnasiums. Ballard High School's home economics teacher, Alice Dodge, organized the 1935–36 bowling activity: thirteen schools competed weekly. In an era before the sport had acquired a wholesome, family-oriented image, the alleys at the private downtown Washington Athletic Club provided a suitable location for the bowlers.[25]

Puget Sound–area mountains and trails had attracted teachers since the turn of the century, but in 1933 the teachers' recreation group sadly admitted that there "was more enthusiasm than participation in the year's walking-for-sport program."[26] Perhaps that program was superfluous given the continuing popularity of the Mountaineers in the city. Organized in 1907 by the photographer Asahel Curtis and a few others, the Sierra Club–like group elected the University of Washington geology professor Henry Landes president. Within a month of its first meeting, "there was standing room only . . . , and 151 people enrolled as charter members," including "forty-two librarians and teachers." The founders hoped to help "in the battle to preserve our natural scenery from wanton destruction, and yet make our spots of supremest beauty accessible to the largest number of mountain lovers." Landes insured the scientific as well as conservationist agenda of the group, and Mountaineer women would contribute in both areas.[27]

Among the librarians and teachers on the list of charter members were Alice Casey, then home economics teacher at B. F. Day; Estelle Chopson, who taught fifth grade at Green Lake until 1932; Bella Fisken, then at Summit, who would retire from Montlake in 1935; and Belle Tellier of Daniel Bagley School, who still taught second grade at John Hay in 1941. Along with the redoubtable Adelaide Pollock, also signing on at the 1907 meeting were Annie C. Brayton, then at Denny School, who went on to help found the Grade Teachers' Club and retired from Fairview in 1931; and Margaret McCarney, girls adviser at Franklin through 1941, who in 1907 was teaching first grade at T. T. Minor.[28]

Other teachers joined within months. Lulie Nettleton, Gertrude Streator, and Winona Bailey became mainstays of the Mountaineers' annual two-to-three-week outings. Until she left to serve with the YMCA in France during World War I, Lulie Nettleton missed very few Mountaineer hikes or annual outings; she served on any number of the club's committees and edited its publications. She made her mark early in 1907 when she reached the top of Mount Si on a climb preparing members for later assaults that summer on peaks in the Olympic range. In 1912, she represented the Mountaineers on the Sierra Club's annual outing in California. Voted one of the best climbers in that party, she reached the summit of five peaks higher than 10,000 feet that summer, including 14,500-foot Mount Whitney. Fittingly, for her wartime service the YMCA assigned her to a rest area for soldiers near Chamonix, France, where she reported being "very happy in leading hikes and making mountaineers out of our boys in the Alps."[29]

Miss Nettleton had arrived in Seattle in 1901 from Fergus Falls, Minnesota. The graduate of Winona State Normal School brought a letter of recommendation praising her as "a hard, conscientious worker [who] through her sincerity gains at once the love of the children and the esteem of [their] parents." The "young lady of neat appearance and excellent character" began teaching fourth grade at B. F. Day. Named a principal in 1921, she did double duty at South Park and Concord until 1929 when she moved to Green Lake for a memorable decade. Already a veteran of thirty-eight years, she was reassigned as principal of J. B. Allen in 1939. Lulie Nettleton was a stalwart in the Grade Teachers' Club and founding member of several of the city's premier organizations. She retired in 1946 at the age of seventy, having, as predicted, "exercised lasting influence" in her community and schools.[30]

In the spring of 1901, Gertrude Streator, a Michigan native, completed a year as the kindergarten teacher at Davenport in eastern Washington, then came west to attend normal school at Bellingham; in March 1902 she applied for a job in Seattle. She also had to her credit two years of study at the Oberlin Kindergarten Training School and two years at

Menomonie, Wisconsin; she also had studied at both Baldwin University and Hiram College in Ohio. Frank Cooper hired her to teach first grade at Green Lake School, and he most likely applauded her taking a leave of absence soon to complete her B.A. at the University of Washington. A woman who took full advantage of the university's presence in Seattle, in 1912 she earned her Master of Arts degree. The B.A. had qualified her for high school teaching, and before retiring in 1945, she had taught English at Broadway, Lincoln, and Roosevelt.[31]

A member of the Mountaineers by 1911, Miss Streator went on many summer outings, wrote accounts of some of them for the *Mountaineer*, and served as the club historian. She also led local walks, another of the club's enduring program traditions; in 1916, for example, she took thirty-five people on a trek from Renton to Maple Valley. With several other teachers, she made the 162-mile hike from Mount Rainier to the Columbia River during the 1911 summer outing, climbing Mount Adams, the state's second highest peak, on the way. It took fifteen days to reach their camp on the north side of Mount Adams at 6,000 feet elevation. The day of the Adams climb, "the rising call sounded before daylight . . . nine hours and twenty minutes later they stood on the summit." Next day, Lulie Nettleton and two male Mountaineers made a second ascent. On reaching the Columbia, the party crossed into Oregon where Gertrude Streator and Mabel Furry, who had also summited Adams, joined Miss Nettleton in climbing Mount Hood.[32]

Mabel Furry, a graduate of Seattle High School with a bachelor's degree in biology and physical education from the University of Washington, had joined the Mountaineers soon after the founding. She began her Seattle teaching career in 1914 as physical education teacher at Queen Anne High School and held that position until she retired in 1959 at the age of sixty-nine. Renowned for her photography, she took part in at least thirty-six of the Mountaineers' summer outings between 1911 and 1952.[33]

One of her colleagues at Queen Anne who also made the Mount Adams climb in 1911 was Winona Bailey, who joined the Mountaineers after going on the first summer outing in 1907. Her family had left Maine for Colorado when she was a child; she graduated from high school in two-mile-high Leadville, where she stayed to teach second grade for two years. After earning a Phi Beta Kappa key and a B.A. in classics at Colorado College in 1896, she taught in Colorado Springs until 1902. With her M.A. from Columbia University in hand, she moved to Puget Sound, taught Latin and algebra in Everett, and applied to teach in Seattle in 1908. After a year at Lincoln High School, she moved to newly opened Queen Anne and spent the rest of her career as its Latin teacher. Although always a hardy individual, she retired in 1933 at the age of sixty because of illness.[34]

Given her Colorado background, it is no wonder that Winona Bailey was drawn to the Mountaineers. That she joined the group after its first summer outing proves her commitment to adventure and the outdoors. That 1907 Olympic expedition involved sailing to Port Angeles by steamer, hiking twenty-one miles into Geyser Valley, and, accompanied by a pack-train, trekking to the main camp at the Elwha basin. Clothing restrictions had been issued for women; those expecting "to go on side trips or climb any of the peaks, must be prepared to wear bloomers or better still knicker-bockers, as on all these trips no skirts will be allowed."[35]

Conquering Mount Olympus was the expedition's ultimate goal. The first attempt to reach the summit was made in brutal weather "only because there was no further time in which to do it." Halfway up the Humbert Glacier, rain changed to wind-driven snow; the party continued on, but soon "a thirty-mile gale was blowing . . . [and] distant cliffs of the main mountain were lost to view." Turning back, the group was half a mile from camp and attempting to go down a steep draw to a snowfield when,

> on the slippery, rain-soaked heather . . . Miss Winona Bailey, lost her foot-ing and in a moment slid and fell over the rocks a hundred feet, until she wedged under the snow at the base of the cliff. That the fall was not fatal seemed miraculous. Dr. Stevens . . . was called forward and was working over the girl within five minutes after she fell. A stretcher was hastily impro-vised . . . around two alpine stocks and as soon as the worst wounds were dressed she was started for camp.

In the shelter of a primitive canvas lean-to Dr. E. F. Stevens treated her wounds, one of which required eleven stitches. It was several days before she could be moved to the main camp, where under the care of Dr. Cora Smith Eaton, Miss Bailey remained for two weeks.[36]

Having failed in that early try for the summit of Washington's Olympus, in 1922 Winona Bailey made history as the first woman to climb Greece's Mount Olympus. She extended her summer vacation that year with a two-month leave of absence. Together with a fellow Latin teacher from Chicago, she sailed from New York and, in the vanguard of air travelers, flew from London to Paris. Of that flight, she wrote: "It is wonderful beyond words. We float on the clouds. The only thing mundane is the noise. We are looking at the cliffs of Dover and the French Coast at the same time." The adventure took the two teachers by way of Rome and Athens through country "infested with bandits" and "off the beaten tourist track." They made their climbing arrangements with difficulty but ultimately accomplished their objective and enjoyed "hospitality of the most delightful kind and . . . [on climbs] had with us nine men, a guide, an interpreter, and Greek soldiery[;] we were always given the finest consideration." By the first week of November, Miss Bailey had resumed drilling students in Latin verb conjugation at Queen Anne, having returned to her "own country with a keener sympathy for the foreigner who is trying to find a niche among us."[37]

Natural splendor routinely attracted teachers to Puget Sound; any number of the interwar cohort felt the lure of life on the water and in the mountains. Florence Keller, a recent graduate of Ypsilanti State Normal School, left Michigan for the Northwest in 1920 with a fellow teacher, Grace Buckbee. They started teaching in Spokane, but when Miss Keller first crossed the Cascades and saw Mount Rainier, she knew she had to move on to Seattle. By September 1922 she had joined Jessie Lockwood's faculty at John Muir. Before long, she and a Longfellow teacher, Lois Glenn, were "up at the Mountain," enjoying "snowshoeing, skiing and tobogganing from the roof of the Inn." The snows were very heavy during their stay at Paradise, and in order to resume their duties in Seattle the amateurs were obliged to snowshoe three miles down the mountain. Florence Keller married John T. Brooke in 1925; widowed in 1942, she returned to teach for two more decades. Lois Glenn continued teaching in Seattle until 1937.[38]

Once in the Northwest, many teachers did not feel the urge to leave even for vacations. Georgetown School's Julia Reible, for one, lived on Capitol Hill with her sister, Amelia, who taught at Rainier School; proclaiming Seattle her home, she said she liked "to remain here the year around." Anna Simmons, a sixth-grade math teacher who went on to junior high teaching, had come to Seattle before the First World War and rarely left "even during the summer."[39]

Indeed, the *Grade Club Magazine* in 1920 offered suggestions for summer activities in the area. Puget Sound had "pastimes and resorts to suit all tastes, and pocketbooks," wrote Lulie Nettleton. She listed the YMCA camp at Yeomalt on Bainbridge Island and "fine camping sites and several delightful boarding places" on Hood Canal; the area around Index was "accessible and the woods [were] lovely," for those to whom "the forest calls." Farther afield was Lake Chelan, where one could reach the head of the lake by boat and "take a splendid trip up to Horseshoe Basin into the real wilderness." Throughout the interwar years, Seattle teachers vacationed, and many eventually owned property, in all those places and others in the state as well.[40]

The Kitsap Peninsula attracted many of the interwar cohort. Nora Plumb had begun teaching primary grades in Seattle before 1907; she moved to McDonald School in 1915, where she still taught first grade in 1941. At some point she bought property on Miller Bay, north of Suquamish; she offered her "5-room modern cottage" with boat, private dock, and beautiful view for rent in the summer of 1934.[41] Alta Wayne, Ethel Bell, and Winifred Ingraham, colleagues at Colman School since before the war, owned a vacation home at Gilberton in the twenties. Miss Wayne retired in 1935; her co-owners still taught in 1941.[42] Elizabeth Anderson, who in 1923 had already taught at Green Lake for at least sixteen years, spent vacations at her summer home at Southworth. Bertha French, longtime second-grade teacher at Cascade School, owned a residence at Indianola that was destroyed during a windstorm in 1923.[43]

Islands proved to the liking of others. Like fellow teachers Nellie Sterret and Louise Rathbun, Josephine Stuart owned property on Orcas Island. The first-grade teacher at Fairview School from 1917 until she retired in 1947, Miss Stuart had begun teaching in Missouri in 1901; she moved to Spokane in 1906. Perhaps summers spent at the normal school in Bellingham awakened a love of the water in the native Kansan. Mary Fullington, a younger colleague at Fairview, had a summer home at Coupeville on Whidbey Island. Having started in Seattle in 1927 as art teacher at the new Cleveland Intermediate School in the south end, she transferred the next year to Fairview just inside the northern city limits; there her consistently outstanding art program led to her elevation to art supervisor for the school district.[44]

As Lulie Nettleton rightly surmised, the forest called many of the interwar cohort. In the midtwenties, woodsy retreats became both attractive and affordable with the advent of the Stillaguamish Fishing and Country Club. Situated on 150 acres near the foot of Whitehorse Mountain on the Stillaguamish River west of Darrington, the club offered rustic living without total isolation. It eventually dropped *fishing* from its name, and by the end of the century many members lived there year-round. But in 1924, when individual lots were laid out and the first cabin built, club members looked forward to weekends and summers without amenities. Electricity reached them in 1928 but remained limited until 1934; telephone service became available in 1931.[45]

Many single women, including teachers from Seattle, bought lots early on. Edna Campbell, who taught at Queen Anne High School, was a charter member and a popular force in the club until 1955. Before her marriage-mandated resignation in 1927, the "born organizer and . . . natural leader" had inspired a colleague, the Spanish teacher and girls adviser Eleanor Iorns, to buy a site. Mrs. Iorns continued as an active member until she retired and moved to California in 1952. Lila Lawrence, Broadway's girls adviser, and Interlake's fifth-grade teacher, June Oakley, numbered among those who acquired property on the Stillaguamish before World War II. Gladys Wilson, who taught English at Ballard High School, bought her view lot in 1936 and moved there when she retired in 1964.[46]

There were more members of the Stillaguamish Country Club from John Muir, with its strong emphasis on nature and conservation, than from any other Seattle school. The father of Muir's sixth-grade teacher, Nina Bonnell, built the first cottage there for a member in 1924 and by the midthirties had built cabins for a number of her Muir colleagues. In 1928, Miss Bonnell herself took the last lot in a newly opened section, a lot on which everyone else had seen "the fallen logs and undergrowth and decided it was too much clearing to bother with." She and her father tackled the tangled patch of forest, and "after many long hours of labor had a building site cleared." The house he created for her stood throughout the century, much as he had built it. A mainstay of the Stillaguamish Country Club, Nina Bonnell served on the board of trustees until 1960.[47]

Helen Haddow came to Seattle from the Midwest in 1918 to teach sixth grade; in 1925 she transferred from Emerson School to John Muir. Two years later she joined the Stillaguamish club, together with her friend and colleague from both Emerson and Muir, Winifred Chaffee. They spent many weekends and summers in her Bonnell-built cabin. Both took an active role on club committees and in its social life. Breast cancer claimed Helen Haddow on March 1, 1957. Winifred Chaffee, a graduate of the normal school in DeKalb, Illinois, had also begun in Seattle in 1918, after teaching two years in Sioux City, Iowa. She retired to the Stillaguamish property in 1959 and died there December 17, 1977.[48]

Mabel Magaard started her Seattle career in 1926. She transferred from Jefferson in West Seattle to Muir the following year and joined its Stillaguamish contingent in 1932, hiring Mr. Bonnell to construct a cabin that she subsequently owned until 1963. Grace Buckbee and Florence Keller had come to Seattle in 1922, Miss Keller to teach at Muir and Miss Buckbee at Jefferson, where she remained throughout the interwar years. She joined the country club in the spring of 1932 and owned her property until she moved to California in 1974. The circle of Muir friends expanded and frequently brought other colleagues, present and former, to the club to visit. Florence Soderback Byers, who returned to teaching after being widowed, joined the Muir faculty in 1937; she and her children spent memorable weekends on the Stillaguamish. Grace Buckbee and Florence Keller Brooke remained lifelong friends, and the Brooke offspring, too, enjoyed many outings at the site on the river.[49]

Another long-tenured teacher joined the Stillaguamish Country Club in 1925. May Phillips had begun teaching in Seattle before the war; she read an advertisement for the club while teaching eighth grade at Coe. She soon had a one-room cabin built, which "just grew like Topsy"; she kept it until 1968. Miss Phillips served continuously on club committees and "was known for her weekend parties for students." Apparently,

some members complained of the noise they made. But not all were aware that a large number of guests were the under privileged or from broken homes. And quite often [Miss Phillips] rewarded her students for outstanding marks with a weekend at the club. She was often seen leading a group [of students] on a hike up French Creek or toward Mt. Higgins.

In the 1930s she transferred to Madison Junior High School in West Seattle, where she remained throughout the interwar years.[50]

For many, if not most, Seattle teachers, summer vacation meant normal
school, college, or university. The *Grade Club Magazine* advised choosing
a "summer school course from a purely selfish motive," whether simply
for "a change of mental atmosphere" or for recreation. It suggested that
one who taught math might enjoy studying a foreign language and
reminded everyone to select "a school with a beautiful campus filled with
inviting nooks." As grade teaching requirements came to include a bachelor's degree, summer study gained greater professional importance than
ever before. More than a few opted for a summer experience unique to
Washington—the Puget Sound Biological Research Station near Friday
Harbor on San Juan Island. The state's normal schools maintained a connection with the station through the thirties, and fees paid by teachers
seeking summer credits played no small part in its financial salvation during the Depression.[51]

May Phillips, for example, spent the summer of 1923 not on the Stillaguamish but at the Friday Harbor station. Ava Chambers, a longtime
science teacher at Bailey Gatzert, studied there in 1922, as did Otie Van
Orsdall, math teacher at West Woodland, who later taught at both Cleveland and Roosevelt high schools. Zela Vieth started her long career at John
Muir in 1927. She wrote glowingly of the San Juans and the six weeks
she spent at the biological station in the summer of 1929: "The hundred
or more tenthouses are scattered among the firs and ferns, while the laboratories and dining hall command a view of the water . . . a summer
paradise—cool, moderate, balmy, invigorating air . . . [with] the study of
marine animal life . . . [and] bird life." A champion of the place and its
programs, she said, "The San Juan Islands offer a variety of interests to
the pleasure seeker, Nature lover, artist or scientist. Since they are so accessible from Seattle, [one] should not overlook them in search of the faraway."[52]

Searching for the faraway remained, however, a favorite summer
undertaking that some of the interwar cohort had begun early in the century. Marion C. French had begun teaching seventh grade at Cascade School
before 1902; she retired from Lowell in 1935. One of the earliest to report
European travel, she attended the Passion Play at Oberammergau in 1910.

She had lodging that summer in the home of Otto Lange, the play's noted portrayer of Christ, who would supply edelweiss seeds for her friend Winona Bailey to plant in Washington's mountains.[53]

After World War I, automobile travel became less exceptional, and many teachers embarked on increasingly long trips by car. More than a few drove the perimeter of the United States, stopping in rudimentary tourist cabins or pitching tents in campgrounds. In 1923, Agnes Eide and a fellow teacher at Bailey Gatzert did just that, covering 12,500 miles in three months. They drove by way of Glacier and Yellowstone national parks to Denver and Pikes Peak, and then through St. Louis to the East Coast, adding Niagara Falls and the Catskills to their scenic list. They proceeded south along the eastern seaboard, explored Florida, then headed west to New Orleans and Dallas. They followed a route through southern New Mexico and Arizona into California, then drove up the coast to home.[54]

Inauguration of the district's sabbatical leave program in 1925 made it possible to combine extensive travel with study. To qualify, a teacher had to have seven years' service in the district; the school board granted no more than twenty leaves a year. A teacher on leave received "the difference between the salary then being earned and that of a . . . substitute teacher," and she had to state "her intention of returning to the Seattle system for the following" year. The plan proved so popular and mutually beneficial that two years later the board increased the number of sabbaticals to thirty; by 1932 sabbatical salaries had become "a flat allowance of $80 per month."[55] Well before that, at least one savings and loan association urged teachers to "Start your 'Sabbatical Leave Savings Account' today!" According to the advertisement, just $5 a week compounding at 5.5 percent interest would in a few years, with the district's stipend, "amount to about $2,000," just shy of the maximum grade salary.[56]

One of the first awarded a sabbatical, Rebecca Waxman of Horace Mann combined her summer vacation with fall semester leave in 1925 for study and travel in Europe. She left Seattle on July 3, devoted the first weeks to touring England's Lake District, and spent eight weeks there with friends and relatives sightseeing in Italy, France, and Switzerland; she then settled in Paris to "put in the next few months at hard work."[57] With only slight variations, this pattern was repeated countless times before World War II.

Ada and Eva McCullough, twins, toured museums in Europe during their sabbatical leaves in 1929 and returned to instill in their students a deep and lasting appreciation of art. Born November 12, 1877, both women earned normal certificates from Iowa's Kossuth Normal School in 1900. Eva McCullough taught six years in Michigan and Minnesota; during the Duluth winter of 1908, she applied to teach in Seattle. She started at Youngstown School the next September; living at the McNaught Hotel on First Hill, she made the streetcar transfer under the pergola in Pioneer Square for the trip to West Seattle. Her sister also abandoned Duluth and joined her at the McNaught that fall; in February 1910 she began four years at Whitworth School. The Capitol Hill apartment they soon moved to was the first of many they shared until Eva's death in 1943. Ada McCullough, who began teaching at Laurelhurst in 1926, remained there until June 1948, when she retired at the age of seventy-one. For decades, her former students benefited from that enriching sabbatical, and they became mainstays of Seattle's volunteer organizations and arts circles.[58]

Even in the depths of the Depression, the school district continued to grant teachers sabbatical leaves. Indeed, the salary of a veteran teacher on sabbatical combined with that for her substitute sometimes saved the district money. Until the United States entered World War II, Seattle teachers traveled the world over while on sabbatical.[59]

In 1939, Cora Forsberg, a second-grade teacher with a full-year sabbatical, sailed in July from San Francisco, aboard a combination passenger-freighter bound for London via the Panama Canal. Germany's invasion of Poland in September forced her to cancel a long-planned stay in London. She spent the remainder of her unforgettable year in neutral Sweden, studying at the universities in both Stockholm and Uppsala, and living for a time on an estate in southern Sweden where she was not spared the intimations of war—soldiers everywhere, occasional blackouts, and bomb shelters in every home. After an arduous bus trip across Finland, she took passage on the S.S. *American Legion*, a refugee ship, in August 1940. By volunteering to help in the ship's hospital, she secured a comfortable hospital bed for herself rather than a bunk in crowded, improvised quarters in the hold. The first two days and night out, the ship sailed in heavy weather through mined waters that became favorite hunting grounds of German U-boats, but she described the rest of the voyage as uneventful. Miss Forsberg had started her Seattle career in 1929 at Concord and moved to E. C. Hughes in 1937; she returned to a class of second-graders at Alki School.[60]

Countless sabbaticals were filled with study and travel in the United States as well. Adelle Wheeler, who had taught third grade at Interlake and Montlake schools since 1907, spent her 1927 leave visiting schools from coast to coast. In Michigan, friends at Ypsilanti State Normal School told her about an honors graduate, a young African-American woman, who now served as principal "of a large public school in New Orleans." With some difficulty, Miss Wheeler located the dilapidated segregated school in a "poverty-stricken part of the city," where she met and observed teachers in their classrooms. She accepted the principal's invitation to inspect a newer, more modern segregated school, which they reached by streetcar, she in the front of the car, her hostess in the back. On her return to Seattle Miss Wheeler wrote an account of her New Orleans experience for the *Grade Club Magazine,* and she sent curriculum material to that principal for her school. She "realiz[ed] perhaps as never before that the true teacher must have a vision . . . [and] faith that progress is the law of humanity."[61]

Over the years, scores of Seattle women studied at Columbia University's Teachers College. Lillian Pryor, a second-grade teacher at Green Lake and district veteran since the midtwenties, spent her 1937 sabbatical in New York. What she said on returning underscores the dividend of teacher loyalty that the school district realized from its sabbatical program. "I'm glad that I teach in Seattle. I've scorned at old furniture, regretted lack of room space, and frowned upon small play areas. Never again!" Having observed living and teaching conditions in Manhattan, she concluded, "We should count our blessings out here—be glad we work in Seattle, our beautiful city. . . . Our western children reflect the influence of a more peaceful and healthful way of living."[62]

Dorothy Crim, one of five who spent part of the 1938–39 school year at Teachers College, echoed Miss Pryor in her report to the superintendent: "I have always felt considerable loyalty for the Seattle Public School system, and my faith in it has increased as I have discovered, in comparing it with schools in other parts of the country, how sound and how consistently progressive has been its program." The girls adviser at Cleveland High School also took courses at the New York School of Social Work to complete a master's degree. She balanced work with entertainment and came back more appreciative of home:

> We saw New York, too!—everything from "Hells a Poppin" to "Henry IV." We thrilled to Grand Opera and went many times to the World Fair. We shopped on Allen Street and Fifth Avenue and went to church in Harlem and on Park Avenue. We found International House a most stimulating place to live during this period of world crises. New York was fun—but I came home firmly convinced that in Seattle one finds a greater degree of gracious living, and sincerely grateful that the school system by which I am employed grants Sabbaticals.

Dorothy Crim was herself a product of the Seattle schools—Lincoln High School class of 1920. After a nine-week normal course in Bellingham, she taught seven years in grade schools in Washington and Alaska. Completing her bachelor's degree at the University of Washington in 1928, she then taught high school English and history in Idaho before joining the Seattle corps in 1930. She declined the opportunity for a principalship in 1952, married that December, and the following spring resigned and moved to California.[63]

Asia began to attract teachers in the midtwenties, and early in the next decade teachers joined tours to Asia led by Henry Landes, then dean at the university and former president of the Mountaineers, and his wife, the former mayor. Before World War II put an end to travel, high school Spanish teachers flocked to South America; both Mexico and Canada remained popular vacation spots, as did Alaska and Hawaii.[64] Europe continued to be a perennial draw, and the summer of 1938 saw perhaps the largest contingent of Seattle teachers to date converge on the continent.

Both Gladys Charles and another recent graduate of Cheney Normal School sang in the Plymouth Church choir. The speaker at an evening program at the church in 1937 touted the joys and advantages of youth hostels, and as Miss Charles recalled, "The next summer, we went on a bicycle hosteling trip to Europe," sailing from New York. Sixty years later she remembered:

> I had borrowed from the credit union—and I still have the statement—
> fifteen hundred dollars for the summer trip. That paid for our train trip to
> New York, our boat trip back and forth across the ocean, our bicycles after
> we got there, the money to stay in the hostels—it cost 25 cents a night and
> you could get your breakfast the next morning. . . . She and I and another
> girl left the group and went down to Italy. . . . [sending] our bikes on to Paris
> where we were going to meet other people. We took the train down to Italy
> and had a wonderful time—took the train back to Paris and then got on the
> ship and came back home . . . [We] went down—by train—to the southern
> part of the country and across and back up the west coast—*on fifteen hun-
> dred dollars!*

Their three-month cycling adventure started in Amsterdam. Taking the bicycles up the Rhine on a riverboat, they pedaled in Germany and Switzerland. An encounter with Hitler Youth lent ominous overtones of the impending war.[65]

Gladys Charles Perry enjoyed further foreign travel in the midsixties. As president of the Washington Education Association, she attended the conference of the World Organization of Teachers in Korea, going by way of Tokyo. Her rise to prominence in professional organizations, first as president of the Seattle Teachers' Association, marked a return of women to leadership positions after a long postwar interval. She frequently found herself the only woman on city committees and public panels.[66]

The prize for most-traveled of the interwar cohort belongs to Sara Luch, physical education teacher at Madison Junior High School from 1936 until her retirement in 1971. The Vancouver, Washington, native and seven colleagues toured Europe during the summer of 1938. She kept a diary and never forgot the details:

> Eight of us girls went together. . . . We went up across Canada by train—
> sailed across to Glasgow . . . then to the Scandinavian Countries. We

crossed the Atlantic on the Athenia, first ship to go down in World War II. Dear old Scotch ladies were stewardesses on the ship and they couldn't understand young girls traveling without a chaperone—I was the youngest, and I was 29 at the time [laughter]. We had fun—

Harbingers of the war were everywhere but presented no serious impediment to travel. Miss Luch recalled anti-Semitic signs throughout Vienna and a waiter in Berlin who "gave us a long song and dance about the wonders of Hitler," but all in all they had warm receptions at every stop. Saying, "everyone was quite taken with the Americans," she remembered Oslo:

In Norway, I met a young fellow who took me dancing at the Royal Yacht Club. He tried to get dates for the other girls—called a lot of friends, but nobody was available. At that time foreign men were delighted to talk to an American, and to take an American girl dancing.[67]

She had borrowed money from her sister to make the trip, but, as she recalled,

I had such a whoop-de-glorious time, I thought "This travel is for me." . . . So I paid my debt as quickly as I could and started saving and borrowed a little more for the summer of 1939 and went to the Orient alone. I had the time of my life.

Never mind that Japan was then waging war in China or that people told her, "You're crazy—there's a war going on," she thought, "If I don't go now I may never get another chance—off I went." She had one regret: "I couldn't go to the Great Wall, which I wanted to see—but I did see it later." Her extensive postwar travels took her back to China and the Great Wall, twice around the world, throughout the United States and Canada, and to 115 countries on every continent but Antarctica.[68]

The group of eight making the European trip in 1938 included Sara Luch's sister, Mary, who taught at Concord School from 1927 until her marriage in 1940. The sisters traveled together again in the 1970s after

Sara retired. The financial end of travel never restrained her; she laughed when she said in 1997, "I don't have any money [now] because I spent it all traveling."[69]

It went almost without saying that the Seattle teacher, at home and abroad, "follow[ed] the dictates of good taste," as admonished by the education philosopher J. Frank Marsh in 1928. Leaving aside the rare report of a missed payment or loud and raucous party, the occasional discovery that a teacher smoked, or the singular accusation that a teacher had alienated the affections of someone's husband, the interwar cohort presented proper models of behavior. These women enriched the city's social, cultural, and recreational organizations with their membership and apparently felt no undo constraint in their extracurricular life. Although not all had a "whoop-de-glorious time," the record is replete with accounts of adventures and activities that brought them great pleasure.

9 / Leaving the Classroom

I have no criticism of our own excellent system
(except for our medieval marriage law!)

—RUTH ISAACS, 1939

Over the years, its "medieval marriage law" cost the Seattle School District dearly in loss of talented teachers and money invested in their careers. Ruth Isaacs, longtime Garfield High School English teacher, remarked on that rule after a year as an exchange teacher in Rochester, New York. Whether Rochester banned married teachers is not clear, but a 1930 survey of 1,500 school systems around the nation showed that 77 percent did, and 63 percent dismissed teachers when they married.[1]

Arguments against married women were tortuous at times, and employment of widows with dependent children should have rendered most of them moot. The most common arguments were regarding whether a woman could serve two masters—husbands and pupils—and whether her own children or her income should come first. An argument made early in the century by eugenicists against women teaching at all lay in the conviction that

> clear probability of harm . . . lies in the prevention of gifted and devoted women from having and rearing children of their own flesh and blood. . . . It is likely the world loses more by the absence from motherhood of women teachers who might otherwise marry than by the absence from the teaching profession of the men who would have their places.

A contributor to *School Executives Magazine* exhumed that notion as late as 1931:

> My chief objection to married women teaching is the fact that it leads almost necessarily to childless homes . . . that really should produce more children. Every time you elect a married teacher, you tacitly endorse and encourage such practices which are the most reprehensible sins of the upper and middle classes.[2]

When World War II produced a severe teacher shortage, the Seattle district resorted to hiring married teachers in "the Emergency Service Classification." Even as it instituted this temporary change, the administration reinforced its long-term commitment to the ban on marriage with the following rationale:

> 1. The public has objected to families' receiving a second salary from the public purse when they already possess one income. . . .
> 2. Marriage implies a home and children. That children of employed mothers suffer is generally recognized. . . .
> 3. Marriage does not necessarily make a good teacher. . . . [Studies] have failed to show . . . any significant superiority of married women teachers over those who are unmarried. On the other hand, such studies suggest that married women may tend to be absent from duty more frequently and that they are less active in improving themselves personally by further study and travel than those who are unmarried.[3]

The school board had always adamantly opposed employing married teachers, but the rare exception had occurred. Two months after the nation entered the war in 1917, a principal faced a personnel problem posed by one of his teachers who "expected to marry a man in the Coast Artillery." He asked the board "whether in case the marriage took place and he was called to the front, she would be retained . . . during the period of his service with the U.S. Army." The board decided "that she be allowed to remain in the Corps, if she marries under the circumstances [described] . . . and 'in the event . . . her husband [be] sent to foreign service' she could be allowed to continue in her teaching position next year."[4]

National emergencies and wartime exigencies could overcome all arguments.

By 1924, as younger women came into Seattle to teach, the board adopted the following statement for all contracts: "Marriage of a woman teacher during the period of her employment shall automatically terminate her contract."[5] Three-quarters of a century later, women's virtually unquestioned acceptance of mandatory resignation seems astonishing. But as the scholar Winifred Wandersee saw the twenties, "The simple truth is that most American women, in opposition to the feminist ideology, regarded their family role as primary, and this view affected their attitudes toward their work."[6] Many never doubted that they should not teach after marrying.

Ruth Isaacs could hardly have been alone in thinking the district policy medieval, yet teachers' letters of resignation seldom went beyond stating that a marriage had already taken place or would on a given date, while expressing enjoyment and satisfaction in the Seattle teaching experience. Among a few exceptions, Gertrude Sennes resigned her position at Hamilton Junior High School in 1930 with some bitterness toward the argument against two-income households:

It is with regret that I tender my resignation . . . my impending marriage . . . automatically terminates my present contract.

I . . . hope some day to be able to resume it when the lay mind recognizes that teaching is more a profession than an economic source of livelihood. There is so much yet to be done in training the benighted mass that leaders may really function!

Mabel Wixon, who resigned to marry in August 1937, made her point the following year when she requested references: "There being no restrictions against married women teaching in Honolulu, I have [applied] for a position."[7]

Regardless of how "lay minds" viewed matters, fellow teachers and students usually cheered news of a wedding. Hazel Milligan, among the lucky few hired in 1934, resigned to be married in 1938. Sixth-graders at John Hay "were just charmed by the idea" of her marrying and would probably have been delighted had the popular teacher continued on in the classroom.[8]

The 1943 wedding of the physical education and dance teacher Helen Hull was the event of the year at Lincoln High School. She recalled that Jessie Orrell, who taught math, interceded with the principal on the behalf of students wanting to celebrate, telling him:

"Mr. Higgins, it is a rare thing for a teacher to be married during her service, and the kids . . . all want to give her a present." And he said, "Well,
if . . . nobody was left out, and it's a volunteer thing." . . . [She told me] "Helen,
now these girls are so excited about your being married. . . . Let them have
their fun . . . you are the only one that they will ever remember having been
married during the school year."

Each of the school's four classes gave her a wedding gift. Fifty-four years later the bride still relished the memory, saying that one class "gave me a tray—a wooden tray. I still have it. And on it they had taped a cookbook, [with] all of their names. . . . I was so pleased."[9]

Most resignations occurred in June, but winter 1925 saw a rash of end-of-semester marriages. Teachers and students at Mercer School honored "Miss Minnie Bagemiel, who was married at the close of the semester . . . the Domestic Science class prepared and served the luncheon." Jefferson School's faculty "gave a luncheon in honor of Miss Marjorie Wilson" on January 22, in advance of her marriage in February.[10]

Some weddings took colleagues by surprise. Mattie Black, who had taught third grade at Gatewood School for ten years, astonished the other teachers on January 12, 1925, "when she did not appear at school until late in the afternoon . . . [and] announced that she had been married to Mr. Broadbent during the day." Presumably Miss Black, and even some faculty friends, had known Mr. Broadbent for some time. Their surprise could hardly have equaled that of Principal Emma Larrabee and the McDonald School faculty in 1930 when they learned of the second-grade teacher's summer vacation: Hazel Alcorn had

sailed immediately following the close of school in June for Manila, osten-
sibly to visit her sister, who is teaching in the Islands. Two days out of Victoria, . . . she met a very fine man. They were married in Manila, and now
as Mr. and Mrs. Edgar C. Powell are on a year's voyage around the world.[11]

According to school district lore and personal recollections, more than a few marriages remained secret. Calling the marriage ban foolish and "a waste of money and talent," Gladys Perry recalled that some continued teaching after marrying and "simply didn't tell the school district." A longtime principal, Arthur Gravrock, concurred, saying that the teachers just never wore their wedding rings.[12]

During the 1933 spring vacation, Alma Wilson, the art teacher at Jefferson School, married Paul Jackson and kept it a secret, continuing to use her maiden name. But at least two people at her school knew. Her husband, a student at the normal school in Bellingham, was doing cadet teaching in that city. "The day Paul and I went to get married at the court house in Bellingham," she recalled, her colleague Jane Mullen "was visiting friends in Bellingham [whose daughter] came home from school and said 'Oh, we had something happen . . . today—a fellow from our school married a Seattle teacher.'" The girl revealed the names, and Miss Mullen, who was a friend of Miss Wilson's, shared the news with another friend, their principal, who "knew from that day on and kept his mouth shut— or I would have lost my job." Alma Wilson, the daughter of Trella Logan, who had come to Seattle with Frank Cooper to teach, continued to live "at home with my parents and [Paul] was still going to school" in Bellingham. She resigned in July a year later and in a succinct letter wrote, "I wish to resign my position as a teacher in the Seattle Schools as I have been married," giving no hint of a wedding date.[13]

Teacher marriages may have been long-anticipated or surprising, celebrated, kept secret, welcomed, or rued by students and colleagues, but more women of the interwar cohort left the classroom to be married than for any other reason. Among 700 women who taught at some point between 1919 and 1941, 58 percent of high school teachers and 65 percent of grade teachers who resigned before retirement age gave marriage as the reason.[14]

Although not all teachers explained their departure, the other reasons for resignation were numerous: health, seeking teaching positions in other school districts, "home conditions," family obligations, and other employment were listed. At least one teacher left to accept a position in Helena, Montana, "because of the financial return, and not due to any dissatisfaction here."[15]

Among resignations to make career changes, that of Ellen Reep stands alone. Her letter to the superintendent, written while on leave, showed courage, humor, gratitude, excitement, and hints of glamour. She had taught history and English at Ballard High School since 1929, and from Norway, on July 12, 1935, she wrote: "I'm applying some . . . frontier courage . . . to limit myself entirely to music as a career. So I hereby tender my resignation from your very fine school system. It is with some regret . . . but I must now make a choice—(before I land in the ol' folks home)." Her field of performance is not known, but she had spent the previous year in New York, "studying, attending 75 concerts, operas, and symphonies, and doing a few concerts myself." Stimulated and encouraged by all that, she sailed for Europe and made her decision:

> I plan to do some study in Germany and Norway but shall return to N.Y. in October. Next spring I may come to the coast for concerts if I can rig up an audience and get a good manager. Needless to say ¾ of the N.Y. population suffers from a career complex but I shall not let that upset me.[16]

Ellen Reep then disappeared from school district records, but undoubtedly her flair and determination kept her in the memories of her students and former colleagues.

Opportunities in other fields offered attractive and tempting possibilities. Retirement prospects, on the other hand, were dismal. Life after retirement had always been a top concern for Seattle's interwar career teachers, both individually and collectively. The district's retirement fund, created in 1917 at the request of an overwhelming majority of teachers, had buoyed them but provided scant comfort and little income for women who had started teaching early in the century.

When Emma Small, district supervisor of drawing since the 1890s, retired in 1922, the grade teachers raised $200 to honor her with a gift. Rather than present something decorative or symbolic, the practical and understanding women sent her the money.[17]

At the time of unionization and organizing battles in 1927, the *Seattle Star* opined that teachers could "never hope to be paid what they earn" but went on to say, "Most could do a better day's work if they could see a saving account piling up against old age." Indeed, the *Seattle Grade Club Magazine* regularly carried advertisements from the city's banks and other thrift institutions that implored teachers to save, citing vacation travel, retirement, and "the wedding day" as worthy goals.[18]

Ethel Y. Phillips, a Seattle investment broker, began promoting retirement annuities in the early thirties. She calculated in 1931 numbers that a teacher could have a lump sum of $18,720 at age sixty by saving "$31 per month now through our Income Bond and at 60 draw $78 per month as long as you live." She advertised in 1935:

> "There will be Gold in your purse
> when there is Silver in your hair"
>
> -IF-
> You secure an Annuity Bond today
> -FROM-
> Ethel Y. Phillips.[19]

Advent of the Seattle Education Auxiliary spoke directly to financial concerns and led to the creation of a retirement home for teachers. In 1930, the venerable Adelaide Pollock put the case to her fellow and future retirees, explaining that the auxiliary

> has for its object the creation of an endowment fund for a home where retired or convalescent teachers may live among congenial friends in pleasant surroundings. . . .
>
> [Some] pioneer teachers have retired. Occasionally one is in need of care. The teaching profession . . . often takes teachers, early in life, from their people and environment. When the time comes to retire, many times teachers have no close relatives and no desire to return to the early home. They love Seattle and the friends . . . here and they desire to make this city their home. They are not happy on the fringe of other homes nor in hotels or apartment houses. They long for the companionship of friends having similar outlooks to their own.
>
> The purpose of the Seattle Education Auxiliary is to serve this group and to prepare a Mecca to which the present corps may turn.

Current and former teachers had already started an endowment fund, and Miss Pollock suggested making their project public, since former students "with pleasant memories of former teachers" might help. She added, however, that the immediate "problem is to get all the present corps to join the Auxiliary and to undertake this publicity."[20]

The idea for an organization dedicated to establishing a retirement home took root at a mass meeting of the entire teaching corps on October 8, 1928, that produced a draft constitution. The group elected Mamie B. Stoecker its first president, Dora Herren recording secretary, and Ida Culver membership secretary; the former superintendent Frank Cooper, Adelaide Pollock, and L. Maxine Kelly constituted the rest of the first board. Other pioneer teachers of the interwar cohort served over time as trustees. In May 1929, the auxiliary filed for incorporation as a nonprofit organization "legally empowered to handle any bequests or legacies it might receive." Bequests in 1932 included $500 from the estate of Eva Dansingburg, who had come to Seattle before 1902, taught and later served as principal at McGilvra School, where she was until the year before her death.[21] The Grade Teachers' Club donated $1,000 that same year.

The auxiliary board, sufficiently encouraged by its constituency and low real estate prices, spent "a great deal of time investigating property," looking specifically for a site "within the city, close to transportation and available for use of all teachers." When a large three-story house with a view, at 1004 Queen Anne Avenue on the south slope of the hill, came on the market in the spring of 1933, the auxiliary bought it. The Seattle Education Auxiliary Residence, as it was first known, soon underwent refurbishing to bring it into code compliance, and two retired teachers moved in even before the work was completed. Operating plans called for teachers to live there "under conditions of comfort and happiness at reasonable rates," and for the building to "become a rendezvous where groups of the teachers may meet and . . . entertain friends."[22]

In 1935, Ida Culver, a noteworthy force in the auxiliary, cohosted an informal reception at the house for a group of retirees. By the end of the afternoon they had formed what they called the Auxiliary Aid. Always in hostess mode, the group agreed that one of its objectives "should be to arrange an annual May Day tea." Those present that afternoon included

Annie Brayton, who in her linen duster had chaired the first meeting of the Grade Teachers' Club in 1912.[23]

Another member of both organizations, Ida Culver had served in the area of finance. She played a role in creation of the Seattle Teachers Credit Union in 1927 and was its first president. She also belonged to the Business and Professional Women's Club and circulated in a wider sphere through the American Association of University Women. She had begun teaching in Seattle in 1911 and for twenty-three years taught third and fourth grades at J. B. Allen School. In 1934 she transferred to Hawthorne in Rainier Valley; perhaps she owned an automobile by then to save her the long streetcar commute from her home in the University District.[24]

Ida Culver was born July 10, 1875, and graduated from high school in Clarion, Iowa. She earned a bachelor's degree in 1904 from the Iowa State Normal School in Cedar Rapids. She taught sixteen years in Iowa and South Dakota and in the course of her long career attended summer sessions in several western states and at the Columbia University Teachers College. Meanwhile, her family moved from Iowa to Holdenville, Oklahoma, near the rich Seminole, Wewoka, and Cromwell oil fields. When her mother died in 1912, Miss Culver, now in Seattle, inherited a house in Iowa, and a one-third share in 120 acres outside Holdenville. She shrewdly parlayed these properties into substantial capital,[25] enhanced her holdings in real property, and made secured loans to fellow teachers and others. In 1935, she bought the mortgage on the teachers home on Queen Anne Avenue from Washington Mutual Savings Bank. When she died January 25, 1936, following a heart attack, the bulk of her estate went to the auxiliary. Fittingly, auxiliary members, with many of whom she had taught, named the retirement property Ida Culver House. When the original house proved too small, the organization built a larger facility in the Ravenna district that opened in July 1950. Although it sold that property to ERA Care, Inc., in 1987, the auxiliary maintained a presence at ERA Care's other retirement home, Ida Culver House–Broadview, where it subsidized the rent of some school-related residents.[26]

That retirees still needed the auxiliary's financial assistance at the end of the century underscores the inadequacy of teacher retirement plans over the years. Many longtime teachers of the interwar cohort petitioned to teach beyond retirement age in order to qualify for slowly improving state programs.

Few approached retirement in circumstances more uncertain than one home economics teacher who had begun her Seattle career at J. B. Allen School in 1936. Because of her declining health, she retired in 1955 at the age of fifty-three. She had contemplated taking a year's leave of absence to regain her strength but did not want to "use up [her] savings to live on." She did "hope to 'take in' sewing." Still, she wanted to be free to work at something else if she could not live on what she earned from sewing.[27]

Even with district retirement fund annuities available across the state, many teachers did not retire when eligible. Of the 172 who retired from the Seattle corps on June 30, 1927, only three had applied for annuities by the end of the year. By late that year, only sixty-nine had applied for annuities in the ten-year life of the fund; five had died and two had returned to teaching. Seattle teachers had begun contributing to the district's fund in 1917, and for twenty-one years, it "never lost a penny on its investments" thanks to "those who shrewdly managed its resources," including such stalwarts as L. Maxine Kelly, who served on the fund's administrative board throughout its history.[28]

The Washington Education Association and other advocacy groups had sought better retirement provisions at the state level since the midtwenties. In 1938, the legislature adopted a plan that consolidated all district retirement funds into a state fund, bringing with them whatever rights had accrued to teachers locally. The new state system operated on an actuarial basis, and "$40 per month was set as the initial amount to be paid [retirees] of 30 years' service at age 60." A paltry annual sum of $480 deterred many from leaving the classroom.[29]

The inadequacy of retirement provisions notwithstanding, in the late thirties the Seattle School District faced the difficult and delicate dilemma presented by an aging corps of veteran teachers. Citing complaints about teachers "no longer capable of doing as effective work as those who are younger," in the spring of 1939, the school board voted to require physical examinations of all teachers older than sixty-five who wished "to continue in service."[30] Further, it announced a plan to lower the compulsory retirement age and to force all teachers reaching age seventy before July 1, 1940, to retire. Thereafter, all who reached age sixty-six during a school year would have to retire July 1. At a public hearing on May 5, an unprecedented number—more than a hundred people—came to argue against the plan. The objections were immediate and both poignant and angry.[31]

A former student reminded the board that "some people are old at 30 and others are young at 60" and that under the proposed plan the district "would lose some of its most valuable instructors." Another citizen agreed, saying "teachers, real teachers, are born, not made" and when found they should "be valued and retained . . . as long as [they are] giving good service." Teachers themselves focused on the financial aspects of impending retirement; one suggested that there be no compulsory retirement in the school district without a system that "will take care of retired teachers properly."[32]

Freda Libbee, who had led the Grade Teachers' Club early in the Depression, pleaded for time while the pension plan was adjusted "so that [teachers] would not have to retire on $40 a month." "Our old teachers are staying awake nights worrying," she declared, "and it isn't fair to them. I propose that we drop the retirement age slowly for their benefit. This can be done over a period of years, and will give those affected time to plan for the future." The PTA firmly supported the teachers. A representative of the Seattle Federation of Women's Clubs spoke in favor of the proposed health examinations, sure that the board "would be fair in all matters."[33]

Four of the board's five members heard the entire discussion on May 5, 1939; three met in special session on June 13 and unanimously adopted a resolution incorporating some of the thoughts expressed the month before. These terms, slightly more lenient than the original proposal, left the age for mandatory retirement at seventy-one, to be lowered gradually to sixty-seven by 1946. However, beginning that September, all who reached age sixty-five would "as a prerequisite to beginning service each year . . . be required to take a physical examination."[34]

The following July, twenty-seven women teachers took physical exams to qualify for the coming year. Six were found in good condition, eighteen in fair, and three in poor. Twelve suffered "moderate heart disease," fourteen had excessively hard arteries, and nine excessively high blood pressure. Three had greater than 10 percent hearing loss, and six showed "slight mental confusion under stress" of the examination.[35]

The case of Ida M. Taylor illustrates the plight of the older teacher with declining physical capacity. Born in 1880, she graduated from Mount Hope Academy in Rogers, Ohio, and normal school in Pennsylvania. One of the quiet, virtually anonymous members of the Seattle corps since 1910, she had brought strength and dedication to the task of teaching fourth grade in several schools from working-class Georgetown to affluent Magnolia before joining the faculty at Coe School in 1922.[36]

Uniformly favorable evaluations show a teacher "very conscientious and painstaking about her work . . . [who helped] every individual child to do his best." One principal said, "Her personal contact and influence with children is a blessing to any community. Her pupils and their parents love her. [But sometimes] . . . I think she comes [to school] too early and stays too late for her [own] best interests." An early report from Elizabeth Tharp, Coe principal, portrayed a self-effacing, dedicated career teacher:

> Miss Taylor lives for her work. Probably too much to get the contact with outside things as she should. . . . She is especially pleasant to work with and never shirks a duty. She is of Quaker parentage and that calmness prevails in her manner. She is somewhat old fashioned in many things she does, but she is faithful and earnest.[37]

Always deferential, in 1927 Miss Taylor had ventured to ask for the "courtesy" of a sabbatical leave, noting that she had "never missed a day except one week which was caused by the illness of my mother." She spent her one-semester sabbatical studying in the field of the developmentally disabled child and returned to teach "adjustment" classes at Warren Avenue and Mercer schools.[38] Several years later, the supervisor Alice Casey evaluated her performance and remarked on her continuing pattern of coming to school early and staying late: she "devotes hours to overtime." Miss Casey then reported the first hint of a problem—Miss Taylor "is slightly handicapped by being deaf at times but her other superior qualities overbalance the handicap." By 1936, increasing hearing loss prompted Ida Taylor to write to the superintendent, "I have always tried to give conscientious, efficient service. . . . [But deafness] is lessening my efficiency so I feel that I should retire at the close of the school year." Only fifty-six years old and worried about how her resignation would be perceived, she "dar[ed] to ask a favor":

> I would like to retire without those who know me thinking that I have been "thrown out" (excuse the boys' phraseology) so, if it can be so arranged, I would like my name placed on the list of those reelected and published in the paper—my retirement made public later.
>
> I sincerely hope this may be granted for it means so very much to me.

Ida Taylor still lived in the First Hill apartment she had called home since 1915. The record does not indicate whether the district honored her request or how she fared after retirement.[39]

From the first implementation of the retirement regulations adopted in 1939, teachers petitioned for exemptions. The board showed a willingness to accommodate them. Kate Adams, who came to Seattle in 1908 for a better salary than her "ideal" situation in Evanston, Illinois, had not grown wealthy teaching at University Heights. Her last recorded salary, $2,400, was reduced by the two Depression-era pay cuts. Scheduled to retire at age sixty-six in 1939, she received an extension until June 1940. On that date she asked "to serve another year for financial reasons" and in 1941 requested "an additional year for the same reason," promising to resign after one semester "if health or decreased efficiency should cause the administrative staff to think it best." On the superintendent's advice, the board voted her a contract for 1941–42, "with the definite understanding that it will be her last year of service." Kate Adams finally retired from her fourth-grade classroom in June 1942.[40]

In spring of 1941, having included the restoration of teachers' salaries to pre-Depression levels in its preliminary budget, the school board found it impossible to increase benefits for retired teachers. The Seattle Association of Classroom Teachers, noting that some retirees received as little as $8 a month, pleaded for some provision, but the board deemed even a token increase "unwise."[41] Teachers nearing retirement endured uncertain futures for two more decades, and they continued to seek the opportunity to teach long enough to take advantage of improving state retirement laws.

In April 1944, Viola J. Lusby resigned, thanking Superintendent McClure "for the excellent treatment I have received through all my years of teaching here." Two months later she wrote again to say, "Because of a probable increase in the teachers' pension I would like to recall the resignation I sent you." Lusby was a graduate of Michigan's Ypsilanti Normal School, and, after teaching ten years in Ann Arbor and Spokane, she started her Seattle career in 1916 under the watchful eye of Adelaide Pollock at West Queen Anne. She immediately "made herself a factor in the district through her cordial manner when parents visit her room, . . . and through her calls to the home." The following year she had transferred to Interlake School in Wallingford where over the next seventeen years she more than lived up to her principal's assessment: "There is perhaps no teacher who secures better response from pupils than Miss Lusby. . . . Her influence in the community is most excellent." In addition to the hope of a better pension, the fact that Julia Reible and Bertha Remley, two longtime colleagues, would teach one more year at Interlake apparently had influenced her. Although the administration had looked "forward to new blood at Interlake," since she had resigned short of the mandatory age, Viola Lusby returned to teach at Interlake until June 1947.[42]

Two decades later, the promise of further improved retirement benefits prompted another veteran to keep teaching. In February 1961, Rubie Carlson Johnstone, teaching first grade at T. T. Minor School, fell "while putting up a bulletin board display and fractured two vertebrae." She resigned in June, but returned five years later, saying: "I am so grateful to . . . the Seattle Public Schools for the opportunity to return for one year. . . . Teaching young children is such a rewarding experience and I shall endeavor to do my very best for the children and the Seattle Public Schools." The Nebraska native's Seattle career had begun in 1926. She received superior evaluations from every principal for whom she taught: in 1929 the seasoned L. Maxine Kelly deemed her "excellent . . . A splendid teacher"; in 1960, Tom Leist considered the veteran of the demonstration school still "a teacher of demonstration quality," adding that "beginning teachers would profit from observing Mrs. Johnstone."[43]

Leist must have rejoiced when she returned to his faculty at T. T. Minor. In the spring of 1968 he asked that she be allowed to teach another year because she "is an excellent primary teacher, in good health." A year later he asked for another extension:

> I hope the review committee will find it possible for Mrs. Rubie Johnstone to teach another year at T. T. Minor School. Mrs. Johnstone is an alert and excellent teacher and one who is current with her teaching techniques. It would be difficult to find a primary teacher of Mrs. Johnstone's abilities.

A third reprieve came in May 1969 after clearance from the medical department. She retired at the age of seventy on June 8, 1970, writing,

> With the new [state] retirement law in effect, I am especially grateful for the opportunity to have remained in service through the 1969–70 school year.
> My many years with the Seattle Schools have been both challenging and rewarding. Kindly convey my thanks to . . . the administrative staff and . . . the school board for the many favors and kindnesses shown me.[44]

The tone of letters of resignation and retirement overwhelmingly reveals the amiable, even affectionate, relationship with the school district that the interwar women teachers had enjoyed since 1902. In the few cases of dismissal, the teacher's reaction is absent from the record, as is any indication of resentment or dissatisfaction on resignation. A notable exception to this otherwise sunny picture is the case of Etta Minnig.

Miss Minnig began her Seattle teaching career in 1911. After twelve years in Queen Anne Hill and Magnolia classrooms, she was assigned to Van Asselt at the far south end of Beacon Hill as head teacher. Van Asselt did not warrant a principal, never having more than five teachers on its roster. For nineteen years Etta Minnig both taught sixth grade there and performed a principal's duties at less than a principal's salary. But when war-related industries brought a flood of people to town and Van Asselt's projected enrollment for autumn 1942 more than tripled, the school board and administration lurched into action: that July, the board ordered twelve portable classrooms moved onto the school grounds and assigned a male principal; the superintendent notified Miss Minnig by special delivery letter to her family home in Erie, Pennsylvania, where she had gone for the summer. On her return to Seattle, the thirty-one-year veteran teacher met with Superintendent McClure and tendered her resignation; he did not accept it and granted her a year's leave of absence, which she proudly declined. Because employment records list her retirement at age sixty-four as June 1943, one can hope the district paid her a year's salary. In a rather condescending footnote, the board said it would "be sympathetic to her application" should she want to return.[45]

But the case of Clara Siggerud is much more representative of the majority of teacher resignations. Among the last in the classic mold of midwestern normal school graduates who came to Seattle to teach, Miss Siggerud had arrived in 1926 with a certificate from the school in Moorhead, Minnesota. She began as a music teacher under Emma Larrabee at McDonald School, who said she "exceeded my expectations. Following Miss Stone, who was so dearly beloved . . . she has kept up the high standard of work. . . . I feel we were fortunate in securing Miss Siggerud." She returned as a substitute two years after retiring and merited an "outstanding substitute" rating. When she resigned in 1962 she wrote to the assistant superintendent, Kenneth Selby:

> "The time has come," the Walrus said—and so it has for me!
>
> I don't know how formal this is supposed to be, but I'm hereby tendering my resignation. . . . effective June '62.
>
> It is a bit confusing to think that I, having been in a school room since age 6, shall now be subjected to a far different daily routine. (I hope not by bells!)
>
> But just to say how very quickly these thirty-five years have passed and how pleasantly!
>
> My associations have been the mostest—every principal and co-worker a very good friend.
>
> My very best wishes go to the Music Department (all close friends) and a deep appreciation to you, Mr. Selby, the administrative Staff and School Board for making teaching in Seattle a very pleasant job![46]

When Dorothy Crim, the girls adviser at Cleveland High School, resigned in 1953, her resignation letter also followed the pattern established by the interwar cohort:

The years I have spent with the Seattle Public schools have been happy ones, filled to the brim with opportunities for professional growth, rewarding experiences, and precious friendships. I have been grateful for the fine leadership afforded by . . . [the schools] and proud of their high standards of achievement. It has always been a source of real personal satisfaction to be a member of the corps.[47]

Perhaps no one summed up her Seattle experience better or more succinctly than Florence Wren Ewart did on her retirement. She had come to Washington from Iowa in 1928 to teach at Aberdeen; two years later she moved to the Seattle district and taught kindergarten at Bryant. She completed her bachelor's degree at Iowa State Teachers College while on sabbatical leave in 1938. Having married at some point after 1948, she remained at Bryant until 1959, then spent one year at Van Asselt before transferring back to the city's north end and Wedgwood School. Her principals' evaluations were uniformly glowing. Even the formidable Bella Perry made such comments as "Loved by all of her pupils and their parents," "A great favorite in the community," and "Mothers all happy when children are placed with Miss Wren. Doing an outstanding piece of work." In 1943, Miss Perry also called her "a power in creating a good spirit in the building and the community," and a year later she wrote, "Fortunate is the child who is placed under the guidance of Miss Wren." Toward the end of Florence Wren Ewart's career, Wedgwood's Arnold Holden, another young postwar principal, wrote, "Mrs. Ewart . . . is a very pleasant surprise to me. Her spirit and enthusiasm for her work is something to behold."[48]

When she retired in 1967, Florence Wren Ewart wrote: "Thirty-seven of the forty-two years that I have taught have been in Seattle. These have been happy and rewarding years. If now deciding upon a career, I would again be a teacher."[49]

Her sentiments were characteristic of the women whose careers included the interwar decades. Dedication and satisfaction are the hallmarks of the cohort who embodied or inherited the Seattle Way.

Epilogue

Women teachers of the interwar cohort came to Seattle for diverse reasons. Their careers in the school district spanned varying lengths of time through more than sixty years that saw changes both in and out of the classroom. Throughout the city they were held in high regard. Not all were paragons, but only a minuscule number ever brought embarrassment or discredit to themselves or the school district, and over the years very few were dismissed or compelled to resign. During the first four decades of the twentieth century, noteworthy women, and, ultimately, their students, accepted teaching positions in Seattle. Together they upheld the tradition of excellence that marked the style and method of education known as the Seattle Way.

World War II was a turning point. Among its enormous effects was an in-migration that increased and altered the city's population; however, few native sons and daughters left Seattle. Men and women who had been schooled by dedicated women in the decades before Pearl Harbor assumed the reins of leadership and steered the city on a prudent postwar course.

Municipal government benefited from the likes of Mayors Dorm Braman and Gordon Clinton, both Roosevelt High School graduates who had attended city grade schools. Daniel J. Evans, another Roosevelt alumnus and product of Laurelhurst Elementary, served an unprecedented three terms as Washington's governor. Any number of city council members and state legislators during the fifties and sixties had come from Seattle classrooms. Joel Pritchard, from Queen Anne High School, and Brock

216

Adams, from Broadway, served Seattle congressional districts in the other Washington. West Seattle and Lafayette schools sent Dietrich Schmitz to the Seattle School Board and his brother, Henry, to the presidency of the University of Washington.

The municipal court bench and the professions as well as volunteer, political, judicial, professional, and service organizations found leaders among women and men who had spent twelve years in the city's public schools. In an era when women seldom made a mark in politics, Janet Powell Tourtelotte, whose education began at the old Lake School, imbibed civics and government from Adella Parker at Broadway High School. She ran for public office and became a force in the Republican Party at state and national levels. Ruby Mar Chow, schooled in the good citizenship atmosphere of Ada Mahon's Bailey Gatzert School, matured into a community leader and, after the restructuring of local government, served on the King County Council.

The League of Women Voters claimed the allegiance of untold numbers of women who had learned both political action and the tradition of volunteer service from girls advisers and their high school girls clubs. Under the direction of an all-woman board filled with the products of the Seattle Public Schools, the Children's Orthopedic Hospital moved into new quarters and began its transition into a renowned regional medical center.

Business and civic leaders educated in Seattle before Pearl Harbor contributed heavily to the success of Century 21, the 1962 world exposition that lifted Seattle from the confines of its insular and parochial interests. Among them, Edward Carlsen had attended Interlake and graduated from Lincoln High School; Al Rochester, who also served on the city council, was a member of the charter class at Isaac I. Stevens School on Capitol Hill and a graduate of Broadway High School. Interwar music teachers had instilled a love and appreciation of music in their students, who as adults both supported and played with the Seattle Symphony Orchestra for decades. Seattle artists such as George Tsutakawa and Morris Graves bore the influence of Broadway High School's legendary art teacher, Matilda J. Piper.

John Muir School's principal, Jessie Lockwood, and its teachers turned out students imbued with the tenets of conservation, and James Ellis went from its classrooms to lead later drives to restore and preserve the city's environment and livability. The Hutchinson brothers capitalized on twelve years at Emerson School and Franklin High School to become late-century icons in the city. Fred won election to baseball's hall of fame and his physician brother, William, spearheaded a drive that created the world-renowned Fred Hutchinson Cancer Research Center in his memory.

Every woman who had taught could take justifiable pride in the postwar urban society created and sustained by former grade pupils and high school students. Those men and women composed an educated citizenry with both a sense of responsibility and a spirit of the common good. They supported progressive measures that preserved the best from the past while laying the foundation for the future.

Any member of the interwar cohort would have delighted in a tribute received by Isa Brown Wilson, one of their number who had begun teaching in 1925 and returned in 1943 to teach under the emergency service provision. The mother of a 1959 Ballard High School graduate wrote that she had come across a paper her son had written for a class and "thought it should be passed on." Assigned to write a short essay on "What Has Widened My Horizons," he wrote:

> Without giving it a single thought I know who widened my horizons the most. It was my first grade teacher, Mrs. Wilson at Loyal Heights School. Mrs. Wilson knew what to do with kids. She knew their abilities and she sure got the most out of them. She gave me an interest in school and pride in my school work, but more important yet is that she taught me how to read well. It is a long time since the first grade, but I can still remember her and thank her for a job well done.[1]

An autobiography, assigned sixteen years earlier, had produced similar thoughts in a freshman English class at Queen Anne.

> Miss Milligan was only the first of a long line of wonderful teachers at John Hay [School]—she was [my] favorite until the 6A, although the Kelly sisters tied for a close second. In 6A [I] changed from Miss Stoy to Miss Olsby. . . . Borghilde Olsby was the best teacher I ever had in grade school. . . . Miss

Olsby could tell simply marvelous stories and crack jokes, too. . . . Miss Olsby treated us like adults, taught us about the public library—suddenly we weren't just little children.[2]

Exceptional women had come to Seattle early in the twentieth century to pursue careers in the teaching profession. Together with their protégées and younger colleagues, they left their imprint on children and young people who absorbed their values and optimism, and shaped the city for decades.

Notes

INTRODUCTION

1. For an account of careers in late nineteenth-century Providence, Rhode Island, see Victoria-Maria MacDonald, "The Paradox of Bureaucratization: New Views on Progressive Era Teachers and the Development of a Woman's Profession," *History of Education Quarterly* 39, no. 4 (Winter 1999). See also Joel Perlmann and Robert A. Margo, *Women's Work? American Schoolteachers, 1650–1920* (Chicago: University of Chicago Press, 2001).

2. Cynthia Fuchs Epstein, *Woman's Place: Options and Limits in Professional Careers* (Berkeley: University of California Press, 1971), p. 157 (quotation); Nancy Hoffman, *Woman's True Profession* (Old Westbury, Conn.: Feminist Press, 1981), p. xix.

3. Susan B. Carter, "Incentives and Rewards to Teaching," in *American Teachers: Histories of a Profession at Work,* ed. Donald Warren (New York: Macmillan Publishing Co., 1989), p. 49.

4. James W. Fraser, "Agents of Democracy," ibid., p. 119.

5. Ibid., pp. 130 and 133.

6. David Tyack, "Future of the Past," ibid., pp. 408–9.

7. Bryce E. Nelson, *Good Schools: The Seattle Public School System, 1901–1930* (Seattle: University of Washington Press, 1988), p. 46. Nelson's book is an excellent account of the Cooper years in Seattle.

8. Ibid., pp. 8 (quotation), 16, and 22. Junior high schools opened in Seattle in 1927.

9. Ibid., p. 24.

10. Lawrence A. Cremin, *American Education: The Metropolitan Experience, 1876–1980* (New York: Harper and Row, 1988), pp. 166 and 169 (first quotations); Nelson, *Good Schools,* pp. 23, 35, and 71 (last quotation).

11. Nelson, *Good Schools*, p. 51.

12. Richard C. Berner, *Seattle 1900–1920: From Boomtown, Urban Turbulence, to Restoration*, vol. 1, *Seattle in the 20th Century* (Seattle: Charles Press, 1991), p. 61.

13. Alma Wilson Jackson, interview by author, May 7, 1997.

14. Seattle School District (SSD) directory, 1902–3; Janice L. Reiff, "Urbanization and the Social Structure: Seattle, Washington, 1852–1910," PhD diss. (University of Washington, 1981), p. 81.

15. Wilson Jackson interview.

16. School board minutes, April 22, 1932, SSD, Record 28, p. 245 (quotation), Seattle Public Schools (SPS) Archives; Doris Chargois Hahn, interview by author, May 3, 1997; Wilson Jackson interview.

17. Reiff, "Urbanization," abstract, unnumbered page (quotations). Reiff says that where documentation is possible, usually seven to thirteen years passed before immigrants to the United States arrived in Seattle, p. 117.

18. Ibid., p. 3.

19. Charles M. Gates, *The First Century at the University of Washington, 1861–1961* (Seattle: University of Washington Press, 1961), p. 13; Reiff, "Urbanization," p. 35.

20. Reiff, "Urbanization," pp. 63 (quotations) and 107.

21. Adelaide Pollock, "The Early Administrative Women in Education of Seattle, Washington" (typescript, 1932), p. 6, Seattle Public Library; *Seattle Grade Club Magazine*, March 1923, pp. 12 and 13 (quotation).

22. Seattle city directory, 1898; SSD records, Micro-C.

23. SSD records, Micro-M.

24. Ibid., Micro-N.

25. Nelson, *Good Schools*, p. 143 (quotation).

26. Ledger of the Primary Teachers' Association, pp. 7–9, Seattle Education Association Archives.

27. Ledger of the Primary Teachers' Association, pp. 9–11.

28. Ibid., pp. 12–15.

29. SSD directories, 1902–3 and 1909–10.

1 / NEW CENTURY, NEW CITY, NEW SCHOOLS

1. Janice L. Reiff, "Urbanization and the Social Structure: Seattle, Washington, 1852–1910," PhD diss. (University of Washington, 1981), pp. 85, 260, and 261 (first and second quotations); Frederick M. Padelford, "The Community," Uni-

versity Congregational Church Fiftieth Anniversary Program, 1941 (third quotation), University Congregational Church archives.

2. Reiff, "Urbanization," pp. 60 and 84; Richard C. Berner, *Seattle 1900–1920: From Boomtown, Urban Turbulence, to Restoration*, vol. 1, *Seattle in the 20th Century* (Seattle: Charles Press, 1991), p. 62.

3. Reiff, "Urbanization," pp. 83 (first quotation) and 84; Berner, vol. 1, p. 14.

4. Reiff, "Urbanization," p. 210; Berner, vol. 1, p. 61. First Hill is now home to the region's hospitals and medical complexes.

5. Florence Soderback Byers, interview by author, February 11, 1997; SSD records, Micro-M and A-96-9-B.

6. Roger Sale, *Seattle Past to Present* (Seattle: University of Washington Press, 1976), pp. 55 (first quotation) and 60 (second quotation).

7. Reiff, "Urbanization," pp. 5, 210, 212, and 215.

8. Ibid., p. 3; Berner, vol. 1, pp. 60, 61, and 62 (quotation).

9. Howard Droker, "Seattle's Jewish Neighborhoods" (typescript, ca. 1998), pp. 1 (first quotation) and 14 (second quotation), copy in Pieroth's possession. For a complete discussion of the neighborhoods, see Molly Cone, Howard Droker, and Jacqueline Williams, *Family of Strangers: Building a Jewish Community in Washington State* (Seattle: University of Washington Press, 2003).

10. Calvin F. Schmid and Wayne McVey, *Growth and Distribution of Minority Races in Seattle, Washington* (Seattle: Seattle Public Schools, 1964), pp. 14 and 15; Calvin F. Schmid and Vincent A. Miller, *Population Trends and Educational Change in the State of Washington* (Seattle: Washington State Census Board, 1960), p. 97; Richard C. Berner, untitled typescript (ca. 1996), copy in Pieroth's possession.

11. Esther Hall Mumford, *Seattle's Black Victorians, 1852–1901* (Seattle: Ananse Press, 1980), pp. 10, 11, and 12.

12. Ibid., pp. 10, 11, 12, 108, 110, 116, 117 (quotation), and 140; Berner, vol. 1, p. 76. For a good understanding of these years, see Horace Cayton, Jr., *Long Old Road: An Autobiography* (Seattle: University of Washington Press, 1970).

13. Florence Adams and Grant Colton, "Seattle's First High School," in "Principals' Exchange," March 1939, p. 13, SPS Archives.

14. Reuben Jones, "How the High Schools Grew," ibid., p. 15.

15. Nancy Hoffman, *Woman's True Profession* (Old Westbury, Conn.: Feminist Press, 1981), pp. xx and xxii (quotations); SSD directory, 1902–3.

16. Frank Cooper, "Twenty-One Years in the Seattle Schools," *Seattle Grade Club Magazine*, March 1923, p. 15; SSD directories, 1902–3 and 1909–10.

17. Cooper, "Twenty-One Years," p. 15.

18. SSD directory, 1909–10.

19. Reiff, "Urbanization," p. 114; John L. Rury, "Who Became Teachers? The Social Characteristics of Teachers in American History," in *American Teachers: Histories of a Profession at Work*, ed. Donald Warren (New York: Macmillan Publishing Co., 1989), p. 33 (quotation).

20. Statistics compiled by author from data in personnel records of 700 women who taught in the Seattle Public Schools at some time between 1919 and 1941—541 grade teachers and 159 high school teachers.

21. SSD records, A-96-9-A. The school district closed Webster School in the 1980s; the building now houses the Nordic Heritage Museum.

22. Ibid., Micro-A.

23. Ibid., Micro-D (second quotation); Janet Powell Tourtelotte, "Powell Family History" (1967), copy in Pieroth's possession (first quotation).

24. SSD records, Micro-K.

25. Ibid., Micro-B; SSD directories, 1915–16 and 1918–19. Greek was dropped from the curriculum in 1916.

26. SSD records, Micro-P.

27. Ibid., Micro-N.

28. Ibid., Micro-M.

29. Henry Landes, "Forward," *Mountaineer*, March 1907, n. p. (quotation); Berner, vol. 1, p. 98. Bailey and Nettleton's long affiliations with the Mountaineers will be discussed in a later chapter.

30. School board minutes, August 26, 1909, SSD Record 8, p. 153.

31. Reiff, "Urbanization," pp. 87 and 3 (quotation).

32. *Annual Report of the Seattle Public Schools*, 1909–10, p. 37 (hereafter cited as SSD, *Annual Report*).

33. Berner, vol. 1, pp. 83 and 106; Sale, *Seattle Past to Present*, p. 83; Seattle Board of Park Commissioners, *First Annual Report, 1884–1904*, pp. 5, 57–66.

34. Doris Pieroth, "No Constitutional Mandate," *Columbia* (Summer 1989).

35. Gary L. Geiger, "Adele Parker: The Case Study of a Woman in the Progressive Era," Master's thesis (Western Washington University, 1979), p. 6; Pieroth statistics. Miss Parker's sister, Maud Parker, M.D., ran unsuccessfully for the Seattle School Board in 1911.

36. Wilbert Nuetzmann, interview by author, June 19, 1998.

37. Berner, vol. 1, pp. 88–90.

38. Ibid., pp. 90–95.

39. Sale, *Seattle Past to Present*, pp. 158–59.

40. SSD records, Micro-J; Sara Luch, interview by author, February 19, 1998.

41. SSD, *Annual Report*, 1909–10, p. 23.

42. Ibid., p. 27 (quotation); Bryce Nelson, *Good Schools: The Seattle Public School System, 1901–1930* (Seattle: University of Washington Press, 1988), p. 94.

43. SSD, *Annual Report*, 1909–10, pp. 26 (first quotation) and 27 (second quotation); Nelson, *Good Schools*, p. 30 (last quotation).

44. SSD, *Annual Report*, 1909–10, pp. 30–31 (quotation); Margaret Houston, interview by author, February 7, 2000.

45. SSD, *Annual Report*, 1909–10, p. 30.

46. Ibid., 1915–16, p. 135.

47. School board minutes, May 26, 1909, SSD Record 8, p. 105 and October 2, 1911, SSD Record 9, p. 188 (quotation); Nelson, *Good Schools*, pp. 54–55.

48. Grade Teachers' Club meeting minutes, October 13, 1913, Grade Club Ledger, p. 34, Seattle Education Association (SEA) Archives; School board minutes, May 26, 1909, SSD Record 8, p. 105, October 2, 1911, SSD Record 9, p. 188 (quotations); Nelson, *Good Schools*, pp. 54–55.

49. Arthur C. Perry, Jr., *The Status of the Teacher* (New York: Houghton Mifflin, 1912), p. 54.

50. SSD records, Micro-M.

51. Ibid., Micro-A and -B (quotations); Nelson, *Good Schools*, p. 49. SSD microfilm records do not contain correspondence, hence the supposition regarding letters of recommendation.

52. School board minutes, May 23, 1917, SSD Record 13, p. 350, and December 20, 1918, SSD Record 15, p. 211.

53. Nelson, *Good Schools*, pp. 77 (quotation) and 50.

54. Nard Jones, *Seattle* (New York: Doubleday, 1972), p. 191 (first quotation); school board minutes, September 17, 1913, SSD Record 10, p. 352.

55. Pieroth statistics; SSD records, A-96-9-F.

56. Nelson, *Good Schools*, p. 71 (first quotation); Broadway High School *Sealth*, 1924; School board minutes, May 14, 1913, SSD Record 10, p. 233 (quotation).

57. Nelson, *Good Schools*, p. 43; Frank Cooper to board, February 13, 1920, SSD records, Superintendent's files, Girls Advisers; school board minutes, February 10, 1915, SSD Record 11, p. 389, February 26, 1915, SSD Record 12, p. 5, and May 7, 1915, SSD Record 12, p. 54.

58. SSD, *Annual Report*, 1915–16, p. 119.

59. Berner, vol. 1, pp. 106 and 136 (quotation).

60. School board minutes, September 8, 1914, SSD Record 11, p. 269.

61. Nard Jones, *Seattle*, p. 203.

62. School board minutes, May 8, 1915, SSD Record 12, p. 14 (first quotation); Nelson, *Good Schools*, p. 49 (second quotation).

63. Nelson, *Good Schools*, p. 116 n. 16; Cooper to board, June 7, 1917, SSD records, Superintendent's files, E28, Retirement Fund (quotation).

64. Cooper to board, June 7, 1917, SSD records, Superintendent's files, E28, Retirement Fund.

65. SSD records, Micro-F.

66. Ibid., Micro-A, -B.

67. Pieroth statistics—all percentages based on SSD records.

68. Adelaide Pollock, "Early Administrative Women," pp. 10 and 15; SSD records, Micro-G.

69. Stephanie Ogle, "Anna Louise Strong," *Notable American Women: The Modern Period* (Cambridge, Mass.: Belknap Press, 1980), p. 664.

70. *Seattle Times* editorial, December 2, 1917 (quotation).

71. Berner, vol. 1, p. 231; Sale, *Seattle Past to Present*, p. 122.

72. Berner, vol. 1, p. 231.

73. School board minutes, March 7, 1918, SSD Record 14, p. 309 (quotation) and April 22, 1918, SSD Record 14, p. 323.

74. Ibid., December 7, 1914, SSD Record 11, p. 334 and May 29, 1918, SSD Record 14, p. 388.

75. Ibid., August 16, 1917–January 4, 1918, SSD Record 14, p. 234; Nelson, *Good Schools*, p. 124.

76. Berner, vol. 1, p. 213.

77. Pollock, "Early Administrative Women," p. 16.

78. *Seattle Times*, January 9, 1966, and November 3, 1975.

79. School board minutes, June 6, 1919, SSD Record 15, p. 358 (quotation); SSD records, Micro-J.

80. Mountaineers, *Bulletin*, January 1918 (quotation); Grade Teachers' Club minutes, April 24, 1917.

81. Ellen Dabney to Cooper, September 28, 1917, SSD records, Superintendent's files, E27; West Seattle High School Scrapbook, SPS Archives.

82. Mary Desimone, interview by author, April 10, 1998 (quotation); School board minutes, October 6, 1915, SSD Record 11, p. 178 (second quotation); Nelson, *Good Schools*, p. 111; and former student interviews.

83. SSD records, Micro-T.

84. Ibid., Micro-H (first quotation); Joanne Youngblood, interview by author, April 8, 1998 (other quotations).

85. School board minutes, November 5, 1920, SSD Record 17, p. 161.

86. Author's interviews with former students and her own recollections.

87. Berner, vol. 1, pp. 234–53 and 285–300, p. 286 (quotation). For accounts of the Seattle General Strike, see also Robert L. Friedheim, *The Seattle General Strike* (Seattle: University of Washington Press, 1964), and Harvey O'Connor, *Revolution in Seattle: A Memoir* (New York: Monthly Review Press, 1964).

88. Berner, vol. 1, p. 291; SSD Record 15, pp. 248–58; Cooper to the board, February 7, 1919 (quotations), SSD records, Superintendent's files.

89. Nelson, *Good Schools*, pp. 130 and 131 (quotations).

90. For an excellent account of the case, see Keith A. Murray, "The Charles Niederhauser Case: Patriotism in the Seattle Schools, 1919" *Pacific Northwest Quarterly* 74, no. 1 (January 1983), pp. 11–17.

91. School board minutes, March 14, 1919, SSD Record 15, p. 284.

92. Richard Berner, *Seattle 1921–1940: From Boom to Bust*, vol. 2, *Seattle in the 20th Century* (Seattle: Charles Press, 1992), pp. 41 and 56.

93. Nelson, *Good Schools*, pp. 150 and 154.

94. School board minutes, May 24, 1921, SSD Record 17, pp. 416, 417 (quotations), and 418. For a detailed account of the taxation and ideological struggles, see Nelson's *Good Schools*, chapter 9, "Doing Less with Less, 1920–22."

95. School board minutes, March 3, 1922, SSD Record 17, p. 293.

96. Nelson, *Good Schools*, pp. 162, 164, and 165.

2 / 1920 AND BEYOND

1. Bryce Nelson, *Good Schools: The Seattle Public School System, 1901–1930* (Seattle: University of Washington Press, 1988), p. 50.

2. Richard Berner, *Seattle 1921–1940: From Boom to Bust*, vol. 2, *Seattle in the 20th Century* (Seattle: Charles Press, 1992), pp. 247–52 and 261–64; Ralph Bushnell Potts, *Seattle Heritage* (Seattle: Superior Publishing Company, 1955), p. 84.

3. Doris H. Pieroth, "Bertha Knight Landes: The Woman Who Was Mayor," in *Women in Pacific Northwest History,* ed. Karen J. Blair (Seattle: University of Washington Press, 2001), pp. 144–51.

4. Roger Sale, *Seattle Past to Present* (Seattle: University of Washington Press, 1976), pp. 140–41.

5. Susan Ware, *Holding Their Own: American Women in the 1930s* (Boston: Twayne Publishers, 1982), p. 72; Patricia A. Schmuck, "Women School Employees in the United States," in *Women Educators: Employees of Schools in Western Countries,* ed. Patricia Schmuck (Albany: State University of New York Press, 1987), pp. 77 and 79 (quotation); Geraldine Clifford, "Man/Woman/Teacher: Gender, Family and Career in American Educational History," in *American Teachers: Histories of a Profession at Work,* ed. Donald Warren (New York: Macmillan Publishing Co., 1989), pp. 308 and 309; Seattle percentages calculated from Pieroth statistics.

6. Velma Laccoarce to Thomas Cole, January 15, 1926, SSD records, A-96-9-L.

7. SSD records, A-96-9-D.

8. George E. Craig to Cole, May 6, 1927, SSD records, A-96-9-L.

9. Estelle Erickson to Cole, March 25, 1925 (quotation) and to Kenneth Selby, June 14, 1946, SSD records, A-96-9-F. Howard E. Erickson was soon named a principal and had a long career in the Seattle district.

10. Kathleen Weiler, *Country Schoolwomen: Teaching in Rural California, 1850–1950* (Stanford: Stanford University Press, 1998), p. 176 (first quotation); Geraldine J. Clifford, "Man/Woman/Teacher," p. 304 (second quotation).

11. Herman Pfeifer, "A Study of Teacher Supply and Demand in the State of Washington," Master's thesis (University of Washington, 1929).

12. SSD records, A-96-9-O.

13. Ibid.

14. School board minutes, January 23, 1925, SSD Record 21, p. 197; Nelson, *Good Schools,* pp. 166 and 167. See also Nelson's chapter 10, "The Triumph of Efficiency, 1922–30."

15. *Seattle Grade Club Magazine,* October 1923, p. 11.

16. Marion McMaster to Samuel Fleming, February 14, 1927, SSD records, A-96-9-M.

17. McMaster to Fleming, February 14, 1927 (first quotation), and May 26, 1936 (second quotation), ibid.

18. *Recent Social Trends in the United States,* vol. 1 (1933; rpt. Westport, Conn.: Greenwood Press, 1980), p. xlvii; *Grade Club Magazine,* May 1928, p. 27 (quotation).

19. *Grade Club Magazine*, October 1922, p. 10.

20. School board minutes, February 23, 1923, SSD Record 19, p. 246.

21. Pieroth statistics.

22. SSD records, A-96-9-B.

23. Ibid.

24. Ibid., A-96-9-K; Dorothy Kwapil, interview by author, April 9, 1997.

25. *Triennial Report of the Public Schools, Seattle, Washington*, 1927–30, p. 119.

26. Francis Neal Morris, "A History of Teacher Unionism in the State of Washington, 1920–45," Master's thesis (University of Washington, 1968), p. 33.

27. School board minutes, April 19, 1929, SSD Record 25, p. 273.

28. SSD directory, 1923–24.

29. Douglas R. Pullen, "The Administration of Washington State Governor Louis F. Hart, 1919–25," PhD diss. (University of Washington, 1974), pp. 204–6.

30. Roland Hartley to Senator Wesley Jones, January 2, 1931, Jones Papers, Box 25, University of Washington Libraries; Bruce D. Blumell, *The Development of Public Assistance in the State of Washington during the Great Depression* (New York: Garland Publishing, 1984), pp. 36 and 37.

31. William H. Mullins, *The Depression and the Urban West Coast, 1929–1933: Los Angeles, San Francisco, Seattle, and Portland* (Bloomington: Indiana University Press, 1991), p. 107.

32. *Washington Public Documents*, 1933–34, vol. 1, pp. 9–17.

33. Ibid., pp. 24 and 25.

34. Blumell, *Public Assistance*, pp. 65 and 66.

35. School board minutes, October 30, 1931, SSD Record 28, p. 108; Dominic Moreo, *Schools in the Great Depression* (New York: Garland Publishing, 1996), p. 172.

36. SSD records, Micro-M.

37. Ibid., A-96-9-O.

38. *Seattle Educational Bulletin*, October 1939, p. 1.

39. Wilbert Nuetzmann, interview by author, June 19, 1998 (first quotation); Gladys Perry, interview by author, January 28, 1997 (second quotation).

40. *Grade Club Magazine*, January 1932, p. 1.

41. SSD, *Financial and Statistical Report*, June 30, 1932, p. 4.

42. Mullins, *Depression and the Urban West Coast*, p. 121.

43. Perry interview.

44. Thelma Chisholm, interview by author, March 6, 1998.

45. Sale, *Seattle Past to Present*, pp. 149 (quotation), 150–52; Berner, vol. 2, pp. 256–64.

46. Pieroth statistics.

47. SSD records, A-96-9-D.

48. Substitute application, August 22, 1932 (quotation), Worth McClure to Iva Trenholme, April 10, 1944, SSD records, A-96-9-T.

49. School board minutes, September 25, 1935, SSD Record 32, p. 68.

50. SSD records, A-96-9-S.

51. SSD directories, 1919–41.

52. School board minutes, March 14, 1941, SSD Record 37, p. 257.

53. Ibid., June 13, 1939, SSD Record 35, pp. 377 and 378.

54. *Washington Public Documents*, 1933–34, vol. 1, p. 17; Clarence Martin to F. C. Harrington, WPA commissioner, November 8, 1939, Martin Papers, Box 35, Washington State Archives, Olympia.

55. SSD records, A-96-9-T.

56. School board minutes, December 3, 1937, SSD Record 34, p. 125.

57. *Seattle Educational Bulletin*, November 1938, p. 2 (quotation).

58. *Seattle Times* and Seattle *Post-Intelligencer*, December 8, 1941; personal recollection of the present writer and numerous interviewees.

59. *Seattle Schools*, vol. 18 (Seattle: Seattle Public Schools, January 1942), p. 3.

60. Ibid., p. 1.

61. *Seattle Times*, October 6, 1974 (first quotation); student writings, Ella Evanson Papers, University of Washington Libraries.

62. Sally Kazama, interview by author, March 19, 1998.

63. Margaret Houston, interview by author, February 10, 1998 (first two quotations); Florence Byers, interview by author, February 11, 1997.

64. Mary Heaton Ingalls, interview by author, June 19, 1998.

65. Chisholm interview; Sara Luch, interview by author, February 19, 1997.

66. Pieroth statistics.

67. School board minutes, May 8 and 29, 1942, SSD Record 38, pp. 300 and 327 (quotation); Chisholm interview; copy of Frankie Close Schmitz's report, August 20, 1943, in Pieroth's possession.

68. Richard Birchfield, interview by author, April 2, 1998; Chisholm interview (quotation).

69. Arthur Gravrock, interview by author, April 2, 1997. Gravrock served as High Point's first principal.

70. Lois Potter to E. W. Campbell, August 10, 1943, and to Lyle Stewart, May 14, 1956 (quotation), SSD records, A-96-9-T.

71. Joan Waldo, Sylvia Tupper, and Mary Bordner (quotation), interview by author, May 6, 1998.

72. SSD records, A-96-9-C.

73. Ibid., Micro-S.

74. Ibid., Micro-W.

75. Ibid., A-96-9-G.

76. For discussion of Seattle's demographic changes, see Quintard Taylor, *The Forging of a Black Community: Seattle's Central District from 1870 through the Civil Rights Era* (Seattle: University of Washington Press, 1994), especially pp. 209–16 on schools, and Doris H. Pieroth, "Desegregating the Public Schools: Seattle, Washington, 1954–68," PhD diss. (University of Washington, 1979).

77. SSD Record 52, p. 315; Frances Owen, interview by author, January 10, 1973.

3 / QUALITY OF LIFE

1. *Seattle Grade Club Magazine,* October 1920, p. 16.

2. Ibid., p. 17.

3. Frances A. Sheridan, "Apartment House Development on Seattle's Queen Anne Hill Prior to World War II," Master's thesis (University of Washington, 1994), pp. 46–48.

4. Seattle *Post-Intelligencer* (hereafter cited as *P-I*), September 1891, quoted in Kay F. Reinartz, *Queen Anne: Community on the Hill* (Seattle: Queen Anne Historical Society, 1993), p. 74.

5. School board minutes, September 17, 1913, SSD Record 10, p. 352; Sheridan, "Apartment House Development," p. 48 (quotations).

6. Sheridan, "Apartment House Development," p. 48. The Lincoln flourished until fire destroyed it in the 1920s, but the Sorrento has existed as a posh hostelry into the twenty-first century.

7. SSD directories. The 1918–19 directory is the last to list teacher addresses.

8. *Grade Club Magazine,* May 1928, p. 34 (quotation); *Seattle Times,* July 2, 2000; Norman S. Haynor, *Hotel Life* (Chapel Hill: University of North Carolina Press, 1936), p. 35. The historian Paul Dorpat reports that at the end of the century the Frye Hotel became part of the city's low income housing stock, with the "marble grandeur of its main floor" restored.

9. Haynor, *Hotel Life*, p. 62.

10. Seattle *P-I*, October 7, 1910 (first quotation); *1913–1914 Washington Gazetteer* (re: Clark Hotel); Gladys Perry, interview by author, January 28, 1997 (quotation); Paul Groth, *Living Downtown: The History of Residential Hotels in the United States* (Berkeley: University of California Press, 1994), p. 62 (last quotation).

11. Groth, *Living Downtown*, pp. 69–72.

12. Haynor, *Hotel Life*, pp. 71 and 72.

13. Groth, *Living Downtown*, p. 63.

14. Doris Chargois Hahn, interview by author, May 3, 1997.

15. Haynor, *Hotel Life*, pp. 98 and 99; SSD directories, 1918–38; Seattle city directories, 1920 and 1930.

16. Perry interview; Roger Sale, *Seattle Past to Present* (Seattle: University of Washington Press, 1976), p. 58.

17. Groth, *Living Downtown*, p. 84; Claremont Hotel brochure, ca. 1934, copy in Pieroth's possession (quotation).

18. Sheridan, "Apartment House Development," pp. 31–32, 52–53, 55, and 83; Lawrence Kreisman, *Made to Last: Historic Preservation in Seattle and King County* (Seattle: University of Washington Press, 1999), p. 55.

19. SSD directories.

20. Ann Sandstrom, interview by author, March 20, 1998.

21. Jennie Carton, "This Old Condo," Windermere Realty publication, number 5, copy in Pieroth's possession.

22. *Grade Club Magazine*, October 1932, p. 39.

23. Jennie Carton, "This Old Condo," number 6, copy in Pieroth's possession.

24. SSD directories, 1918–41; Seattle city directories, 1920 and 1969.

25. Ibid., 1909–10, 1914–15, and 1918–19.

26. Ibid., 1909–10 and 1918–19.

27. SSD records, A-96-9-S; SSD directories, 1910–41; Seattle city directories, 1901, 1930–47, and 1998.

28. Margaret Houston, interview by author, February 10, 1998.

29. SSD records, Micro-A; SSD directories, 1907–41; *Grade Club Magazine*, June 1926, p. 46.

30. Jeanne DeFriel Gardiner, interview by author, May 14, 1998 (quotation); Puget Sound Traction Company map, Special Collections, University of Washington Libraries.

31. DeFriel Gardiner interview; SSD directories, 1915–16 and 1918–19.

32. *Grade Club Magazine,* February 1922, p. 18; SSD records, A-96-9-H; SSD directories, 1902–33.

33. SSD records, Micro-M and A-96-9-K; SSD directories, 1902–18; *Grade Club Magazine,* March 1922, p. 30.

34. Frank Willard to Grace McCauley and Myrtle Kiger, June 20, 1940, and principal's evaluation, May 25, 1931, SSD records, A-96-9-K; *Seattle Times,* July 27, 1960.

35. Lynn Dumenil, "Re-Shifting Perspectives on the 1920s," in *Calvin Coolidge and the Coolidge Era,* ed. John Earl Haynes (Washington, D.C.: Library of Congress, 1998), p. 86 (first two quotations); Sandstrom interview (third quotation); Mary Desimone, interview by author, April 10, 1998.

36. Virginia Scharff, *Taking the Wheel: Women and the Coming of the Motor Age* (New York: Free Press, 1991), pp. 102–108.

37. James J. Flink, *The Car Culture* (Cambridge: Massachusetts Institute of Technology Press, 1975), p. 243.

38. Ibid., p. 171.

39. Scharff, *Taking the Wheel,* pp. 114 and 115 (quotation); Flink, *The Car Culture,* p. 173.

40. *Grade Club Magazine,* March 1931, p. 45.

41. Ibid., May 1934, pp. 15 and 24, and October 1934, *passim.*

42. School board minutes, September 5, 1924, SSD Record 21, p. 44.

43. Phoebe Gilbert, interview by author, October 15, 1997 (quotation); Richard Birchfield, interview by author, April 2, 1998.

44. Perry interview.

45. Sara Luch, interview by author, February 19, 1997.

46. *Grade Club Magazine,* March 1925, p. 44.

47. Ibid., March 1925, p. 44.

48. Perry interview; Nard Jones, *Seattle* (New York: Doubleday, 1972), p. 195 (quotation); Birchfield interview.

49. Seattle *P-I,* March 3, 1924, November 22, 1924, April 30, 1928, and January 9, 1937.

50. Edith Davidson to Virgil Smith, March 25, 1946, SSD records, A-96-9-D.

51. For a telling, delightful account of a teacher's 1917 experience in a one-room school, see "Sagebrush Schoolmarm" in *Washington Schools in the Good Old Days,* ed. Zita Lichtenberg (Olympia: Office of the State Superintendent of Public Instruction, 1969).

52. Jeffrey Ochsner, "Architecture for Seattle Schools, 1880–1900," *Pacific Northwest Quarterly* 83, no. 3 (October 1992), p. 129.

53. Ibid., p. 131.

54. Seattle Public Schools, *School Histories* (Seattle, 1951), n. pag.; SSD directories, 1902–40.

55. Grade Teachers' Club minutes, February 25, May 27, and October 13, 1913, and April 23, 1914, Grade Club Ledger, Seattle Education Association (SEA) Archives.

56. School board minutes, June 6, 1919, SSD Record 15, p. 371 and October 24, 1924, SSD Record 21.

57. School board minutes, January 11, 1911, SSD Record 9, p. 6; *Grade Club Magazine*, May 1935, p. 24.

58. School board minutes, March 9, 1914, SSD Record 11, p. 92, May 7, 1915, SSD Record 12, p. 54, February 8, 1915, SSD Record 11, p. 384, and November 17, 1917, SSD Record 14, p. 177.

59. Ibid., January 11, 1911, SSD Record 9, p. 6 (first quotation), January 27, 1911, SSD Record 9, p. 11 (second quotation), and August 22, 1922, SSD Record 19, p. 90.

60. Ibid., January 6, 1915, SSD Record 11, p. 359 (first quotation); Dominic W. Moreo, *Schools in the Great Depression* (New York: Garland Publishing, 1996), pp. 83 (editorial quotation) and 93 (last quotation).

61. School board minutes, January 9, 1911, SSD Record 9, p. 3 and January 24, 1915, SSD Record 11, p. 372 (first quotation); Willard to board, December 15, 1915, SSD records, Superintendent's files, E27 (second quotation).

62. "Report on Lighting of School Buildings," December 15, 1915, SSD records, Superintendent's files, E27.

63. Ibid.

64. School board minutes, October 18, 1916, SSD Record 13, p. 135 (first quotation), March 28, 1917, SSD Record 13, p. 288 (second quotation), and December 16, 1921, SSD Record 17, p. 207.

65. Ibid., January 16, 1917, SSD Record 13, p. 251.

66. Nelson, *Good Schools*, p. 60 (first quotation); school board minutes, December 29, 1917, SSD Record 14, p. 227, June 25, 1918, SSD Record 14, p. 34 (second quotation); Grade Teachers' Club minutes, May 21, 1919, p. 24 (last quotation).

67. School board minutes, January 23, 1920, SSD Record 16, p. 255 (first

quotation); Wilbert Nuetzmann, interview by author, June 19, 1998 (second quotation).

68. Paul Dorpat, *Seattle Now and Then,* vol. 2 [Seattle, ca. 1986], features 54 and 55; Helen Hamilton, interview by author, April 14, 1998.

69. SSD records, A-96-9-A; SSD directories, 1917–40; Seattle city directories, 1917–40.

70. SSD directories, 1918–40; Seattle city directories, 1918–40.

71. SSD records, Micro-C; SSD directories, 1919–40; Seattle city directories, 1919–40.

72. SSD directories, 1918–40; Seattle city directories, 1918–40.

73. SSD records, Micro-H; SSD directories, 1913–40; Seattle city directories, 1913–40.

74. *Grade Club Magazine,* May 1931, p. 44.

4 / PERPETUATING THE SEATTLE WAY

1. Gladys Perry, interview by author, January 28, 1997, and Wilbert Nuetzmann, interview by author, June 19, 1998 (quotation).

2. School board minutes, May 23, 1917, SSD Record 13, p. 349.

3. Ibid., September 7, 1917, SSD Record 14, p. 58; SSD directories, 1918–41.

4. School board minutes, October 23, 1918, SSD Record 15, p. 160; SSD directories, 1918–41.

5. Mary Grupe to Thomas Cole, May 2, 1923 (first quotation), SSD records, A-96-9-T; SSD records, A-96-9-M (second quotation); Cornelia Jenner to Almina George, March 22, 1927, SSD records, A-96-9-L.

6. Jenner to George, March 20, 1926, SSD records, A-96-9-S.

7. Ibid.

8. SSD directories, 1926–45; Emerson supervisor evaluation, November 12, 1926, and Minor principal evaluation, November 13, 1928, SSD records, A-96-9-S.

9. SSD records, A-96-9-W.

10. Pieroth statistics.

11. Marguerite Siggelko to Worth McClure, February 17, 1936, SSD records, A-96-9-S.

12. *Triennial Report of the Public Schools, Seattle, Washington,* 1927–30, pp. 35 and 36 (hereafter cited as SSD, *Triennial Report*).

13. Amelia Telban, interview by Olaf Kvamme, July 18, 1989, tape and transcript in Pieroth's possession.

14. Ibid.

15. SSD, *Triennial Report*, 1927–30, p. 34.

16. Nuetzmann interview.

17. Perry interview.

18. Ibid.

19. *Educational Secretary* 13 (February 1966), p. 1.

20. SSD records, A-96-9-S.

21. Ibid. The present writer has fond memories of Miss Doris Patrick, the wonderful red-haired first-grade teacher who taught her to read and write.

22. Copeland to Cooper, May 4, 1922, SSD records A-96-9-D (first quotation); Allen Dale, "The Little Red School House Grows Up," *Town Crier* 30 (March 1935), pp. 12–13.

23. *Seattle Grade Club Magazine*, October 1926, p. 34.

24. SSD directories, 1918–41; SSD records, Micro-L.

25. School board minutes, May 24, 1918, SSD Record 14, p. 382; SSD records, Micro-L.

26. SSD records, Micro-H; interviews with former teachers and cadets.

27. Nuetzmann interview.

28. Margaret Houston, interview by author, February 10, 1998.

29. SSD records, A-96-9-W.

30. Helen Reynolds to Frank Cooper, May 19, 1922, ibid., A-96-9-S.

31. Bertha King to Reynolds, May 20, 1941, ibid., A-96-9-V.

32. Helen Roberts to Virgil Smith, April 1, 1941 (quotation), ibid., A-96-9-R.

33. Houston interview.

34. Cecil Dryden, *Light for an Empire: The Story of Eastern Washington State College* (Spokane: Eastern Washington State College, 1965), pp. 99 and 100; *Washington State Normal School at Ellensburg Catalog*, 1920, p. 20.

35. Dryden, *Light for an Empire*, p. 99; *Washington State Normal School at Ellensburg Catalog*, 1904, p. 20, and 1925, pp. 22–28.

36. Arthur C. Hicks, *Western at 75* (Bellingham: Western Washington State College Foundation, 1974), p. 35.

37. Dryden, *Light for an Empire*, pp. 181, 182, and 185; Hicks, *Western at 75*, p. 47 (quotation).

38. Mary Heaton Ingalls, interview by author, June 18, 1998.

39. SSD directories, 1937–38 and 1940–41; *Seattle Education Bulletin,* October 1936, p. 1.

40. School board minutes, April 7, 1926, SSD Record 22, p. 311 (quotations); SSD, *Triennial Report,* 1924–27, p. 58.

41. SSD, *Triennial Report,* 1924–27, p. 58.

42. SSD directories, 1918–41; school board minutes, August 10, 1929, SSD Record 26, p. 50.

43. Ida Vetting, "The Seward Demonstration School," *Grade Club Magazine,* December 1931, p. 17.

44. Telban, in Kvamme interview; SSD, *Triennial Report,* 1924–27, p. 59 (second quotation); *Seattle Education Bulletin,* December 1926, p. 1; school board minutes, December 13, 1929, SSD Record 26, p. 178.

45. SSD, *Triennial Report,* 1924–27, p. 60 (quotations) and 61.

46. Ibid., p. 59 (first quotation); Nuetzmann interview (second quotation).

47. Houston interview. Some students from the 1930s recall teachers rehearsing their lessons the day before presenting them in demonstration.

48. Perry interview.

49. SSD records, Micro-M.

50. Ibid., Micro-T.

51. Nuetzmann interview.

5 / PRINCIPALS

1. SSD directories, 1919–41.

2. Wilbert Nuetzmann, interview by author, June 19, 1998. No Seattle secondary school had a woman principal until 1978, when Roberta Byrd Barr was named principal of Lincoln High School.

3. Margaret Gribskov, "Adelaide Pollock and the Founding of the NCAWE," in *Women Educators: Employees of Schools in Western Countries,* ed. Patricia A. Schmuck (Albany: State University of New York Press, 1987), pp. 127–33.

4. SSD directory, 1903–4; Margaret Gribskov, "Adelaide Pollock and the NCAWE," p. 133.

5. School board minutes, August 9, 1940, SSD Record 37, p. 47; SSD directories, 1930–40; Seattle Public Schools, *School Histories* (Seattle, 1951), n. pag.

6. Adelaide Pollock, "The Early Administrative Women in Education of Seattle, Washington" (typescript, 1932), Seattle Public Library; Margaret Gribskov, "Adelaide Pollock and the NCAWE," p. 134.

7. *Triennial Report of the Public Schools, Seattle, Washington*, 1927–30, p. 113 (quotation) (hereafter cited as SSD *Triennial Report*); "Principals' Exchange," June 10, 1937, SPS Archives.

8. SSD *Triennial Report*, 1924–27, p. 81.

9. Ibid., p. 82.

10. SSD records, Micro-G; school board minutes, August 28, 1936, SSD Record 33, p. 46. The name of Lake School soon changed to McGilvra.

11. School board minutes, May 6 (quotation) and May 24, 1921, SSD Record 17, pp. 383 and 416.

12. Jessie How, interview by Joan Coffey, February 19, 1990, transcript in Pieroth's possession (quotations); SSD records, Micro-N and others, for examples of evaluations.

13. How, in Coffey interview.

14. Ibid. (first quotation); Constance Pitter Thomas, interview by Marcia Greenlee, August 17, 1977, transcript in Black Women's Oral History Project file, Special Collections, University of Washington Libraries (second and third quotations); Maxine Pitter Haynes, interview by author, May 12, 1998.

15. How, in Coffey interview (first quotation); school board minutes, June 9, 1933, SSD Record 29, p. 348 (second quotation).

16. School board minutes, August 28, 1936, SSD Record 33, p. 46. By the time Annie Gifford retired, the Longfellow building had grown to twenty rooms; five years later it became Edmund Meany Junior High.

17. SSD records, Micro-K; SSD directories, 1902–40.

18. SSD directories 1910–19 and Seattle city directories, 1920–40.

19. Mary Desimone, interview by author, April 10, 1998.

20. Ibid.

21. Ibid.

22. Joseph Patricelli, interview by author, December 31, 1999.

23. Horace Cayton, Jr., *Long Old Road: An Autobiography* (Seattle: University of Washington Press, 1970), p. 28.

24. Eva Ott to Frank Cooper, July 21, 1920, and Anna Kane evaluations, February 19, 1920, November 17, 1929, and March 1930, SSD records, A-96-9-O and -W.

25. Evaluation dated December 18, 1939, SSD records, A-96-9-T.

26. School board minutes, June 14, 1940, SSD Record 36, p. 365; re: closure of Rainier School, Seattle Public Schools, *School Histories*, n. pag.

27. SSD records, Micro-K; school board minutes, May 29, 1907, SSD Record 7, p. 146. All who knew her referred to her as L. Maxine Kelly, with emphasis on the first initial.

28. SSD records, Micro-K; Pollock, "Early Administrative Women," p. 9.

29. *Seattle Times*, March 6, 1948 (first quotation); Seattle Public Schools, *School Histories*, n. pag. (second and third quotations).

30. Frances A. Sheridan, "A Brief History of Interbay," *Queen Anne and Magnolia Almanac '97*, pp. 32 and 33; *Seattle Times*, March 6, 1948.

31. *Seattle Times*, March 6, 1948 (quotation); author's conversation with Jim Tracy, April 12, 2000.

32. Author's conversations at reunion of former Interbay students, Everett, Washington, April 12, 2000.

33. Florence Byers, interview by author, February 11, 1997.

34. Nuetzmann interview.

35. Seattle Public Schools, *School Histories*, n. pag.

36. SSD records, A-96-9-J.

37. Ibid., Micro-K; *Seattle Educational Bulletin*, April 1935; Shelton, James, Sandra L. Barker and Stephanie L. Bravmann, *The Ida Culver Story* (Seattle, 1998), pp. 14 and 18; Seattle city directories, 1903–51.

38. School board minutes, May 15, 1915, SSD Record 11, p. 49 (first quotation), September 23, 1938, SSD Record 35, p. 66 (second quotation), and November 18, 1932, SSD Record 29, p. 154.

39. Pollock, "Early Administrative Women," p. 10.

40. School board minutes, June 29, 1923, SSD Record 19, p. 406, September 1, 1922, SSD Record 19, p. 47 (quotation), and May 4, 1923, SSD Record 19, p. 315.

41. Ibid., October 23, 1918, SSD Record 15, p. 163 (first quotation), and October 7, 1919, SSD Record 16, p. 149 (second quotation).

42. Seattle Public Schools, *School Histories*, n. pag.; school board minutes, May 9, 1910, SSD Record 8, p. 269, and May 16, 1919, SSD Record 15, p. 345.

43. School board minutes, March 20, 1925, SSD Record 21, p. 247, November 21, 1927, SSD Record 24, p. 175, and March 2, 1928, SSD Record 24, p. 284.

44. Helen Shelton, interview by author, November 19, 1997.

45. Mary Jo Dvorak, interview by author, March 3, 1998.

46. Jim Shelton, interview by author, June 8, 1998. Shelton was quoting Tony Allasina, who succeeded Miss Mahon as Bailey Gatzert principal.

47. Mary Lou Strandoo, interview by author, July 2, 1998; countless others reported the same list of possible punishments.

48. Bertha King, primary assistant, to Helen Reynolds, May 20, 1941, SSD records, A-96-9-V.

49. Maude Sexton, interview by Lois Benson, November 28, 1989, transcript in Pieroth's possession.

50. Amelia Telban, interview by Olaf Kvamme, July 18, 1989, tape and transcript in Pieroth's possession.

51. Mary Heaton Ingalls, interview by author, June 18, 1998.

52. SSD records, A-96-9-L and -N.

53. Joan Waldo (first quotation), Sylvia Tupper, and Mary Bordner, interview by author with former Bryant students, May 6, 1998; Nuetzmann interview.

54. Byers interview.

55. Jim Shelton interview.

56. School board minutes, May 4, 1923, SSD Record 19, p. 315; Byers interview.

57. SSD records, A-96-9-L and -R.

58. Genevieve Rogers to Frank Willard, June 19, 1940 (third quotation), SSD records, A-96-9-R; Mary Hootman to Samuel Fleming, March 27, 1947 (last quotation), ibid., A-96-9-H.

59. Jim Shelton interview (first quotation); Jeanne DeFriel Gardiner, interview by author, May 14, 1998 (second quotation).

60. Nuetzmann interview.

61. SSD directories, 1907–37; school board minutes, June 8, 1911, SSD Record 9, p. 17; Nuetzmann interview.

62. Nuetzmann interview.

63. Ibid.

64. Waldo, Tupper, Bordner interview.

65. Nuetzmann interview.

66. Ibid. For Hilder Erickson's union involvement, see Elmer Miller Papers, University of Washington Libraries.

67. SSD records, A-96-9-F (first quotation); Nuetzmann interview (other quotations).

68. Emma Groves, interview by James Ferris, August 1, 1989, tape and transcript in Pieroth's possession.

69. Richard Birchfield, interview by author, May 15, 2000.

70. Agatha Shook, to Worth McClure, December 19, 1938, SSD records, A-96-9-S.

71. Sara Luch, interview by author, February 19, 1997 (Mary Luch quotation); school board minutes, August 28, 1936, SSD Record 33, p. 45; Houston interview (remaining quotations).

72. School board minutes, May 14, 1937, SSD Record 33, p. 311.

73. Jim Shelton interview.

74. Houston interview.

75. Ibid.; Rene Rice, interview by author, May 14, 1998 (quotation).

76. Dora Herren to Fleming, April 3, 1946 (first quotation); 28 Ravenna teachers to Fleming, May 18, 1953 (second quotation); Ravenna PTA to Fleming, June 1, 1953, all in SSD records, A-96-9-R.

77. Ellen Creelman to Cooper, May 10, 1921 (first quotation); Annie Gifford to Cooper, May 10, 1921 (second quotation); Janet Dewhurst to Reuben Jones, May 12, 1924, all in ibid., A-96-9-D.

78. *Seattle Grade Club Magazine*, October 1924, p. 39; Teacher's Service Report for Janet Dewhurst, April 1, 1943, SSD records, A-96-9-D.

79. Francis Neal Morris, "A History of Teacher Unionism in the State of Washington, 1920–45," Master's thesis (University of Washington, 1968), pp. 138 and 139.

80. Copy of Dewhurst statements in McClure to school board, January 14, 1945, SSD records, A-96-9-D; *Annual Report of the Seattle Public Schools for the Year Ending June 30, 1943*, p. 15 (last quotation).

81. SSD records, A-96-9-D.

82. SSD Record 62, p. 52; Wade Vaughn, *Seattle-Leschi Diary*, 2nd ed., (Seattle, 1988), pp. 200 (first quotation) and 201; Loren Troxel to Fred Breit, July 16, 1965, SSD file, 521-VRT, re: reassignment program, SPS Archives; Dewhurst to Ernest Campbell, May 11, 1964, SSD records, A-96-9-D (last quotation).

83. "The Janet Dewhurst Fund: Appreciating Yesterday, Understanding Tomorrow," brochure of the Seattle Education Auxiliary, copy in Pieroth's possession.

84. SSD records, Micro-L; Seattle Public Schools, *School Histories*, n. pag.

85. Katie Dolan, interview by author, July 22, 1998.

86. School board minutes, December 4, 1936, SSD Record 33, p. 140 (first quotation); Dolan interview (other quotations).

87. Dolan interview. Author's interviews with former students in those other schools confirm the snob label.

88. Program for evening session, National Education Association convention, July 6, 1927, Education/Seattle File, Special Collections, University of Washington Libraries.

89. School board minutes, May 3, 1935, SSD Record 31, p. 279.

90. *Seattle Times*, June 7, 2000 (quotations).

91. School board minutes, December 4, 1936, SSD Record 33, p. 140.

92. The beautiful window weathered the near-violent social upheavals of the 1960s and 1970s and can still be viewed in the John Muir building.

6 / DEALING WITH DIVERSITY

1. Frank Cooper to school board, January 20, 1922, SSD records, Superintendent's files. In the twenties the district provided adult evening classes in English at Bailey Gatzert and Pacific.

2. Frank Miyamoto, "An Immigrant Community in America," *East across the Pacific: Historical and Sociological Studies of Japanese Immigration and Assimilation,* ed. Hilary Conroy and T. Scott Miyakawa (Santa Barbara: ABC Clio, 1972), p. 222 (quotation).

3. Howard Droker, "Seattle's Jewish Neighborhoods" (typescript, ca. 1998), pp. 3 and 4.

4. School board minutes, April 9, 1914, SSD Record 11, p. 90.

5. SSD records, Micro-W.

6. June Rose Droker, interview by author, May 18, 1998.

7. Droker, "Seattle's Jewish Neighborhoods," p. 4.

8. No African American taught in the district until the board hired Mrs. Thelma Dewitty in 1947; it hired the first teacher of Asian extraction in April 1949, May Higa.

9. Reva Twersky, interview by author, April 27, 1998.

10. Vivian Austen Spearman, March 5, 1968, interview tape, Acc. 4905–001, Special Collections, University of Washington Libraries.

11. SSD directories, 1902–41.

12. Maxine Pitter Haynes, interview by author, May 12, 1998.

13. Elsie Hill Fell to Pieroth, April 15, 2000; Barbara Byers Howard, interview by author, December 10, 1999.

14. Janet E. Rasmussen, *New Lands, New Lives: Scandinavian Immigrants in the Pacific Northwest* (Seattle: University of Washington Press, 1993), pp. 126–31 (quotation); SSD directories, 1910–41.

15. Rasmussen, *New Lands, New Lives,* p. 135 (quotation); SSD directories, 1921–41.

16. Margaret J. Thomas, "Pupils from Other Lands," *Seattle Grade Club Magazine,* December 1923, p. 13 (quotations); SSD directories, 1918–25.

17. "Americanization in the Seattle Grade Schools," *Grade Club Magazine,* April 1920, p. 12.

18. Laverne Anderson, interview by author, June 15, 1998.

19. Joan Waldo, Sylvia Tupper, and Mary Bordner, interview by author, May 6, 1998 (quotations); *Seattle Times,* December 20, 1999.

20. *Grade Club Magazine,* April 1920, p. 13 (song lyrics); Jeanne DeFriel Gardiner, interview by author, May 14, 1998; SSD directories, 1904–41.

21. "Americanization in the Seattle Grade Schools," p. 12.

22. Ibid.

23. William Hosokawa, *Nisei: The Quiet Americans* (New York: William Morrow and Co., 1969), p. xii.

24. SSD records, Micro-B.

25. Yoon K. Pak, "'Wherever I Go I Will Be a Loyal American': Democracy and Dissonance in the Lives of Seattle's Nisei," PhD diss. (University of Washington, 1999), pp. 8 (first quotation) and 160 (second quotation); SSD directories, 1907–41. The Pak dissertation presents thorough coverage of the Seattle district's emphasis on democracy in the schools; it was published by Routledge/Falmer Press in 2001.

26. Hosokawa, *Nisei,* p. xv.

27. SSD directories, 1910–41.

28. Maud Thompson, "Children of the Orient," *Grade Club Magazine,* December 1929, pp. 18, 34, and 35.

29. Worth McClure, "America's Melting Pot," ibid., May 1932, p. 8.

30. Huldah E. Olein, "Conflict Produced in Pupils by Divergent Aims of Home and School," ibid., October 1932, pp. 19 and 45; SSD directories, 1902–37.

31. Mary E. Knight, "New Social Science Changes Successful," *Seattle Educational Bulletin,* May 1926, p. 2.

32. Richard Berner, *Seattle Transformed: World War II to Cold War*, vol. 3, *Seattle in the 20th Century* (Seattle: Charles Press, 1991), p. 19.

33. Frank Miyamoto, "An Immigrant Community in America," p. 234.

34. SSD directories, 1902–41; SSD records, Micro-M; Seattle Public Schools, *School Histories* (Seattle, 1951), n. pag. The old school stood on Main Street, one block north of Jackson Street, between Fifth and Sixth avenues, on the present site of Kobe Terrace and just beyond the end of the restored street car line that runs east from the waterfront.

35. Shigeko Uno, interview by Louis Fiset, September 14, 1995, copy of transcript in Pieroth's possession; Henry Itoi to Pieroth, March 11, 1999.

36. Monica Sone, *Nisei Daughter* (Boston: Little, Brown and Company, 1953; rpt. Seattle: University of Washington Press, 1979), p. 18.

37. Frank Miyamoto, "An Immigrant Community in America," pp. 234–35.

38. Hosokawa, *Nisei*, p. 168.

39. Uno, in Fiset interview; Itoi to Pieroth.

40. Aki Kurose, interview by author, February 23, 1998.

41. Frank Miyamoto, "An Immigrant Community in America," p. 235 (quotation); Itoi to Pieroth.

42. Ada J. Mahon, "Intimate Glimpses of Japan," *Grade Club Magazine*, October 1931, pp. 11–14.

43. William Mar, interview by author, September 28, 2000.

44. SSD records, Micro-M.

45. Ibid.; Seattle city directories, 1910–40.

46. SSD records, A-96-9-H.

47. Amelia Telban, interview by Olaf Kvamme, July 18, 1989, tape and transcript in Pieroth's possession.

48. Mar interview. Ruby Mar Chow went on to become a leader in the international community and to serve as a member of the King County Council.

49. John Corbally, "Orientals in the Seattle Schools," *Sociology and Social Research* 16, no.1 (October–September 1931), p. 63.

50. Ibid., p. 66 (first quotation), and 63 (second quotation).

51. Sone, *Nisei Daughter*, p.78.

52. Sally Kazama, Testimony before Congressional Re-dress Hearing, Seattle, Washington, August 21, 1981 (quotations); Sally Kazama, interview by author, March 19, 1998.

53. Itoi to Pieroth (first quotation); Ethel Telban, interview by author, April 23, 1998 (second and third quotations).

54. Louis Fiset interview with Sharon Aburano, August 10, 1995 (quotations) (copy of transcript in Pieroth's possession); Mar interview.

55. *Grade Club Magazine*, June 1930, pp. 33 and 34.

56. Mahon, "Intimate Glimpses of Japan," p. 14 (first quotation); Atsushi Kiuchi in the *Seattle Times*, July 19, 1998 (second quotation).

57. David A. Takami, *Divided Destiny: A History of Japanese Americans in Seattle* (Seattle: University of Washington Press, 1998), p. 50.

58. Itoi to Pieroth. For an account of Seattle's reception of the returning Nikkei, see Howard Droker, "Seattle Race Relations during the Second World War," *Pacific Northwest Quarterly* 67 (October 1976).

59. SSD records, Micro-M; Seattle *Post-Intelligencer*, June 19, 1951.

60. Kay Reinartz, *Queen Anne: Community on the Hill* (Seattle: Queen Anne Historical Society, 1993), p. 113 (first quotation); Louis Fiset, "Redress for Nisei Public Employees in Washington State after World War II," *Pacific Northwest Quarterly* 88 (Winter 1996–97), pp. 22 (second quotation) and 23 (third quotation).

61. Scrapbook, pp. 61 and 71, Ella Evanson Papers, University of Washington Libraries; *Seattle Times*, October 6, 1974.

62. *Seattle Times*, October 6, 1974 (first quotation); student writings, Evanson Papers (second quotation).

63. SSD records, Micro-E.

64. Rikimatand Hideshima to Ella Evanson, February 24, 1942, Evanson Papers.

65. *Seattle Times*, October 6, 1974.

66. Doris H. Pieroth, "Desegregating the Public Schools: Seattle, Washington, 1954–68," PhD diss. (University of Washington, 1979), pp. 21 and 48.

7 / GENTEEL MILITANTS

1. *Seattle Grade Club Magazine*, October 1930, p. 10.

2. Bryce Nelson, *Good Schools: The Seattle Public School System, 1901–1930* (Seattle: University of Washington Press, 1988), p. 56.

3. *Grade Club Magazine*, December 1922, pp. 11, 12, and 38.

4. Ibid., p. 11. Unfortunately, no copy of the original constitution can be found.

5. School board minutes, November 20, 1912, SSD Record 10, p. 110.

6. *Grade Club Magazine,* May 1931, p. 28 (quotation).

7. Grade Teachers' Club meeting minutes, November 22, 1912, Grade Club Ledger, Seattle Education Association (SEA) Archives.

8. *Grade Club Magazine,* May 1931, p. 28 (first quotation); *Annual Report of the Seattle Public Schools for the Year Ending June 30, 1915,* p. 136 (second quotation); Grade Teachers' Club minutes, December 17, 1912.

9. Grade Teachers' Club minutes, February 25, 1913.

10. Ibid., March 31, 1913.

11. Ibid., May 27, 1913.

12. Ibid., December 2, 1913.

13. Ibid., April 23, 1914.

14. Ibid., October 12, 1914.

15. *Grade Club Magazine,* April 1920, p. 16.

16. Grade Teachers' Club minutes, April 23, 1914 (quotation), and April 24, 1915.

17. *Grade Club Magazine,* May 1935, p. 17; SSD directories, 1902–35.

18. SSD records, Micro-B (first quotation); Helen Shelton, interview by author, November 19, 1997 (second quotation).

19. *Grade Club Magazine,* December 1922, p. 11 (quotation); Grade Teachers' Club minutes, April 24, 1917.

20. Grade Teachers' Club minutes, October 24, 1916; *Grade Club Magazine,* December 1922, p. 12 (quotations).

21. Grade Teachers' Club minutes, May 31, 1917, and November 17, 1921 (quotation).

22. Ibid., April 4, 1917.

23. *Grade Club Magazine,* April 1920, pp. 10 and 11.

24. School board minutes, October 3, 1903, SSD Record 6, p. 49, April 20, 1906, SSD Record 6, p. 377, and May 9, 1910, SSD Record 8, p. 268.

25. Seattle *Post-Intelligencer (P-I),* September 1–October 10, 1910 (quotations, October 10).

26. Susan B. Carter, "Incentives and Rewards to Teaching," in *American Teachers: Histories of a Profession at Work,* ed. Donald Warren (New York: Macmillan Publishing Co., 1989), p. 53; School board minutes, April 30, 1917, SSD Record 13, p. 317, May 14, 1917, SSD Record 13, p. 341, and May 23, 1917, SSD Record 13, p. 350. According to one conversion calculation, a World War I–era

minimum salary of $840 would have yielded $16,060 in end-of-the-century dollars.

27. School board minutes, December 7, 1917, SSD Record 14, p. 204, and January 8, 1917, SSD Record 13, p. 209.

28. Committee of Minimum Teachers, memo to Cooper, December 15, 1917, quoted in Nelson, *Good Schools*, p. 115.

29. School board minutes, January 7, 1918, SSD Record 14, pp. 241 and 242.

30. Grade Teachers' Club minutes, February 1, 1918; school board minutes, January 7, 1918, SSD Record 14, p. 242.

31. Grade Teachers' Club minutes, April 5, 1918. Survey results were not found in the records.

32. School board minutes, May 7, 1918, SSD Record 14, p. 361, May 1, 1918, SSD Record 14, p. 353.

33. Ibid., May 20, 1918, SSD Record 14, p. 371.

34. Ibid., p. 372.

35. Grade Teachers' Club minutes, May 22, 1918; school board minutes, May 23, 1918, SSD Record 14, p. 381, and May 24, 1918, SSD Record 14, p. 384.

36. Seattle *P-I*, October 5, 1918.

37. School board minutes, November 7, 1918, SSD Record 15, p. 168, and November 22, 1918, SSD Record 15, pp. 180–81 (quotations).

38. Grade Teachers' Club minutes, May 22, 1918 (quotation), June 13, and September 16, 1918; school board minutes, June 25, 1918, SSD Record 15, p. 31. The school district directory for 1918–19 shows that nineteen men taught full time at elementary school industrial shop centers and nine rotated part time through buildings with elementary "bench work" centers.

39. School board minutes, January 17, 1919, SSD Record 15, p. 236, March 14, 1919, SSD Record 15, p. 284 (quotation), and March 28, 1919, SSD Record 15, p. 293.

40. School board minutes, May 7, 1919, SSD Record 15, p. 337; Grade Teachers' Club minutes, May 11, 1919 (quotations). Agnes Parker left the grade ranks before elimination of the differential, completed her bachelor's degree in 1926, and taught history at Broadway High School until retiring in 1945.

41. Cooper to school board, August 7, 1916, SSD records, Superintendent's files, E27, Outside Employment file (first quotation); Nelson, *Good Schools*, p. 128 (second quotation).

42. Cooper to school board, December 8, 1919, SSD records, Superintendent's files, E27, Outside Employment file; Nelson, *Good Schools*, p. 140.

43. School board minutes, June 11, 1920, SSD Record 16, p. 412.

44. SSD directories, 1910–41.

45. Cooper to school board, February 11, 1921, SSD records, Superintendent's files, E28; school board minutes, April 6, 1921, SSD Record 17, p. 347 (quotations).

46. School board minutes, October 4, 1926, SSD Record 23, p. 107.

47. Ibid., March 14, 1919, SSD Record 15, p. 284, and May 21, 1920, SSD Record 16, p. 392; Dominic W. Moreo, *Schools in the Great Depression* (New York: Garland Publishing, 1996) (re: inflation percentage).

48. Grade Teachers' Club, minutes of executive committee meeting, March 27, 1922, SEA Archives; Grade Teachers' Club minutes, April, 1922, quoted in *Grade Club Magazine*, May 1933, p. 49.

49. School board minutes, June 9, 1922, SSD Record 18, p. 375, April 7, 1922, SSD Record 17, p. 318, and June 16, 1922, SSD Record 18, p. 394.

50. Tax Reduction Council communiqué to the school district, quoted in Nelson, *Good Schools*, p. 159; school board minutes, June 30, 1922, SSD Record 18, p. 421 (last quotation).

51. School board minutes, February 1, 1924, SSD Record 20, p. 213, May 16, 1924, SSD Record 20, pp. 329–40, and August 11, 1922, SSD Record 19, p. 41 (quotation).

52. *Grade Club Magazine*, June 1925, p. 19 (quotation); school board minutes, March 20, 1925, SSD Record 21, p. 247.

53. *Grade Club Magazine*, June 1925, pp. 19 (quotations) and 21, and December 1924, p. 27; Francis Neal Morris, "A History of Teacher Unionism in the State of Washington, 1920–45," Master's thesis (University of Washington, 1968), p. 27.

54. *Grade Club Magazine*, June 1920, e.g., p. 9; Grade Teachers' Club minutes, April 12, 1920 (first quotation), and March 13, 1920 (second quotation).

55. *Grade Club Magazine*, March 1926, p. 33 (first two quotations), and December 1927, p. 33 (last quotation).

56. Morris, "History of Teacher Unionism," pp. 43–44.

57. School board minutes, November 21 and 27, 1927, SSD Record 24, pp. 160 and 177 (quotation); Morris, "History of Teacher Unionism," p. 48.

58. Morris, "History of Teacher Unionism," pp. 51, 52 (quotation), and 56.

59. School board minutes, February 17, 1928, SSD Record 24, p. 266.

60. Morris, "History of Teacher Unionism," p. 57 (quotation).

61. School board minutes, May 4, 1928, SSD Record 24, p. 364. In Morris, "History of Teacher Unionism," see especially chapter 4, "The Seattle High School Teachers' Union and the 'Yellow-dog Rule.'"

62. *Grade Club Magazine,* December 1920, p. 39.

63. Ibid., May 1931, p. 51 (quotations); SSD directories, 1915–20.

64. Agnes Winn, "Reminiscences," and Amy Estep, "When I Was Editor," *Grade Club Magazine,* March 1928, pp. 20 (first quotation), 25 (second quotation), and 45 (third quotation).

65. Grade Teachers' Club minutes, April 12, 1920; *Grade Club Magazine,* December 1920, p. 38 (first quotation), June 1921, p. 47 (last quotations), and May 1931, p. 29.

66. Jeanne DeFriel Gardiner, interview by author, May 14, 1998.

67. Ibid. (quotation); SSD records, Micro-S.

68. DeFriel Gardiner interview.

69. *Grade Club Magazine,* May 1931, p. 29.

70. SSD directories, 1915–41; *Grade Club Magazine,* May 1931, p. 29 (first quotation); Myra Snow, "Third Class through Bandit Land," *Grade Club Magazine,* May 1929, pp. 26–29 (quotations).

71. SSD records, Micro-H.

72. Joseph T. Hazard, *Pioneer Teachers of Washington State* (Seattle: Seattle Retired Teachers Association, 1955), p. 128.

73. SSD records, Micro-H; *Grade Club Magazine,* May 1931, p. 51 (quotations).

74. SSD records, Micro-H; Hazard, *Pioneer Teachers,* p. 128.

75. *Grade Club Magazine,* June 1925, p. 21 and December 1925, p. 50.

76. Ibid., March 1925, p. 23.

77. SSD records, Micro-W; *Grade Club Magazine,* May 1931, p. 52.

78. SSD records, A-96-9-S (first two quotations); Joanne Youngblood, interview by author, April 8, 1998, and Phoebe Quigley Gilbert, interview by author, October 15, 1997 (last quotation).

79. SSD records, A-96-9-W (quotation); *Grade Club Magazine,* December 1929, p. 32; school board minutes, October 3, 1929, SSD Record 27, p. 101.

80. *Seattle Grade Club Magazine,* May 1932, p. 52.

81. SSD records, A-96-9-S; Seattle Public Schools, *School Histories* (Seattle, 1951), n. pag.

82. *Grade Club Magazine,* May 1928, pp. 28, 29 (quotations), and 46.

83. Ibid., May 1929, p. 10, and May 1931; SSD directories, 1918–41.

84. *Grade Club Magazine,* October 1930, p. 10 (first two quotations) and October 1931, p. 9 (last quotation).

85. Ibid., May 1933, p. 28 (quotation); SSD directories, 1910–41.

86. Morris, "History of Teacher Unionism," pp. 100 and 101; Daniel Patrick Riley, "An Analysis of the Structure and Function of the Seattle Association of Classroom Teachers from 1936 to 1958," Master's thesis (University of Washington, 1959), pp. 65 and 66.

87. *Grade Club Magazine,* May 1924, p. 13.

8 / BEYOND THE CLASSROOM

1. *Seattle Grade Club Magazine,* May 1934, p. 25.

2. *History of the Women's University Club* (Seattle, n.d.), p. 1 (quotation), Special Collections, University of Washington Libraries; "Women's University Club Handbook," ca. 1998, p. 6, photocopy in Pieroth's possession.

3. *History of the Women's University Club,* pp. 4 and 5; "Handbook," ca. 1998, p. 6, (quotation), and 1915–16, p. 25–39, Special Collections, University of Washington Libraries.

4. "Handbook," 1915–16, pp. 25–39; *Seattle Times,* November 11, 1975.

5. *History of the Women's University Club,* pp. 10, 11 (quotation), 16 and 18.

6. Mountaineers, *Bulletin,* June 1919, p. 3; SSD records, A-96-9-C.

7. *Seattle Times,* January 13, 1973; SSD records, A-96-9-C; Mountaineers, *Bulletin,* September 1913, p. 9.

8. Broadway High School, *Sealth,* 1923, p. 4, SPS Archives. Any number of Seattle women could recite the creed from memory decades after graduating.

9. SSD records, Micro-G.

10. Seattle *Post-Intelligencer (P-I),* May 21, 1918.

11. Roosevelt High School, *The Strenuous Life,* 1929, p. 72, SPS Archives; Joanne Youngblood, interview by author, April 8, 1998; Phoebe Quigley Gilbert, interview by author, October 15, 1997 (quotation).

12. *The Strenuous Life,* 1927, p. 68; Jeanne DeFriel Gardiner, interview by author, May 14, 1998 (quotation).

13. *Seattle Times,* January 12, 1964.

14. Seattle Soroptimist Club yearbooks, 1925–40, photocopies in Pieroth's possession; *American Soroptimist,* September 1960, p. 4.

15. Alice D. Rayner, *The Path We Came By: A History of Plymouth Congregational Church, Seattle, Washington, 1869–1937* (Seattle, n.d.), pp. 39 and 40.

16. "Order of Worship," September 15, 1935, Plymouth Congregational Church Archives; Mildred T. Andrews, *Seeking to Serve: The Legacy of Seattle's Plymouth Congregational Church* (Dubuque, Iowa: Kendal Hunt, 1988), p. 105.

17. "Order of Worship," February 18, 1923, January 3, 1926, April 18, 1926, and January 13, 1929.

18. "Order of Worship," October 31, 1926 (quotation) and October 7, 1923; 1913 membership list, Plymouth Congregational Church Archives; SSD directories, 1925–41.

19. SSD records, A-96-9-B; Andrews, *Seeking to Serve*, p. 227; author's conversation with Marcia Almquist, Plymouth church archivist, January 29, 2001; Seattle *P-I*, March 23, 1999.

20. *Grade Club Magazine*, December 1920, pp. 26–27.

21. Ibid., May 1934, p. 16; Amelia Telban, interview by Olaf Kvamme, July 18, 1989, tape and transcript in Pieroth's possession.

22. *Grade Club Magazine*, May 1933, pp. 34 (first quotation) and 37 (second quotation).

23. Ibid., May 1934, pp. 15 and 16 (quotations).

24. Ibid., May 1931, p. 37 (quotation), and October 1936, pp. 13 and 14.

25. Ibid., May 1934, p. 23, March 1935, p. 21, May 1933, p. 37, May 1935, p. 21, March 1936, p. 25.

26. Ibid., May 1933, p. 37.

27. Jim Kjeldsen, *The Mountaineers: A History* (Seattle: Mountaineers Books, 1998), p. 13 (first two quotations); *Mountaineer*, March 1907, n. pag. (last quotation).

28. *Mountaineer*, March 1907, p. 26; SSD directories, 1907–41.

29. Mountaineers, *Bulletin*, August 1912, p. 2, and May 1919, p. 3 (quotation).

30. SSD records, Micro-N.

31. Ibid., Micro-S.

32. *Mountaineer*, 1916, n. pag., and 1911, pp. 15, 20, 21 (quotation), 23, and 24.

33. SSD records, Micro-F; Kjeldsen, *The Mountaineers*, pp. 167 and 170.

34. Washington, D.C., *Herald*, October 22, 1922; SSD records, Micro-B.

35. *Mountaineer*, June 1907, pp. 46 and 47 (quotation).

36. Ibid., September 1907, pp. 69, 70 (first two quotations), 71 (last quotation), and 72; Kjeldsen, *The Mountaineers*, pp. 21 and 26. Cora Smith Eaton, one

of a number of women physicians in Seattle early in the twentieth century, was the Mountaineers' first secretary and on that first Mount Olympus trek had been coleader with Asahel Curtis.

37. Winona Bailey to Iranilla Caskin, quoted in undated clipping, biography file, Special Collections, University of Washington Libraries (first quotation); Washington, D.C., *Times*, June 27, 1922 (second quotation); Washington, D.C., *Herald*, October 22, 1922 (last quotations).

38. Jack Brooke (Keller's son), interview by author, September 15, 1999; *Grade Club Magazine*, May 1924, p. 47 (quotations); SSD directories, 1922–41.

39. *Grade Club Magazine*, March 1924, p. 28.

40. Ibid., June 1920, pp. 24 and 25 (quotations), and 1920–41, *passim*.

41. Ibid., May 1934, p. 19 (quotation); SSD directories, 1902–41.

42. *Grade Club Magazine*, May 1924, p. 47; SSD directories, 1915–41.

43. *Grade Club Magazine*, March 1923, pp. 23 and 34.

44. Ibid., October 1929, p. 32; SSD directories, 1902–41.

45. Joan Mann and Meg Rafanelli, eds., "Stillaguamish Country Club, 1924–99" (photocopy, n.p., n.d.), pp. 7–15; Stillaguamish Country Club, "Anniversary Book" (n.d.).

46. Mann and Rafanelli, "Stillaguamish Country Club," p. 3; Stillaguamish Country Club, "Anniversary Book," pp. 7, 23 (quotation), 27, 38, 40, and 47.

47. Mann and Rafanelli, "Stillaguamish Country Club," pp. 3 and 42; Stillaguamish Country Club, "Anniversary Book," pp. 13 and 42 (quotations).

48. Stillaguamish Country Club, "Anniversary Book," pp. 18 and 43; SSD records, Micro-C; SSD directories, 1918–41.

49. Stillaguamish Country Club, "Anniversary Book," pp. 22 and 31; SSD directories, 1918–41; Barbara Byers Howard, interview by author, December 10, 1999; Brooke interview.

50. Stillaguamish Country Club, "Anniversary Book," p. 30 (quotations); SSD directories, 1915–41.

51. *Grade Club Magazine*, May 1924, p. 42.

52. Ibid., October 1922, p. 44, December 1922, p. 38, March 1923, p. 42, and March 1930, pp. 19 and 39 (quotations); SSD directories, 1915–41.

53. Mountaineers, *Bulletin*, April 1912.

54. *Grade Club Magazine*, May 1924, p. 44.

55. School board minutes, February 13, 1925, SSD Record 21, p. 214 (first two

quotations); school board minutes, April 1, 1927, SSD Record 23, p. 284 (last quotation); school board minutes, May 6, 1932, SSD Record 28, p. 275.

56. *Grade Club Magazine*, October 1926, p. 44.

57. School board minutes, April 20, 1925, SSD Record 21, p. 297; *Grade Club Magazine*, October 1925, p. 31 (quotation).

58. *Seattle Education Bulletin*, May 1928; Laurelhurst alumnae, interviews by author; SSD directories, 1909–26; SSD records, Micro-M.

59. School board minutes, December 6, 1935, SSD Record 32, p. 126.

60. *Seattle Educational Bulletin*, January 1941; SSD directories, 1927–41.

61. *Grade Club Magazine*, May 1928, pp. 14 (first two quotations) and 34 (last quotation); SSD directories, 1907–30.

62. *Seattle Education Bulletin*, February 1938, p. 2 (quotations); SSD directories, 1927–41.

63. *Seattle Education Bulletin*, December 1939; Dorothy Crim to Worth McClure, October 2, 1939 (quotations), and to Samuel Fleming, March 8, 1953, SSD records, A-96-9-R.

64. *Grade Club Magazine*, October 1927, pp. 18–26, October 1931, p. 40, and December 1931, p. 42.

65. Gladys Perry, interview by author, January 28, 1997.

66. Ibid.

67. Sara Luch, interview by author, February 19, 1997; Luch's 1938 diary, photocopy in Pieroth's possession.

68. Luch interview.

69. Ibid.

9 / LEAVING THE CLASSROOM

1. Ruth Isaacs to Samuel Fleming, February 14, 1939, SSD records, A-96-9-I; Susan Ware, *Holding Their Own: American Women in the 1930s* (Boston: Twayne Publishers, 1982), p. 28.

2. Geraldine J. Clifford, "Man/Woman/Teacher: Gender, Family and Career in American Educational History," in *American Teachers: Histories of a Profession at Work*, ed. Donald Warren (New York: Macmillan Publishing Co., 1989), p. 305 (quotations). See also Dina M. Copelman, *London's Women Teachers: Gender, Class and Feminism, 1870–1930* (London: Routledge, 1996).

3. *Annual Report of the Seattle Public Schools for the Year Ending June 30, 1943,* pp. 15 and 16.

4. School board minutes, June 11 and 13, 1917, SSD Record 13, pp. 385 (first quotation) and 397 (second quotation).

5. Ibid., April 4, 1924, SSD Record 20, p. 276.

6. Winifred Wandersee, *Women's Work and Family Values* (Cambridge, Mass.: Harvard University Press, 1981), p. 118.

7. Gertrude Sennes to Thomas Cole, June 4, 1930, SSD records, A-96-9-S; Mabel Wixson to Worth McClure, December 14, 1938, SSD records, A-96-9-W.

8. Ann Sandstrom, interview by author, March 20, 1998.

9. Helen Hull Larsen, interview by author, April 1, 1997.

10. *Seattle Grade Club Magazine,* March 1925, p. 44.

11. Ibid., October 1930, p. 33.

12. Gladys Perry, interview by author, January 28, 1997; Arthur Gravrock, interview by author, April 2, 1997.

13. Alma Wilson Jackson, interview by author, May 7, 1997; SSD records, A-96-9-W.

14. Percentages calculated from Pieroth statistics.

15. SSD records, A-96-9-N.

16. Ellen Reep to Fleming, July 12, 1935, ibid., A-96-9-R.

17. Grade Teachers' Club minutes, June 6, 1922, Grade Club Ledger, Seattle Education Association Archives.

18. Seattle *Star,* November 29, 1927; *Grade Club Magazine,* 1920–41, *passim.*

19. *Grade Club Magazine,* May 1931, p. 44, and October 1935, p. 25.

20. Adelaide Pollock, "A New Venture," ibid., March 1930, pp. 8–9.

21. Ida Culver, "The Seattle Education Auxiliary, Inc.," ibid., October 1932, p. 48 (quotation), May 1929, p. 46; "Principals' Exchange," November 5, 1937, SPS Archives.

22. Ida Culver, "S.A.E. Residence," *Grade Club Magazine,* May 1934, p. 14.

23. Ibid., May 1935, p. 30.

24. SSD records, Micro-C; *Grade Club Magazine,* October 1927, p. 23, and 1920–36 *passim;* James Shelton, Sandra Barker and Stephanie Bravmann, *The Ida Culver Story* (Seattle, 1998). pp. 8–10; "Principals' Exchange," November 5, 1937.

25. SSD records, Micro-C; Shelton, Barker, and Bravmann, *The Ida Culver Story,* p. 6. Contrary to rumors of oil money as the source of Miss Culver's assets, nothing indicates any drilling on her Oklahoma acreage.

26. SSD records, Micro-C; Shelton, Barker, and Bravmann, *The Ida Culver Story*, pp. 6, 15–21, 28, and 33.

27. M—— S—— to Lyle Stewart, February 28, 1955, SSD records, A-96-9-S.

28. Herman Pfeifer, "A Study of Teacher Supply and Demand in the State of Washington," Master's thesis (University of Washington, 1929), p. 37; *Grade Club Magazine*, December 1927, p. 27; Seattle Public Schools, *A Decade of School History: 1930–1940* (Seattle, Seattle Public Schools 1940), p. 25 (quotation).

29. *Grade Club Magazine*, December 1927, p. 19; Seattle *Post-Intelligencer (P-I)*, June 8, 1938 (quotations).

30. School board minutes, May 5, 1939, SSD Record 35, pp. 305 and 306 (quotations); *Seattle Times*, April 30, 1939.

31. School board minutes, May 5, 1939, SSD Record 35, p. 306; Seattle *P-I*, May 6, 1939.

32. School board minutes, May 5, 1939, SSD Record 35, p. 308.

33. Ibid.; Seattle *P-I*, May 6, 1939 (last quotation).

34. School board minutes, June 13, 1939, SSD Record 35, pp. 377 and 378.

35. Ibid., July 11, 1940, SSD Record 37, p. 25.

36. SSD records, A-96-9-T; SSD directories, 1910–36.

37. Evaluations by Charles Potter, March 10, 1917 (first quotation), Dio Richardson, July 14, 1921 (second quotation), and Elizabeth Tharp, March 22, 1922 (third quotation), SSD records, A-96-9-T.

38. Ida Taylor to McClure, February 14, 1927, ibid., A-96-9-T; SSD directories, 1928–36.

39. Casey evaluation, May 1934, Taylor to McClure, March 11, 1936 (second quotation), and April 21, 1936 (third quotation), SSD records, A-96-9-T.

40. Ibid., A-96-9-A; school board minutes, June 6, 1941, SSD Record 37, p. 381, and April 10, 1942, SSD Record 38, p. 270.

41. School board minutes, April 9, 1941, SSD Record 37, pp. 291–93.

42. Viola Lusby to McClure, April 9, 1944, and June 6, 1944; Pollock evaluation, December 9, 1916; Austin (Interlake) evaluation, February 24, 1922; E. W. Campbell to McClure, June 8, 1944, all in ibid., A-96-9-L.

43. Billy Fogg to Superintendent's Conference, April 3, 1961, ibid., A-96-9-J (first quotation), Rubie Johnstone to J. B. Chichester, May 4, 1967 (second quotation), Kelly evaluation, 1929, and Leist evaluation, February 18, 1960, all in ibid., A-96-9-J.

44. Tom Leist to Chichester, April 17, 1968 (first quotation), and February 10,

1969 (second quotation), Charlotte Bansmer to Chichester, May 1, 1969, Rubie Johnstone to Chichester, February 24, 1970 (third quotation), ibid., A-96-9-J.

45. Ibid., A-96-9-M; school board minutes, September 11, 1942, SSD Record 39, pp. 88 and 89, and October 16, 1942, p. 140 (quotations).

46. Substitute evaluation, April 1964, and Clara Siggerud to Kenneth Selby, March 24, 1962, SSD records, A-96-9-S. Throughout district records, correspondence shows that Selby, assistant superintendent for elementary schools, was highly respected and a true favorite of the interwar cohort of women teachers.

47. Dorothy Crim to Fleming, March 8, 1953, ibid., A-96-9-R.

48. Perry evaluations, 1939–44, and Holden evaluation, December 1960, SSD records, A-96-9-E.

49. Florence Wren Ewart to Chichester, March 27, 1967, ibid.

EPILOGUE

1. Essay enclosed in letter, Kenneth Selby to Isa Wilson, October 6, 1958, SSD records, A-96-9-W.

2. Freshman English paper, read aloud during author's interview with Ann Sandstrom, March 20, 1998.

Bibliography

PUBLISHED WORKS

Andrews, Mildred T. *Seeking to Serve: The Legacy of Seattle's Plymouth Congregational Church.* Dubuque, Iowa: Kendal Hunt, 1988.

Aron, Cindy S. *Working at Play: A History of Vacations in the United States.* New York: Oxford University Press, 1999.

Beard, Charles A., and Mary P. Beard. *America at Mid-passage.* Vol. 3, *The Rise of Civilization.* New York: The Macmillan Company, 1939.

Belasco, Warren J. *Americans on the Road: From Auto Camp to Motel, 1910–1945.* Cambridge: Massachusetts Institute of Technology Press, 1979.

Bellman, William Goodrich. *Montlake—2021 and Way Beyond: The Years 1912 to 1994.* Seattle: self-published.

Berner, Richard C. *Seattle 1900–1920: From Boomtown, Urban Turbulence, to Restoration.* Vol. 1, *Seattle in the 20th Century.* Seattle: Charles Press, 1991.

———. *Seattle 1921–1940: From Boom to Bust.* Vol. 2, *Seattle in the 20th Century.* Seattle: Charles Press, 1992.

Bird, Caroline. *Born Female: The High Cost of Keeping Women Down.* Rev. ed. New York: David McKay Company, Inc., 1970.

———. *The Invisible Woman.* New York: David McKay Company, Inc., 1966.

Blumell, Bruce D. *The Development of Public Assistance in the State of Washington during the Great Depression.* New York: Garland Publishing, 1984.

Boorstin, Daniel J. *The Americans: The National Experience.* New York: Random House, 1965.

Broderick, Henry. *The "HB" Story: Henry Broderick Relates Seattle's Yesterdays with Some Other Thoughts By the Way.* Seattle: McCaffrey Publishers, 1969.

Brown, Dorothy M. *Setting a Course: American Women in the 1920s.* Boston: Twayne Publishers, 1987.

Campbell, D'Ann. *Women at War with America: Private Lives in a Patriotic Era.* Cambridge, Mass.: Harvard University Press, 1984.

Carter, Paul A. *Another Part of the Twenties.* New York: Columbia University Press, 1977.

Carter, Susan B. "Incentives and Rewards to Teaching," Donald Warren, ed. *American Teachers: Histories of a Profession at Work.* New York: Macmillan Publishing Co., 1989.

Cayton, Jr., Horace. *Long Old Road: An Autobiography.* Seattle: University of Washington Press, 1970.

Clifford, Geraldine J. "Man/Woman/Teacher: Gender, Family and Career in American Educational History." In *American Teachers: Histories of a Profession at Work,* ed. by Donald Warren. New York: Macmillan Publishing Co., 1989.

Cone, Molly, Howard Droker, and Jacqueline Williams. *Family of Strangers: Building a Jewish Community in Washington State.* Seattle: University of Washington Press, 2003.

Copelman, Dina M. *London's Women Teachers: Gender, Class and Feminism, 1870–1930.* London: Routledge, 1996.

Corbally, John. "Orientals in the Seattle Schools." In *Sociology and Social Research* 16, no. 1 (October–September, 1931), 61–66.

Cremin, Lawrence A. *American Education: The Metropolitan Experience, 1876–1980.* New York: Harper and Row, 1988.

Crunden, Robert M. *From Self to Society, 1919–1941.* Englewood Cliffs: Prentice Hall, 1971.

Dorpat, Paul. *Seattle Now and Then.* Vol. 2, [Seattle: ca. 1986].

Droker, Howard. "Seattle Race Relations During the Second World War." *Pacific Northwest Quarterly* 67 (October 1976).

Dryden, Cecil. *Light for an Empire: The Story of Eastern Washington State College.* Spokane: Eastern Washington State College, 1965.

Dumenil, Lynn. "Re-shifting Perspectives on the 1920s." In *Calvin Coolidge and the Coolidge Era,* ed. by John Earl Haynes. Washington, D.C.: Library of Congress, 1998.

Epstein, Cynthia Fuchs. *Woman's Place: Options and Limits in Professional Careers.* Berkeley: University of California Press, 1971.

Erigero, Patricia C. *Seattle Public Schools Historic Building Survey Report.* Seattle: Historic Seattle Preservation and Development Authority, 1989.

Faderman, Lillian. *Odd Girls and Twilight Lovers: A History of Lesbian Life in Twentieth-century America.* New York: Penguin, 1991.

Fass, Paula S. *The Damned and the Beautiful: American Youth in the 1920s.* New York: Oxford University Press, 1977.

Flanagan, Maureen A. "Women in the City, Women of the City: Where Do Women Fit in Urban History?" *Journal of Urban History* 23, no. 3, (March, 1997), 251–59.

Flink, James J. *The Car Culture.* Cambridge: Massachusetts Institute of Technology Press, 1975.

Frare, Alena L. *Magnolia Yesterday and Today.* Seattle: Magnolia Community Club, 1975.

Fraser, James W. "Agents of Democracy: Urban Elementary School Teachers and the Conditions of Teaching." In *American Teachers: Histories of a Profession at Work,* ed. by Donald Warren. New York: Macmillan Publishing Co., 1989.

Friedheim, Robert L. *The Seattle General Strike.* Seattle: University of Washington Press, 1964.

Gates, Charles M. *The First Century at the University of Washington, 1861–1961.* Seattle: University of Washington Press, 1961.

Gribskov, Margaret. "Adelaide Pollock and the Founding of the NCAWE." In *Women Educators: Employees of Schools in Western Countries,* ed. by Patricia A. Schmuck. Albany: State University of New York Press, 1987.

Groth, Paul. *Living Downtown: The History of Residential Hotels in the United States.* Berkeley: University of California Press, 1994.

Harris, Barbara J. *Beyond Her Sphere: Women and the Professions in American History.* Westport: Greenwood Press, 1978.

Hartmann, Susan M. *The Home Front and Beyond: American Women in the 1940s.* Boston: Twayne Publishers, 1982.

Haynor, Norman S. *Hotel Life.* Chapel Hill: University of North Carolina Press, 1936.

Hazard, Joseph T. *Pioneer Teachers of Washington.* Seattle: Seattle Retired Teachers Association, 1955.

Hicks, Arthur C. *Western at 75.* Bellingham: Western Washington State College Foundation, 1974.

Hoffman, Nancy. *Woman's True Profession.* Old Westbury, Conn.: The Feminist Press, 1981.

Hosokawa, William. *Nisei: The Quiet Americans.* New York: William Morrow and Co., 1969.

———. *Out of the Frying Pan: Reflections of a Japanese American.* Niwot: University Press of Colorado, 1998.

Jeffries, John W. *Wartime America: The World War II Home Front.* Chicago: Ivan R. Dee, 1996.

Jones, Nard. *Seattle.* New York: Doubleday, 1972.

Kaufman, Polly Welts. *National Parks and the Woman's Voice: A History.* Albuquerque: University of New Mexico Press, 1996.

Kennedy, David M. *Freedom from Fear: The American People in Depression and War, 1929–1945.* New York: Oxford University Press, 1999.

Kjedlsen, Jim. *The Mountaineers: A History.* Seattle: Mountaineers Books, 1998.

Kreisman, Lawrence. *Made to Last: Historic Preservation in Seattle and King County.* Seattle: University of Washington Press, 1999.

Levine, Lawrence W. *The Unpredictable Past: Explorations in American Cultural History.* New York: Oxford University Press, 1993.

Lichtenberg, Zita, ed. *Washington Schools in the Good Old Days.* Olympia: Office of the State Superintendent of Public Instruction, 1969.

MacDonald, Victoria-Maria. "The Paradox of Bureaucratization: New Views on Progressive Era Teachers and the Development of a Woman's Profession." In *History of Education Quarterly* 39, no. 4 (Winter 1999).

Marsh, J. Frank. *The Teacher Outside the School.* New York: World Book Company, 1928.

Miyamoto, Frank. "An Immigrant Community in America." In *East Across the Pacific: Historical and Sociological Studies of Japanese Immigration and Assimilation,* ed. by Hilary Conroy and T. Scott Miyakawa. Santa Barbara: ABC Clio, 1972.

Modell, John. *Into One's Own: From Youth to Adulthood in the United States, 1920–1975.* Berkeley: University of California Press, 1989.

Moreo, Dominic W. *Schools in the Great Depression.* New York: Garland Publishing, 1996.

Mullins, William H. *The Depression and the Urban West Coast, 1929–1933: Los Angeles, San Francisco, Seattle, and Portland.* Bloomington: Indiana University Press, 1991.

Mumford, Esther Hall. *Seattle's Black Victorians, 1852–1901.* Seattle: Ananse Press, 1980.

Murray, Keith A. "The Charles Niederhauser Case: Patriotism in the Seattle Schools, 1919." *Pacific Northwest Quarterly* 74, no. 1 (January 1983), 11–17.

Nelson, Bryce E. *Good Schools: The Seattle Public School System, 1901–1930.* Seattle: University of Washington Press, 1988.

Ochsner, Jeffrey K. "Architecture for Seattle Schools, 1880–1900." *Pacific Northwest Quarterly* 83, no. 3 (October 1992), 128–43.

O'Connor, Harvey. *Revolution in Seattle: A Memoir.* New York: Monthly Review Press, 1964.

Ogle, Stephanie, "Anna Louise Strong." In *Notable American Women: The Modern Period.* Cambridge, Mass.: Belknap Press, 1980.

Palladino, Grace. *Teenagers: An American History.* New York: Basic Books (Harper Collins), 1996.

Palmer, George H. *The Ideal Teacher.* Riverside Educational Monographs. New York: Houghton Mifflin, 1910.

Parrish, Michael E. *Anxious Decades: America in Prosperity and Depression.* New York: W.W. Norton, 1992.

Perlmann, Joel, and Robert A. Margo. *Women's Work? American Schoolteachers, 1650–1920.* Chicago: University of Chicago Press, 2001.

Perry, Arthur C., Jr. *The Status of the Teacher.* Riverside Educational Monographs. New York: Houghton Mifflin Company, 1912.

Pieroth, Doris H. "Bertha Knight Landes: the Woman Who Was Mayor." In *Women in Pacific Northwest History,* ed. by Karen J. Blair. Seattle: University of Washington Press, 2000.

Potts, Ralph Bushnell. *Seattle Heritage.* Seattle: Superior Publishing Company, 1955.

Rasmussen, Janet E. *New Land, New Lives: Scandinavian Immigrants in the Pacific Northwest.* Seattle: University of Washington Press, 1993.

Rayner, Alice D. *The Path We Came By: A History of Plymouth Congregational Church, Seattle, Washington, 1869–1937.* Seattle: 1937.

Recent Social Trends in the United States. Vol. 1. New York: McGraw-Hill, 1933. Reprint, Westport: Greenwood Press, 1980.

Reese, William J. *Power and the Promise of School Reform: Grassroots Movements During the Progressive Era.* Rev. ed. New York: Teachers College Press, 2001.

Reinartz, Kay F. *Queen Anne: Community on the Hill.* Seattle: Queen Anne Historical Society, 1993.

Reynolds, Cecelia. "Limited Liberation: A Policy on Married Women Teachers."

In *Women Educators: Employees of Schools in Western Countries*, ed. by Patricia A. Schmuck. Albany: State University of New York Press, 1987.

Rousmaniere, Kate. *City Teachers: Teaching and School Reform in Historical Perspective*. New York: Teachers College Press, 1997.

Rury, John L. *Education and Women's Work: Female Schooling and the Division of Labor in Urban America, 1870–1930*. Albany: State University of New York Press, 1991.

———. "Who Became Teachers? The Social Characteristics of Teachers in American History." In *American Teachers: Histories of a Profession at Work*, ed. by Donald Warren. New York: Macmillan Publishing Co., 1989.

Sale, Roger. *Seattle Past to Present*. Seattle: University of Washington Press, 1976.

Scharff, Virginia. *Taking the Wheel: Women and the Coming of the Motor Age*. New York: Free Press, 1991.

———. *To Work and To Wed: Female Employment, Feminism, and the Great Depression*. West Port: Greenwood Press, 1980.

Schmid, Calvin F., and Wayne McVey. *Growth and Distribution of Minority Races in Seattle, Washington*. Seattle: Seattle Public Schools, 1964.

Schmid, Calvin F., and Vincent A. Miller. *Population Trends and Educational Change in the State of Washington*. Seattle: Washington State Census Board, 1960.

Schmuck, Patricia A. "Women School Employees in the United States." In *Women Educators: Employees of Schools in Western Countries*. Albany: State University of New York Press, 1987.

Seattle Educational Bulletin. Vols. 1-17, no. 4 (January, 1941).

Seattle Grade Club Magazine. Vols. 1-21 (1920–1941).

Seattle Public Schools. *Annual Report of the Seattle Public Schools*, 1909–40.

Seattle Public Schools. *A Decade of School History: 1930–1940*. Seattle: Seattle Public Schools, 1940.

Shelton, James, Sandra Barker, and Stephanie Bravmann. *The Ida Culver Story*. Seattle: 1998.

Sone, Monica. *Nisei Daughter*. Boston: Little, Brown and Company, 1953. Reprint, Seattle: University of Washington Press, 1979.

Stage, Sarah, and Virginia B. Vincenti, eds. *Rethinking Home Economics: Women and the History of a Profession*. Ithaca: Cornell University Press, 1997.

Takami, David A. *Divided Destiny: A History of Japanese Americans in Seattle*. Seattle: University of Washington Press, 1998.

Taylor, Quintard. *The Forging of a Black Community: Seattle's Central District from 1870 through the Civil Rights Era*. Seattle: University of Washington Press, 1994.

Thornton, Tamara Plakins. *Handwriting in America*. New Haven: Yale University Press, 1996.

Tuttle, William, Jr. *"Daddy's Gone to War": The Second World War in the Lives of America's Children*. New York: Oxford University Press, 1993.

Tyack, David. "The Future of the Past: What Do We Need to Know About the History of Teaching?" In *American Teachers: Histories of a Profession at Work*, ed. by Donald Warren. New York: Macmillan Publishing Co., 1989.

Underwood, Kathleen. "The Pace of Their Own Lives: Teacher Training and the Life Course of Western Women." *Pacific Historical Review* 55, no. 4 (November 1986).

Walthew, Margaret, ed. *Duwamish Diary*. Seattle: Seattle Public Schools, 1996.

Wandersee, Winifred. *Women's Work and Family Values*. Cambridge, Mass.: Harvard University Press, 1981.

Ware, Susan. *Holding Their Own: American Women in the 1930s*. Boston: Twayne Publishers, 1982.

Warren, Donald, ed. *American Teachers: Histories of a Profession at Work*. New York: Macmillan Publishing Co., 1989.

Weiler, Kathleen. *Country Schoolwomen: Teaching in Rural California, 1850–1950*. Stanford: Stanford University Press, 1998.

West, Elliott, and Paula Petrik, eds. *Small Worlds: Children and Adolescents in America, 1850–1950*. Lawrence: University Press of Kansas, 1992.

Westin, Jeane. *Making Do: How Women Survived the '30s*. Chicago: Follett Publishing Company, 1976.

UNPUBLISHED WORKS

Carton, Jennie. "This Old Condo." Windermere Realty publication, n.d., numbers 5 and 6.

Geiger, Gary L. "Adele Parker: The Case Study of a Woman in the Progressive Era." Master's thesis, Western Washington University, 1979.

Gunns, Albert F. "Roland Hill Hartley and the Politics of Washington State." Master's thesis, University of Washington, 1963.

Mann, Joan, and Meg Rafanelli, eds., "Stillaguamish Country Club, 1924–99." Photocopy.

Morris, Francis Neal. "A History of Teacher Unionism in the State of Washington, 1920–45." Master's thesis, University of Washington, 1968.

Pak, Yoon K. "'Wherever I Go I Will Be a Loyal American'; Democracy and Dissonance in the Lives of Seattle's Nisei." PhD diss., University of Washington, 1999.

Pfeifer, Herman. "A Study of Teacher Supply and Demand in the State of Washington." Master's thesis, University of Washington, 1929.

Pieroth, Doris H. "Desegregating the Public Schools: Seattle, Washington, 1954–68." PhD diss., University of Washington, 1979.

Pollock, Adelaide, "The Early Administrative Women in Education of Seattle, Washington." Typescript in Seattle Public Library, 1932.

Pullen, Douglas R. "The Administration of Washington State Governor Louis F. Hart, 1919–25." PhD diss., University of Washington, 1974.

Reiff, Janice L. "Urbanization and the Social Structure: Seattle, Washington, 1852–1910." PhD diss., University of Washington, 1981.

———. "Seattle: The First Fifty-five Years; A Study in Urban Growth." Master's thesis, University of Washington, 1973.

Riley, Daniel Patrick. "An Analysis of the Structure and Function of the Seattle Association of Classroom Teachers from 1936 to 1958." Master's thesis, University of Washington, 1959.

Sheridan, Frances A. "Apartment House Development on Seattle's Queen Anne Hill Prior to World War II." Master's thesis, University of Washington, 1994.

———. "A Brief History of Interbay." *Queen Anne and Magnolia Almanac '97.*

Stillaguamish Country Club. "Anniversary Book." Mimeograph, n.d.

Stout, Areil E. "The Life and Leadership of Mary Gross Hutchinson." Master's thesis, University of Washington, 1972.

ARCHIVAL AND MANUSCRIPT COLLECTIONS

Plymouth Congregational Church Archives

"Orders of Worship," 1926–35.

Seattle Education Association Archives

Ledger of the Primary Teachers' Association.

Meeting Minutes, Seattle Grade Teachers' Club, Grade Club Ledger, November 1912–April 1922.

Seattle Public Schools Archives

Assorted scrapbooks and (published) high school yearbooks.
Seattle School District record (board minutes), 1-67.
Seattle School District records (personnel files), A-96-9 and Microfilm A-Z.
Seattle School District records (superintendent's files).
Seattle Public Schools annual and triennial reports, etc. (published).

University of Washington Libraries, Special Collections

Black Women's Oral History Project transcripts.
Ella Evanson Papers.
Elmer Miller Papers.
The Mountaineers Papers.

INTERVIEWS

Special Collections, University of Washington Libraries

Spearman, Vivian Austen. March 5, 1968. Acc. 4905-001.
Thomas, Constance Pitter. August 17, 1977. Black Women's Oral History Project.

Retired Teachers Oral History Project, courtesy of Olaf Kvamme and Paul Horlein

Groves, Emma. Interview by James Ferris. August 1, 1989.
How, Jessie. Interview by Joan Coffey. February 19, 1990.
Sexton, Maude. Interview by Lois Benson. November 28, 1989.
Telban, Amelia. Interview by Olaf Kvamme. July 1989.

Louis Fiset, historian

Aburano, Sharon. August 10, 1995.
Uno, Shigeko. September 14, 1995.

Doris H. Pieroth

Members of the Interwar Teacher Cohort

Byers, Florence Soderback. February 11, 1997.

Chisholm, Thelma. March 6, 1998.

Hahn, Doris Chargois. May 3, 1997.

Houston, Margaret. February 10, 1998, and February 7, 2000.

Ingalls, Mary Heaton. June 18, 1998.

Jackson, Alma Wilson. May 7, 1998.

Kwapil, Dorothy. April 9, 1997.

Larsen, Helen Hull. April 1, 1997.

Luch, Sara. February 19, 1997, and February 19, 1998.

Nuetzmann, Wilbert. June 19, 1998.

Pearce, Beulah. February 26, 1998.

Perry, Gladys Charles. January 28, 1997.

Shelton, Helen. November 19, 1997.

Later Colleagues of the Interwar Cohort

Bedford, Elva. May 5, 1998.

Cohrs, Kay. April 22, 1998.

Cohrs, Ray. April 22, 1998.

Rice, Rene. May 14, 1998.

Saari, Viola. June 12, 1998.

Shelton, Jim. June 8, 1998.

Other Teachers and School Personnel

Gravrock, Arthur. April 2, 1997.

Kurose, Aki. February 23, 1998.

Stalder, Virginia. June 25, 1998.

Telban, Ethel. April 23, 1998, and May 29, 1999.

Watson, Lyle. May 15, 1998.

Students of the Interwar Cohort

Anderson, Ernest. June 15, 1998.

Anderson, Laverne Nelson. June 15, 1998.

Belare, Kinneta J. May 12, 1998.

Berner, Richard. March 4, 1998.

Birchfield, Richard. April 2, 1998, and May 15, 2000.

Blumenthal, Stanley. June 11, 1998.

Bordner, Mary. May 6, 1998.

Brier, Nancy. April 15, 1998.

Brolin, Dorcas Finn. October 22, 1997.

Buckley, Michael. June 10, 1998.

Buckley, Mona Firnstahl. June 10, 1998.

Burton, Joan. April 15, 1998.

Danz, Carolyn Blumenthal. June 11, 1998.

Dolan, Katie Houlihan. July 22, 1998.

Drebin, Priscilla Blumenthal. June 11, 1998.

Droker, June Rose. May 18, 1998.

Dvorak, Mary Jo. March 3, 1998.

Eberharter, Betty. April 1, 1998.

Evans, Hazel. March 26, 1998.

Gardiner, Jeanne DeFriel. May 14, 1998.

Gastfield, Vera Hall. March 29, 1998.

Gilbert, Phoebe Quigley. October 15, 1997.

Greene, Mary Randolph. July 14, 1998.

Greene, Richard. July 14, 1998.

Hamilton, Helen. April 16, 1998.

Haynes, Maxine Pitter. May 12, 1998.

Hittman, Suzanne. May 13, 1998.

Howard, Barbara Byers. December 10, 1999.

Kazama, Sally. March 19, 1998.

Lucas, Joy. May 27, 1998.

McLellan, Bruce. April 14, 1998.

Moldrem, Anne. April 13, 1998.

Nolte, Betty Jo. April 3, 1998.

O'Conner, John. June 3, 1998.

Pheasant, Helen. April 17, 1998.

Roberts, Frances. May 29, 1998.

Roe, Ellen Tallman. April 19, 1999.

Roe, Hal. April 19, 1999.

Sandstrom, Ann Loman. March 20, 1998.

Shuman, Edith. May 7, 1998.

Sorenson, Janice. February 27, 1998.

Spear, Sonia. April 20, 1999.

Strandoo, Mary Lou. July 2, 1998.

Thomas, Constance Pitter. July 23, 1998.

Thompson, Lucile. June 29, 1998.

Tupper, Sylvia. May 6, 1998.

Twersky, Reva K. April 27, 1998.

Van Arsdel, Rosemary. May 19, 1998.

Waldo, Joan Campbell. May 6, 1998.

Watson, Betty Lea. April 14, 1998.

Wedermeyer, Rowena. June 8, 1998.

Wright, Sharon. December 4, 1997.

Youngblood, Joanne. April 8, 1998.

Group discussion, April 12, 2000, former Interbay School pupils

Christensen, Elaine Blake.

Fell, Elsie Hill.

Ferguson, Helen.

Lord, Lila Blake.

Nichols, Irene.

Poltz, Tae Tsubota.

Raymond, Dorothy.

Tracy, Evelyn Myers.

Tracy, Jim.

Vaughn, Bonnie Jean.

Yonemura, Emiko Tsubota.

Index

Aburano, Sharon, 145
Adams, Brock, 216
Adams, Florence, 14
Adams, Kate, 17, 211
Adams School, 77, 82, 131, 138
African Americans, 14, 61, 108, 127, 131, 133, 150, 194; teachers, 242n8. *See also* desegregation
age, of teachers, 16, 17, 51, 52, 89, 90; aging corps, 43, 54, 208, 209. *See also under* retirement
Ahlgren, Ida, 17
Aiken, Effie, 73
Aiken, Mary, 73
Alaska gold rush, 7
Alaska Yukon Pacific Exposition, 20, 60, 65, 68, 85, 175
Albright, Ella, 24, 25
Alcorn, Hazel (Powell), 202
Alki Point, 183
Alki School, 41, 71, 85, 113, 194
Allen, Mary, 84
Allen, Zella, 182
American Association of University Women, 107
American Federation of Teachers, 165, 166
Anderson, Cora, 77
Anderson, Elizabeth, 188

Anderson, Evelyn, 77
Anderson, Laverne Nelson, 135
apartment buildings, 68–70; Kinnear, 69; Malloy Manor, 70
Arctic Club, 175
Asian Americans. *See* Chinese Americans; Nikkei
Asian-American teachers, 242n8
Attebury, Hester, 65
Austen, Vivian (Spearman), 133
automobile ownership, 63, 74–78, 86, 116, 169

bachelors degree: percentage of teachers holding, 16, 29, 44, 51; required for grade teachers, 191; required for high school teachers, 17, 159
Bagemiel, Minnie, 202
Bagley School, 22, 119, 120, 125, 183
Bailey, Winona, 20, 31, 184, 185, 192, photo
Bailey Gatzert School, 14, 44, 56, 90, 116, 117, 131, 137, 141–49, 172, 181, 191, 192, 217, 244n34, photo. *See also* Good American Citizenship Club
Ballard district, 11, 13, 71, 132, 134
Ballard High School, 15, 28, 39, 81, 92, 131, 178, 183, 189, 204, 218

Bankhead, Bessie, 32
bans: on married teachers *(see under*
    marriage); on outside employment
    (see outside employment); on tutor-
    ing, 163
Beacon Hill district, 116, 213
Beacon Hill School, 145
Beairsto, Mary, 117
Belden, Fannie, 78
Bell, Ethel, 188
Bellingham Normal School, 16, 19, 22,
    25, 44, 77, 88, 91, 95, 101, 125, 178,
    184, 188, 195, 203
Bennett, Edith Page, 18, 19
Benson, Alli, 134
Bergstrom, Delia, 181
Better Schools Council, 126
B. F. Day School, 70, 71, 89, 101, 105,
    136, 168, 183, 184
Bigelow, Mabel, 65
Black, Mattie (Broadbent), 202
boarding houses, 25, 64
board of education. See Seattle School
    Board
Boeing Airplane Company, 57
Bohan, Julia K., 137, 138
Bon Marché department store, 157
Bonnell, Nina, 189
Bottomly, Forbes, 61
Braman, Dorm, 216
Brayton, Annie C., 152, 183, 207
Breen, Margaret, 93
Brighton School, 60, 71, 107, 162, 171
Broadway High School, photo; begin-
    nings, 10, 14, 15; first girls club in
    city, 26; staff, 19, 20, 31, 46, 159, 175,
    176, 183, 185; students, 106, 139, 141,
    217; teachers graduated from, 17, 28,
    72, 94, 101, 125
Brown, Evelyn, 45
Brown, Ira C., 22
Brown, Lulu A., 162
Bryant Elementary School, 39, 59, 70,

91, 117, 120–22, 126, 127, 135,
    215
Buchanan, Nina O., 81, 83, 155, 166,
    168
Buckbee, Grace, 187, 190
Buckley, Catherine, 28
Buckley, Nellie, 28, 41
business and professional women's
    clubs, 107
Byers, Florence Soderback, 12, 57, 111,
    119, 190

cadet program, 42, 49, 87–98 passim,
    125, 144; criteria for selection, 87,
    88, 96; salaries, 39, 88, 89, 97, 160;
    supervisors, 88, 90, 91, 93–95, 97,
    98, 100; youthful element, 89, 90
Calder, Mary, 138, 139
Campbell, Edna, 189
Campbell, Ernest, 61
Capitol Hill, 13, 18, 68–70, 72–74, 78,
    81, 85, 98, 105, 131, 134, 157, 187, 193
Carlsen, Edward, 217
Carlson, Rubie (Johnstone). See John-
    stone, Rubie Carlson
Carson, Mabel M., 162
Cascade School, 18, 23, 74, 107, 113, 115,
    182, 188
Casey, Alice, 183, 210
Castonia, Minnie, 85
Cayton, Horace, 108
Central district, 14, 61
Central Labor Council, 164, 166
Central School, 9, 10, 14, 28, 64, 65,
    139, 140
Century 21 Exposition, 217
certification, 96, 97
Chaffee, Winifred, 190
Chambers, Ava, 146, 191
Chargois, Doris (Hahn), 67
Chargois, Mildred (Tanner), 67
Charles, Gladys. See Perry, Gladys
    Charles

Cheney Normal School, 39, 40, 47, 52, 59, 79, 91, 94, 97, 195
Chilberg, Mabel, 175, 176
child labor laws, 156
Children's Orthopedic Hospital, 23, 68, 177, 217
Child Study Laboratory, 23, 179
Chinese Americans, 143, 144, 217
Chisholm, Thelma, 51, 58
Chopson, Estelle, 183
Chow, Ruby Mar, 144, 217
church membership. See religious institutions
civil rights movement. See desegregation; Leschi Improvement Council
Clarahan, Elizabeth, 176
class size, 35, 122, 154
Cleveland High School, 191, 195
Clinton, Gordon, 216
clubs, 103, 104. See also Grade Teachers' Club; Plymouth Girls' Club; women's clubs
Coe School, 69, 89, 115, 147, 155, 167, 176, 182, 190, 210
Coffey, Tennie, 59
Cole, Thomas, 36, 41, 43, 46, 77, 98, 114, 162, 164, 170
Coleson, Bertha, 153
colleges and universities. See bachelors degree; doctorate; masters degree; normal schools/colleges of education; Phi Beta Kappa; Teachers College, Columbia University; University of Washington; Washington State University/College
colleges of education. See normal schools/colleges of education
Colman School, 13, 18, 32, 82, 107–9, 131, 137, 140, 188, photo
Columbia City, 11, 71, 172
Columbia School, 19, 50, 71, 77, 91, 123, 172
Commonwealth Builders, Inc., 47

Communism, 33, 34, 47, 60. See also dismissal of teachers; loyalty oaths
commuting. See transportation, to school
Concord School, 19, 50, 71, 77, 91, 123, 182, 184, 194, 197
conduct/standards of behavior for teachers, 25, 40, 198, 216
Cooper, Frank, 4–6, 9, 11–36 passim, 61, 102, 103, 110, 124, 206, photo; and curriculum, 5, 6, 22, 30; disciples, 127; early years in Seattle, 15, 16; educational philosophy, 22 (see also Seattle Way); and Grade Teachers' Club, 153; legacy, 87; resignation, 35, 36, 163; salary advocacy, 23, 34; Teachers' superintendent, 4, 20, 34; and women principals, 103, 110, 113, 124
Copeland, Eunice, 9, 10, 72, 92, 93, 103, 117, 125, 127
Copeland, Fannie, 72
Cornish School, 21, 22
cost of living, 157, 165. See also under World War I
Coughlin, Mary W., 88
Coyle, Marion, 53
Crim, Dorothy, 194, 195, 214
Culver, Ida, 113, 206, 207, 254n25. See also Ida Culver House
cultural opportunities and activities, 19–22, 37, 51, 180, 217
curriculum, 5, 6, 60, 104; frills, 35; German, dropped and reinstated, 30, 41; Pacific Rim history course, 42, 140; physical education and dance, 21, 22; retail selling, 42; retrenchment, 41; vocational education, 42, 161
Curtis, Asahel, 183
custodians, 34, 108

Dabney, Ellen Powell, 17, 18, 31
Dahl, Florence, 78
Dansingburg, Eva, 206

Dartt, Pearl, 73
Davidson, Edith (Lind), 79
Delano, Lila, 65
demonstration schools, 45, 87, 90, 98–101, 126, 171, 212, 237n47
Denishawn Dance Troupe, 22
Denny regrade, 12, 84
Denny School, 10, 14, 80, 84, 85, 143, 183, photo
Depression era, 25, 46–52, 54, 76, 82, 106, 173, 193; few teachers hired during, 49, 96; lunch programs, 50, 51; needy students, 50, 51, 106, 145, 146; salary cuts, 172, 211
desegregation, of schools, 51, 61, 127, 150; Voluntary Racial Transfer Program, 61, 127
Desimone, Mary P., 32
Dewey, John, 5, 6, 144
Dewhurst, Janet, 125–28, 150, 181, photo.
Dick, Bessie, 181
discipline, 106, 111, 116, 123, 142, 144; corporal punishment, 108, 111, 116, 121, 142, 155
dismissal of teachers, 25, 26, 30, 109, 213
doctorate, 58
Dodge, Alice, 183
Dolan, Katie Houlihan, 129
Dresser, Iva, 85
Droker, June Rose, 132
Dunlap School, 49, 71
Dust Bowl refugees, 54

Eastern Washington College of Education, 97. See also Cheney Normal School
Eaton, Dr. Cora Smith, 186, 251n36
E. C. Hughes School, 38, 171, 194
Eckstein, Nathan, 160
educational philosophy. See Cooper, Frank; Dewey, John; progressive education; Seattle Way

Eide, Agnes, 192
Ellensburg Normal School, 16, 45, 90, 95, 181
Ellis, James, 129, 217
emergency service. See under World War II
Emerson School, 53, 65, 77, 89, 122, 125, 181, 190, 217
environmental activism, 128, 129, 183, 217, 218
ERA Care, Inc., 207
Erickson, Estelle (Flohr), 40
Erickson, Hilder, 121, 240n66
Erickson, Howard E., 40, 228n9
Estep, Amy, 167
ethnic and immigrant groups, 13, 14, 131; Americanization of, 135, 136, 145, 146; arrival in Seattle of, 222n17; English language acquisition of, 131–36, 242n1; foreign classes at Pacific School for, 131–35, 137; multicultural approach to education, 139, 140, 145, 150; racial intolerance, 57, 108, 133, 138, 147, 148; schools with high concentration of, 13, 14, 111, 131, 137–41. See also individual groups
Evans, Daniel J., 216
Evanson, Ella, 56, 148, 149
exceptional students. See special education
exchange teachers/programs, 45, 194, 199, photo

Fahey, Ella, 28
Fairview School, 72, 92, 97, 98, 117, 188
family obligations, 203; care of sick or elderly parents, 18, 210; return home for vacations, 21, 174, 213
Farrell, Harriet, 71
Fauntleroy School, 72, 94, 123, 172
Fell, Elsie Hill, 134
Felzer, Genevieve, 122
Finch, Helen, 85

First Hill, 12–14, 69, 71, 77, 85, 98, 131, 211; residential hotels, 65, 138, 193
Fisher, Clide O., 111
Fisken, Bella, 10, 183
flag exercises, 32, 146
Fleming, Samuel, 42, 61
Forsberg, Cora, 193, 194
Fortnightly Club, 104
Foss, Laura, 134
Franklin High School, 15, 18, 26, 43, 65, 95, 141, 175, 184, 217
Frantz Coe School. See Coe School
Frederick and Nelson department store, 157
Fremont Bridge, 70
French, Bertha, 188
French, Marion C., 191
Fullington, Mary, 188
Furry, Mabel, 185

Gannon, Josephine, 65
Garfield High School, 22, 28, 42, 140, 141, 164, 199
Gasperich, Mary, 118
Gatewood School, 52, 57, 148, 202
Gatzert School. See Bailey Gatzert School
Gayton, Gertrude, 81
George, Almina, 29, 81
Georgetown district, 11, 13
Georgetown School, 187, 210
German, Marion, 77
Gifford, Annie L., 103–7, 113, 120, 125, 129
girls advisers, 26, 51, 176, 177, 184, 189, 195, 214
girls clubs, 26, 177–79; creed, 177
Glass, Rose, 176, 178, 179
Gleason, Belle, 180
Glenn, Lois, 187
Good American Citizenship Club, 145, 146, photo
Goodhue, Nellie, 179

Gourlay, Edith, 81
Grade Club Magazine. See *Seattle Grade Club Magazine*
Grade Teachers' Club, 31, 37, 81, 151–73; building and working conditions, 153–54; class size, 154; founding, 151–53; and Frank Cooper, 153–58; loans to teachers, 156, 169; magazine (see *Seattle Grade Club Magazine*); membership, 153, 154, 156, 167; presidents, 153–55, 166–72; professional and intellectual development, 168; retirement, 154, 156; salary, 153, 158–59, 161, 165, 169; and Seattle School Board, 153, 156; social and recreational emphasis, 155, 168, 181–83
Graham, Charlotte, 114, 122, 123, 130
Graves, Morris, 217
Gravrock, Arthur, 203, 230n69
Great Depression. See Depression era
Green Lake district, 11, 14
Green Lake School, 53, 107, 135, 170, 172, 183–85, 188, 194
Greenwood School, 156
Griffin, Leah, 165
Groves, Emma, 122, 123

Haddow, Helen, 190
Haley, Margaret, 4, 9
Hamilton Junior High School, 42, 74, 201
handicapped students. See special education
Hanson, Ole, 159
Harding, Constance, photo
Hargraves, Alice, 85
Harper, Ella, photo
Harper, Evangeline C., 30, 160, 161
Harris, Mattie Vinyerd, 14
Harrison School, 119, 125, 138
Hart, Emma C., 81, 103, 104, 141
Hart, Nell, 10, 80
Hartley, Roland Hill, 47, 97

Hawkins, Alma, 32
Hawthorne School, 71, 83, 120, 124, 207
Haynes, Maxine Pitter. *See* Pitter, Maxine (Haynes)
head teachers, 114, 116, 124, 213. *See also* women principals
Heaton, Mary (Ingalls), 97, 98, 117
Henson, Ethel, 162
Hermann, Ida, 93, 95, 124, 130
Hermanson, Clara, 143, 144
Herren, Dora, 77, 104, 115, 125, 169–71, 181, 206
Highland Park School, 57, 72, 73, 123
High School Teachers' League, 164, 165, 173
High School Women's League, 26
hiking, 20, 183–5, 187
Hillman City, 80
hiring considerations: best teachers regardless of origin, 15, 164; experience, 16, 25, 28, 90; graduates of Seattle schools and Washington normal schools, 16, 17, 41, 164; women at lower salaries, 3
hiring statistics, 44, 51, 52, 89, 164
Hodges, Jo, 93, 95, 98
Holden, Arnold, 215
Holmes, E. B., 166
home ownership, 72–75. *See also* vacation property
Hootman, Mary, 119
Horace Mann School, 24, 85, 131, 132, 143, 173, 192
Hosokawa, William, 137, 138, 142
hotels. *See* Olympic Hotel; residential hotels; Sarah B. Yesler Women's Hotel
housing arrangements, of teachers. *See* apartment buildings; boarding houses; home ownership; living arrangements; residential hotels
housing projects, 58, 59
Houston, Margaret, 57, 72, 94, 96, 100, 123, 124, 150, photo

How, Jessie K., 105
Hull, Helen (Larsen), 202
Hunter, Lilah, 165
Hurd, May, 73, 74
Hutchinson, Fred, 218
Hutchinson, William, 218

Ida Culver House, 113, 127, 128, 206, 207
immigrant and ethnic communities. *See* ethnic and immigrant groups
inflation. *See* cost of living
influenza epidemic (1918), 34, 161, 162
Ingalls, Fred, 117
Ingraham, Winifred, 188
in-service training. *See* cadet program; demonstration schools
insurance, 151, 172
Interbay district, 110–13
Interbay School, 12, 69, 81, 88, 89, 103, 110–13, 131, 134, 135, photos
Inter-Club dinner, 175
Interlake School, 70, 73, 74, 78, 81, 94, 189, 194, 212
International district, 137
Iorns, Eleanor, 189
Isaacs, Ruth, 199, 201, photo
Italian Americans, 13, 32, 107, 108, 131
Itoi, Henry, 141, 142, 147

Jackson, Alma Wilson. *See* Wilson, Alma Jackson
Jackson, Dorothea, 93, 100
Janet Dewhurst Fund, 128
Japanese Americans. *See* Nikkei
Japanese internment. *See under* World War II
J. B. Allen School, 74, 78, 184, 207, 208
Jefferson School, 28, 190, 202
Jenner, Cornelia, 88, 89
Jewish population, 13, 131, 132, 133, 137, 159, 192
John Hay School, 49, 69, 171, 201, 218

John Marshall Junior High School, 42, 168

John Muir School, 57, 119, 128–30, 187, 189, 190, 217, photo

Johns, Alma, 52

Johnstone, Rubie Carlson, 113, 212

Jones, Lydia, 182

Judd, Elsie, 81, 133

Judges, Louise, 135

junior high schools, creation of, 42

Jurgensohn, Eva, 22, 31, 180

juvenile delinquents. *See* parental schools

Kane, Anna B, 18, 32, 82, 104, 105, 107–9, 113, photo

Kane, Margaret, 18, 107

Kaye, A. L., 164

Kazama, Sally, 145

Keegan, Sara, 39

Keller, Florence (Brooke), 129, 187, 190

Kelly, L. Maxine, 69, 103–5, 110–15, 130, 206, 208, 212, 239n27, photo

Kelly, Marion, 182

Kennedy, Julia A., 8, 64

Kernan, Frances, 182

Kiger, Myrtle, 74, 75, 113

King County Council, 217

Kirk, Priscilla Maunder, 14

Knight, Mary E., 140

Knight, Rebecca S., 162

Koch, Rabbi Samuel, 159

Kurose, Aki, 142

Kwapil, Dorothy, 45

laboratories for democracy, schools as, 6, 92, 93, 138

labor unrest, 33, 34

Laccoarce, Velma, 38

Ladies Musical Club, 20, 51

Lafayette School, 59, 71, 217

Lake Union, 13, 15, 70, 73, 99

Landes, Bertha Knight, 37, 78, 195

Landes, Henry, 183, 195

Larrabee, Emma D., 53, 54, 71, 83, 202, 214

Latona School, 70, 71, 73, 83

Laurelhurst School, 28, 40, 77, 80, 170, 171, 193, 215

Laurie, Helen, 93–95, 98, 127, 144

Lawrence, Lila, 26, 189

League of Women Voters, 217

Leist, Tom, 212, 213

leisure activities, 174–98 passim. *See also* cultural opportunities and activities; social life; sports and recreation; travel; women's clubs

lesbianism, 75

Leschi district, 127

Leschi Improvement Council, 127

Leschi School, 127, 150

Lewis, Dora, 179

Lewis, Rae, 144

Lewiston Normal School, 38

Libee, Freda, 151, 172, 173, 175, 209

Lincoln High School, 15, 18, 28, 32, 37, 41, 44, 45, 60, 65, 89, 176, 178, 185, 195, 217; boarding in a private home, 25, 64, 66, 67, 70

living arrangements, 63; with other teachers, 74, 75, 111; with parents/ siblings, 18, 72, 78, 85, 132, 143, 170, 179, 187, 203; proximity to school, 63, 69, 71, 74, 79, 84, 86, 138; *Seattle Times* survey, 64. *See also* apartment buildings; boarding houses; home ownership; residential hotels

Local 200, 165, 166

Lockwood, Jessie, 104, 128–30, 187, 217

Logan, Trella Belle (Wilson), 6, 7, 10, 64, 203

Loman, Guy, 56

Longfellow School, 103, 105, 107, 120, 125, 131, 133, photo

Lovering, Lydia, 104

Lowell School, 45, 81, 131, 134, 139, 176

Loyal Heights School, 218
loyalty oaths, 60
Luch, Mary, 77, 78, 123, 197
Luch, Sara, 78, 196, 197
Lusby, Viola, 212

Machmeier, Theresa, 147
Madison Junior High School, 72, 74, 78, 191, 196
Madison Park district, 105, 172
Madrona School, 124, 170
Magaard, Mabel, 190
Magnolia district, 111, 213
Magnolia School, 77, 85, 181, 182, 210
Mahon, Ada J., 9, 10, 56, 83, 90, 116, 117, 141–50, 181, 217, photo
Main Street School, 13, 83, 137, 141, photo
Maloney, Minnie, 48
Maple School, 82
Mar, William, 144
Marie, Queen of Romania, 179
marriage: ban on married teachers, 199, 200, 201; emergency service (see under World War II); equal status for married teachers, 126; repeal of ban, 40, 43, 58; resignations to marry, 17, 29, 39, 40, 43, 44, 52, 53, 90, 92, 95, 103, 117, 119, 123, 129, 144, 189, 195, 201–3; return to teaching, 92, 187, 190, 218; statistics, 90, 203; undisclosed, 203; widows, 18, 170, 187, 190, 199
Marshall, Walter, 127
Martin, Clarence, 47, 48, 97
masters degree, 17, 29, 126, 185, 195
Mattheson, Anna Mae, 104, 119, 122
Matthews, Reverend Mark, 153
McCarney, Margaret, 26, 184
McCauley, Grace, 74, 75, 113
McClure, Letha, 69
McClure, Worth, 46, 49, 54, 61, 106, 128, 129, 139, 214
McConnel, Mary, 78
McCullough, Ada, 78, 193

McCullough, Eva, 193
McDonald School, 53, 70, 71, 78, 83, 85, 94, 124, 169, 188, 202, 214
McGilvra School, 65, 172, 206
McKean, Lou, 176
McKechnie, Grace, 156
McKenzie, Belle, 166
McManis, Georgia, 15
McMaster, Marion, 42, 43
Meany, Edmond, 178
medical inspection in schools, 22, 82
Mercer School, 7, 14, 45, 202, 210
Merrick, Jessie, 129
Milligan, Hazel, 201, 218
Mills, Henrietta, 104
Minnig, Etta, 24, 116, 213, 214
minorities. See ethnic and immigrant groups
Miyamoto, Frank, 141
Moffet, Mildred V., 89
Monday Night Study Club, 104
Montague, Frances, 101
Montlake district, 72
Montlake School, 74, 115, 170, 181, 183, 194
moonlighting. See outside employment
Moore, Maud, 88
Moore, Nina, 12, 111
morale, 6, 94, 95, 113, 158, 163, 165
moral instruction, 6, 26, 34, 35
Moran, Margaret, 78
mountain climbing, 20, 183–5, 187
Mountaineers, The, 19, 31, 177, 183–87, 195, photo
Mount Baker district, 15
Mount Olympus, 186, 187
Mount Rainier, 180, 182, 185, 187
Mowry, Lavinia, 19
Muir, John, 128, 129
Mullen, Jane, 203
Municipal League. See Seattle Municipal League
Myers, Hazel, 93, 98

Nason, Letta, 9, 10
National Council of Administrative Women in Education, 29, 104
National Education Association, 4, 104, 176; convention in Seattle, 129, 171
Netterer, Elizabeth, 91, 93, 98, 181
Netterer, Jeremiah, 98
Nettleton, Lulie, 20, 104, 114, 176, 184, 185, 189, photo
Nettleton, Marie, 19, 182
Nicol, Jean, 117
Niederhauser, Charles, 34
Nikkei, 13, 14, 55, 57, 90, 131, 133–38, 141–49
normal schools/colleges of education: change to colleges of education, 97; curriculum, 96; East/New England, 73, 74, 128, 132, 210; Idaho, 38; Midwest, 8, 9, 16–19, 28, 53, 60, 84, 93, 101, 105, 107, 149, 168, 170, 171, 184, 187, 193, 207, 212, 214; teachers from, statistics, 51; Washington, 28, 29, 41, 44, 51, 88, 96, 97, 103, 191 (see also Bellingham Normal School; Cheney Normal School; Ellensburg Normal School)
Northgate School, 124, 150
North Queen Anne School, 134
novitiate program. See cadet program
Nuetzmann, Wilbert, 94, 118, 122

Oakley, June, 189
O'Hearn, Juliet, 176
Olein, Hulda, 139, 140
Olmsted Brothers, 20
Olsby, Borghilde, 49, 218
Olson, Inga, 88
Olympic Hotel, 176
organization of teachers, 3, 9, 126, 127, 151, 165, 166, 240n66; community support, 204; labor union support, 166; reluctance to orga-

nize, 45, 152. See also Grade Teachers' Club
Orrell, Jessie, 41
Ostle, Ruth, 41
Ott, Eva, 109
outdoor recreation. See sports and recreation
outside employment, 161–63. See also under World War II

Pacific Rim history course. See under curriculum
Pacific School, 14, 59, 65, 85, 131, 132, 134, 136, 137, 172
Padelford, Frederick, 11, 178
parental schools, 22
parents of teachers, ill or aged. See family obligations
parent-teacher associations, 37, 50, 64, 106, 154, 164, 209; Child Welfare Board, 50
Pariseau, Eugenie, 114, 119, 120
Parker, Adella, 20, 21, 159, 217, 224n35
Parker, Agnes, 19, 161, 247n35
parks, 20; Cowen, 73; Jefferson, 116, 145, 183; Lincoln, 183; Ravenna, 70; Volunteer, 13, 131
Passage, Margaret, 44
Patrick, Doris, 92, 236n21
patriotism, 29, 30, 33, 34, 135. See also Communism; flag exercises; loyalty oaths; and under World War I
Pelton, Anna, 68
Pennington, Harriet, 67, 68
Percival, Dorothy, 94, 95
Perry, Bella, 83, 117, 120–22, 126, 127, 130, 215
Perry, Gladys Charles, 68, 77, 91, 100, 195, 196, 203
Perry, H. Jeannette, 175
personal finances, 156, 162, 192, 196, 197, 205, 207
Phi Beta Kappa, 41, 103, 169, 170, 177, 185

Phillips, May, 78, 190
Pioneer Square/Place, 26, 65, 71, 79,
    131, 141, 193, photo
Piper, Matilda J., 217
Pitter, Constance (Thomas), 106
Pitter, Edward, 106
Pitter, Marjorie Allen, 106
Pitter, Maxine (Haynes), 106, 133
platoon system, 99, 120
Plumb, Nora, 188
Plymouth Congregational Church, 169,
    177, 180, 181, 195
Plymouth Girls' Club, 180, 181
political activism of teachers and princi-
    pals, 21, 81, 83, 126, 127, 154–56, 165,
    166
Pollock, Adelaide, 31, 65, 69, 83, 102,
    103, 107, 110, 175, 180, 183, 205, 206,
    212
Portage Bay, 70
Porter, Florence, 135, 136
Porter, George, 164
Potter, Lois, 59
Powell, John H., 18
Preston, Josephine Corliss, 155
Primary Teachers' Association, 9, 10, 151
principals. See women principals
Pritchard, Joel, 216
progressive education, 5, 6, 22, 144.
    See also Dewey, John; laboratories for
    democracy; Seattle Way
Progressive Era and values, 4, 5, 15, 22,
    29, 110
proximity to school. See under living
    arrangements
Pryor, Lillian, 194
public schools. See Seattle Public Schools
Puget Sound Biological Research Sta-
    tion, 191

qualifications. See certification; hiring
    considerations
Queen Anne High School, 15, 28, 41, 57,
58, 82, 165, 176, 185–87, 189, 216,
    218
Queen Anne Hill, 12, 13, 14, 65, 68–
    70, 84, 111, 112, 134, 171, 213

race relations. See desegregation; ethnic
    and immigrant groups
railroads, 21, 111
Rainier School, 110, 131, 133, 187
Rainier Valley, 13, 79, 108, 131, 207
Randall, Thelma Thompson, 124, 125
Rathbun, Louise, 136, 168
Ravenna district, 11, 113, 207
Ravenna School, 28, 39, 70, 73, 77, 78,
    125, 126
Red Cross, 31, 103, 157, 176
Reep, Ellen, 204
Reible, Amelia, 133, 187
Reible, Julia, 187, 212
religious institutions, 169, 179, 180;
    First Presbyterian Church, 152,
    180; University Congregational
    Church, 180; University Methodist
    Church, 169. See also Plymouth
    Congregational Church; Temple
    de Hirsch
Remley, Bertha, 212
residential hotels, 64–69; Frye, 65,
    231n8; Lincoln, 65, 231n8; Mission
    Inn, 67; Otis, 65, 107, photo; Sorrento,
    65, 231n8; Wintonia, 65, 168
resignations, 203, 214; for marriage
    (see under marriage); for other
    employment, 52, 53, 203, 204; war-
    related, 31–33, 59, 75, 149, 176, 178,
    184
retirement: age at, 44, 51, 52, 60, 101,
    110, 168, 170, 184, 185, 186, 193, 208,
    120, 213, 214; homes for teachers,
    127, 128, 205–7; mandatory, 54, 208,
    209, 211–13; physical examinations
    required, 54, 208, 209; state enabling
    legislation, 27, 28, 156; state system/

pension, 54, 208, 209, 211, 212; teachers' fund (Seattle), 154, 155, 204

Reynolds, Clara, 15, 179

Reynolds, Helen, 95, 98, 127, 179

Roberts, Helen, 95, 96

Robertson, Alice, 132

Rochester, Al, 217

Rogers, Genevieve, 119

Roosevelt High School, 32, 42, 65, 136, 165, 176, 178, 179, 185, 191, 216

Ross School, 19, 84, 119, 131, 138

Rowell, Elizabeth, 26, 176

rural schools, 80, 96

Russell Sage Foundation, 29

sabbaticals, 19, 32, 45, 59, 93, 192, 194, 195, 210, 215

salary, 17, 19, 23, 24, 153; of cadets, 39, 88, 89, 97, 160; community support for increase of, 159, 164; competitive with other regions, 151, 160; cuts, 25, 54, 59, 163–65, 172, 211; data, 24, 25, 34, 48, 49, 52, 59, 60, 114, 115, 157, 159, 160, 163, 164, 166, 211; inequities (grade/high school), 24, 34, 97, 158, 159, 161, 163; inequities (men/women), 3, 4, 30, 33, 160, 161; single scale, 46, 97, 126, 159, 161, 165, 166, 169; state minimum, 49; of substitute teachers, 25, 52; of women principals, 114, 115. *See also* sick leave and compensation

Salmon Bay School, 131

Santmyer, Walter, 161

Sarah B. Yesler Women's Hotel, 64

savings. *See* personal finances

Sawhill, Mary Louise, 72

Scandinavian Americans, 13, 131, 132, 134, 135

scenic attractions of Seattle and Northwest, 16, 19, 187–89, 191

Schmitz, Dietrich, 217

Schmitz, Frankie Close, 58

Schmitz, Henry, 217

school architecture, 80

school board. *See* Seattle School Board

school building conditions, 79–81, 153, 154, 194; heating, 81, 153; lighting, 82, 83; plumbing, 81–82; restrooms, 81–83; portables, 81–83, 213, photos; telephones, 83, 84

school closures and relocations, 48, 85, 141

school counselors, 41, 59, 98

school day/hours, 35, 36, 57

school funding, 46–49

school legislation, 27, 28, 32, 97, 154, 156

school nurse program, 22

Sears, Arthur G., 56, 138

Seattle: annexations/boundaries, 11, 14, 15, 71, 81, maps; ethnic and immigrant migration patterns, 12, 13, 26, 99, 127; frontier characteristics, 7, 11, 20; population characteristics and statistics, 6–8, 16, 26, 27, 54, 58; ratio of men to women, 8, 16; regrading projects, 12, 84; schools (*see* Seattle Public Schools; Seattle School Board); stability of, 11, 12, 38

Seattle Art Museum, 51

Seattle Association of Classroom Teachers, 126, 173, 211

Seattle Chamber of Commerce Bureau of Taxation, 35

Seattle Education Association, 173

Seattle Education Auxiliary and Residence, 127, 205, 206

Seattle Federation of Women's Clubs, 26, 30, 37, 154, 155, 159, 209

Seattle Fine Arts Society, 20

Seattle general strike, 33, 34

Seattle Grade Club Magazine, 73, 74, 76, 85, 92, 117, 136, 165, 167, 169, 181, 188, 191, 194, 205

Seattle Grade Teachers' Club. *See* Grade Teachers' Club

Seattle High School, 143, 177, 185
Seattle High School Teachers Union, 46
Seattle Housing Authority, 58, 59
Seattle Kindergarten Training School, 125
Seattle Municipal League, 48
Seattle Post-Intelligencer, 153
Seattle Principals' Association, 114, 164, 165
Seattle Public Schools: administration/ Central Office, 46, 83, 91, 98, 101, 105, 109, 170, 213; Department of Primary Method, 95; Department of Research, 41; first school, 8; graduates as future Seattle leaders, 20, 21, 37, 62, 106, 129, 137, 138, 147, 164, 216–18; graduates as future Seattle teachers, 9, 12, 14, 17, 19, 28, 41, 45, 94, 58, 91, 92, 94, 115, 125, 143, 176, 185, 195, 203; number of schools, 10, 16; number of teachers, 15, 26; ratio of men to women teachers, 15, 16, 38, 40, 53, 161, 247n38; superintendents of (see Bottomly, Forbes; Campbell, Ernest; Cole, Thomas; Cooper, Frank; Fleming, Samuel; McClure, Worth). *See also individual schools by name*
Seattle Repertory Playhouse, 51
Seattle Republican, 108
Seattle Retired Teachers Association, 170
Seattle School Board, 5, 9, 23, 98; anti-union position, 166, 167; budget cuts, 35, 47, 114; composition and elections, 5, 29, 30, 34, 35, 126, 160, 161, 166; hiring practices, 15, 27, 131; men principals preferred, 113, 213; opposition to married teachers, 200, 201; outside employment of teachers, 161–63; parsimony of, 35, 36, 83, 84, 91, 105, 152, 154, 160, 163, 164, 211; program cuts, 35–36; reactionary trends, 29, 30, 34, 35; salary cuts, 36, 48, 114, 163–65; staff cuts, 35–36; and teacher living arrangements, 25, 64; teacher

petitions to, 24, 84, 153, 166; women on, 29, 30; World War I salaries/ bonuses, 158
Seattle Star, 204
Seattle Symphony Orchestra, 20, 217
Seattle Teachers' Association, 23, 151, 155, 196
Seattle Teachers Credit Union, 207
Seattle Teachers' League, 173
Seattle Times, 63, 64, 81
Seattle Way, 5, 6, 22, 29, 37, 42, 89, 91, 92, 98, 131, 215
Selby, Kenneth, 214, 256n46
Sennes, Gertrude, 201
Seven Devils, 118–24
Seward School, 65, 73, 88, 98–100, 132
sexual harassment, 7
Shannon, James F., 110
Sharples, Casper, 166
Shelton, Helen, 115
Shelton, James, 120
Shephardson, Iva (Trenholme), 52
Shook, Agatha, 123
Shorrett, John, 166
Shorrock, Ebenezer, 29, 35, 160, 161
sick leave and compensation, 10, 23, 151, 156
Sierra Club, 183, 184
Siggelko, Marguerite, 89, 90, 214
Siggerud, Clara, 214
Simmons, Anna, 187
Skartvedt, Agnes, 182
Small, Emma, 15, 204
Smith, J. Allen, 178
Smith, W. Virgil, 99
Smith, Zula, 60
Snow, Myra, 114, 163, 168
social life, 174–98
Sone, Monica, 141, 145
Soroptimist Club, 179
South Park district, 12
South Park School, 71, 79, 84, 138, 184
special education, 23, 39, 59, 210

Spencer, George, 160
sports and recreation, 19, 178, 180–82, 183, 187. *See also* Grade Teachers' Club; hiking; mountain climbing; Mountaineers, The
standards of behavior for teachers, 25, 40, 198, 216
Starks, Marjorie, 39
Sterrett, Nellie B., 153–55, 168, 180, 188
Stevens, Carolyn, 103
Stevens School, 131, 217
Stillaguamish Country Club, 189–91
Stoecker, Mamie B., 166, 171, 172, 203
Streator, Gertrude, 31, 184, 185
Strong, Anna Louise, 5, 29, 30, 33, 87, 160
Stuart, Josephine, 188
student government, 128
student memories, 32, 69, 73, 75, 77, 106–8, 111, 115, 120, 123, 128, 129, 132–34, 136–38, 141, 142, 145, 146, 155, 161, 169, 209, 218
substitute teachers, 25, 52, 60, 214
summer employment. *See* outside employment
summer study, 19, 42, 44, 53, 103, 191, 207
summer vacations. *See* vacations
Summit School, 88, 98, 119, 139, 183
Suzzallo, Henry, 47

Taake, Irene B., 32
Tanagi, George, 135, 136
Tanner, Blanche, 114, 123, 124
Tax Reduction Council, 35, 46, 163, 164
Taylor, Ida M., 209–11
teacher deaths before retirement, 53, 60, 78, 101, 113, 120, 138
teacher evaluations, 39, 75, 88, 89, 92, 94, 95, 105, 109, 117, 119, 122, 125, 127, 143, 171, 184, 210, 212, 214, 215
Teachers College, Columbia University, 18, 125, 144, 178, 181, 194, 207
teacher shortages, 19, 40, 60, 149, 200

Teachers Institute, 23, photo
teachers' organizations. *See* American Federation of Teachers; Grade Teachers' Club; High School Teachers' League; Primary Teachers' Association; Seattle Association of Classroom Teachers; Seattle Education Association; Seattle High School Teachers Union; Seattle Teachers' Association; Seattle Teachers' League; Washington Education Association; Washington State Federation of Teachers; World Federation of Education Associations; World Organization of Teachers
teacher supply and demand, 40, 52, 96
teacher training. *See* cadet program; colleges and universities; demonstration schools; normal schools/colleges of education; sabbaticals; summer study
teaching, as a profession, 4, 151
teaching conditions. *See* class size; school building conditions; school day/hours
Telban, Amelia, 90, 99, 116, 117, 145, photos
Telban, Ethel, 145
Tellier, Belle, 183
Temple de Hirsch, 131, 132, 159
tenure: length of, 16, 17, 19, 24, 28, 29, 41, 44, 60, 71, 95, 101, 103, 105, 113, 127, 132, 133; job security, 165, 170
Tharp, Elizabeth, 69, 83, 89, 104, 115, 210
Thomas, Margaret J., 134, 135, 172, 173
Thompson, Maud, 138, 139, 157
Tobey, Mark, 37
Tompkins, Helen, 101
Tormey, Gertrude, 54
Tourtelotte, Janet Powell, 217
transportation, to school: automobile, 63, 77, 78, 116; bus, 78; horse and buggy, 8, 64; jitneys, 73, 77; streetcars, 12, 69–71, 77–79, 85, 110, photo

travel: airplane, 187; automobile, 74–77, 78, 192; foreign, 45, 59, 139, 140, 142, 149, 169, 177, 179, 187, 191–93, 195–97, 202, 204; ship, 149, 193–97, train, 21, 111; in United States, 77, 78, 192, 194, 195. *See also* sabbaticals

Tsutakawa, George, 217

T. T. Minor School, 19, 60, 72, 81, 89, 107, 131, 133, 155, 161, 184, 212, 213

Tucker, Edith, 91, 94, 97, 98

tutoring, 163

Tyack, David, 4

Unemployed Citizens League, 47

unemployment, 47, 50, 52

unionization of teachers. *See* organization of teachers

University district, 11, 19, 70, 85, 207

University Heights School, 17–19, 37, 45, 70, 73, 122, 211

University of Washington, 8, 139; significance for teachers, 17, 19, 25, 28, 29, 52, 97, 158, 168, 170, 178, 185

University Village, 136

Uno, Shigeko, 141, 142

vacation employment. *See* outside employment

vacation property, 117, 147, 169, 182, 188–91

vacations, 21, 154. *See also* family obligations; sabbaticals; summer study; travel

Van Asselt district, 11

Van Asselt School, 24, 71, 116, 213, 215

Van Orsdall, Otie, 191

Vaupell, Helen, 176, 181

Vetting, Ida, 88, 95, 98, 99, 124, 126, 127

Vieth, Zela, 191

Vopni, Sylvia, 58

Voters Information League, 35, 163, 164

Waller, Vera, 183

Wallingford district, 11, 68, 71, 73

Wandersee, Winifred, 201

Warren Avenue School, 14, 27, 88, 153, 210, photo

Washington Commonwealth Federation, 47

Washington Education Association, 29, 87, 91, 171, 196, 208

Washington School, 13, 14, 56, 67, 131, 137–39, 142, 148

Washington State Federation of Teachers, 121, 126

Washington State Legislature. *See* school funding; school legislation

Washington State University/College, 44, 92

Waughop, Sara, 10

Waxman, Rebecca, 132, 192

Wayne, Alta, 188

Webster School, 17, 78, 81, 85, 88

Wedgwood School, 215

Wenner, Blanche, 31, 176

Westin, Margaret, 89

West Queen Anne School, 31, 45, 65, 83, 175, 177, 212

West Seattle district, 71, 72, 79, 85, 193

West Seattle High School, 15, 32, 41, 45, 57, 61, 162, 176

West Woodland School, 60, 162, 191

Wheeler, Adelle, 73, 74, 194

Wheeler, Gladys, 134

White, Lillie P., 133

Whittier School, 56

Whitworth School, 80, 193

Wilcox, Elizabeth, 65

Willard, Frank E., 74, 90, 110

Wilson, Alma (Jackson), 7, 203

Wilson, Gladys, 189

Wilson, Isa Brown, 218

Wilson, Mabel V., 164, 170, 171, 173

Wilson, Marjorie, 202

Wilson, Trella Belle Logan. *See* Logan, Trella Belle
Winn, Agnes, 167, 168
Winsor, Robert, 87, 158, 160
Witham, Myrtle, 60
Wixson, Mabel, 201
women principals, 9, 16, 18, 53, 92, 94, 102–30 passim, 143, 144, 170, 172, 202, 210, 237n2, photos; autonomy of, 105; community relations, 102, 111, 141, 142; lasting influence of, 54, 106, 142, 184; number of, 102; and parents, 102, 105, 111, 120, 121, 124; professionalism and organizations, 103, 104; qualifications and recruitment of, 103, 110, 124, 125, 128; ratio of men to women, 102; replaced by men, 113, 213; salaries, 114, 115; and teachers, 102, 105, 112, 116, 123 (*see also* Seven Devils; teacher evaluations); tributes to, 54, 106, 130. *See also* head teachers
women's clubs. *See* American Association of University Women; business and professional women's clubs; Ladies Musical Club; Plymouth Girls' Club; Seattle Federation of Women's Clubs; Soroptimist Club; Women's University Club of Seattle
women's hotels. *See* Sarah B. Yesler Women's Hotel
Women's Legislative Council, 159, 179
Women's Legislative Federation, King County, 156
Women's Overseas Service League, 31, 179
women's suffrage, 20, 21
Women's University Club of Seattle, 175–78
women supervisors, 18, 79, 88, 93, 179, 189, 204, 210

working-class neighborhoods, 13, 50, 65, 71, 79, 84, 106, 111–13
working conditions. *See* class size; school building conditions; school day/hours
World Federation of Education Associations, 139
World Organization of Teachers, 196
World War I, 27, 31, 37, 75, 156, 157; anti-German sentiment, 30; Armistice Day, 33; cost of living/inflation, 25, 27, 33, 46, 157, 158, 246n26; male teachers, recruitment and bonus, 25, 27, 30, 33, 158–60; nativism, 29, 30; patriotism of teachers, 33; teacher shortage, 40; textbook purges, 30; wartime service of women teachers, 31–33, 75, 149, 176, 178, 184
World War II, 52, 57, 59, 122, 193, 194, 216, photos; air raid drills in schools, 55, photo; civil defense, 57, photo; emergency service of married teachers, 40, 45, 52, 53, 57, 126, 200, 218; Japanese internment, 55–57, 147–49, 172, 173; military service of teachers, 59; mobilization for, 54, 55; outside employment of teachers during, 57; Pearl Harbor, 55, 146–48, 216; population increase, 58; rationing, 57, photo; teacher shortage, 19, 60, 149, 200, V-2 training programs, 58; Women's Army Corps, 59
Wren, Florence (Ewart), 215

yellow dog contracts, 167
Young Men's/Women's Christian associations, 26, 31, 32, 64, 168, 178, 184, 188
Youngstown School, 46, 52, 71, 117, 120, 193

LIBRARY OF CONGRESS CATALOGING-IN-PUBLICATION DATA

Pieroth, Doris Hinson.
Seattle's women teachers of the interwar years :
shapers of a livable city / Doris Hinson Pieroth.
p. cm.
"A McLellan book."
Includes bibliographical references and index.
ISBN 0-295-98445-7 (hardback : alk. paper)
1. Women teachers—Washington (State)—
Seattle—History—20th century.
2. Teachers—Washington (State)—Seattle—
History—20th century.
3. Education—Washington (State)—Seattle—
History—20th century.
I. Title.
LB1775.3.W2P54 2004
371.1'009797'772—dc22
2004010769